Aristophanic Comedy
and the Challenge of
Democratic Citizenship

T0339226

ARISTOPHANIC COMEDY
AND THE CHALLENGE OF
DEMOCRATIC CITIZENSHIP

John Zumbrunnen

UNIVERSITY OF ROCHESTER PRESS

First published 2012
Transferred to digital printing and reprinted in paperback 2017

University of Rochester Press
668 Mt. Hope Avenue, Rochester, NY 14620, USA
www.urpress.com
and Boydell & Brewer Limited
PO Box 9, Woodbridge, Suffolk IP12 3DF, UK
www.boydellandbrewer.com

Hardcover ISBN: 978-1-58046-417-8
Paperback ISBN: 978-1-58046-588-5

Library of Congress Cataloging-in-Publication Data
Zumbrunnen, John.
 Aristophanic comedy and the challenge of democratic citizenship / John Zumbrunnen.
  p. cm.
 Includes bibliographical references and index.
 ISBN 978-1-58046-417-8 (hardcover : alk. paper) 1. Citizenship. 2. Democracy. 3. Aristophanes—Criticism and interpretation. 4. Citizenship in literature. 5. Democracy in literature. I. Title.
 JF801.Z86 2012
 323.601—dc23

2011048876

A catalogue record for this title is available from the British Library.
This publication is printed on acid-free paper.
Printed in the United States of America

Parts of chapter 2 appeared in my "Comedy, the Ordinary Citizen, and the Salvation of the City," in *When Worlds Elide: Political Theory, Cultural Studies and the Effects of Hellenism*, ed. J. Peter Euben and Karen Bassi (Lanham, MD: Lexington Books, 2010), 229–52, and are reprinted here with permission of Rowman and Littlefield.

An earlier version of chapter 4 appeared as "Elite Domination and the Ordinary Citizen: Aristophanes' *Acharnians* and *Knights*," in *Political Theory* 23, no. 5 (October 2004): 656–77, and is reprinted here with permission of Sage Publications.

An earlier version of chapter 5 appeared as "Fantasy, Irony, and Economic Justice in Aristophanes' *Assemblywomen* and *Wealth*," in *American Political Science Review* 100, no. 3 (August 2006): 319–33, and is reprinted here with permission of Cambridge University Press.

CONTENTS

Acknowledgments   vii

Introduction   1

1   Peaceful Voyages: *Peace* and *Lysistrata*   21

2   Ordinary Citizens, High Culture, and the Salvation of the
City: *Clouds, Women at the Thesmophoria,* and *Frogs*   41

3   *Archē* and the Anger of the Ordinary Citizen: *Wasps* and *Birds*   60

4   Elite Domination and the Clever Citizen:
Acharnians and *Knights*   81

5   Fantasy, Irony, and Economic Justice:
Assemblywomen and *Wealth*   99

Conclusion: Democratic Possibilities   123

Notes   137

Bibliography   153

Index   163

ACKNOWLEDGMENTS

I started this project at Union College, thinking of it as something like comic relief from my book on Thucydides. My early work on Aristophanes benefitted from Union's generous sabbatical policy and from the professional and personal support of my colleagues at the college, especially Richard Fox, Lori Marso, and Zoe Oxley. My new colleagues at the University of Wisconsin have been encouraging from the start, particularly my department chair John Coleman, my good friend Kathy Cramer Walsh, and my fellow political theorists Rick Avramenko, Helen Kinsella, and Jimmy Casas Klausen. Special thanks to Howard Schweber, who offered insightful comments on various drafts of the manuscript. I am grateful as well for summer research support provided by the University of Wisconsin Graduate School.

I have presented various versions of different parts of this book on panels at annual meetings of the American Political Science Association, the Midwest Political Science Association, the Western Political Science Association, and the Southern Political Science Association. I thank the other participants on those panels, as well as my fellow conferees at a 2007 Liberty Fund conference on "Aristophanes on War and Peace." Thanks, too, to the many colleagues with whom I've talked about Aristophanes and Greek political thought more generally over the last several years. They include Karen Bassi, Peter Euben, Jill Frank, Dustin Gish, Seth Jaffe, Dan Kapust, Gerry Mara, Liz Markovits, Arlene Saxonhouse, Joel Schlosser, Michael Svoboda, Christina Tarnopolsky, Rachel Templer, John Wallach, David Williams, Catherine Zuckert, and Michael Zuckert.

I have been fortunate to again have Sandy Thatcher as my editor. Sandy's commitment to the highest standards of scholarly publishing and to the field of political theory are well known. I deeply appreciate his continued support of my work. I am grateful as well to Suzanne Guiod, who guided this manuscript through the publication process at the University of Rochester Press. Two anonymous readers for the press offered suggestions that substantially improved the final product.

Continued thanks to my family. My mother is a constant source of support in my life, and she patiently tolerates my children's seemingly unending interest in that buffalo place southeast of Des Moines. Along those lines, I am incredibly fortunate to live with my very own rowdy and raucous comic chorus: Abby, Charlie, Maggie, and Ben. To varying degrees they share my love of donuts, Looney Tunes, Brewers baseball, and Badger hockey. They decidedly do not share my interest in politics, much less political theory or political science. Though they know that I've been finishing up a book, they could not care less what that book is about. They never want to talk about Aristophanes. They just want to hang out, even when my mind is on work. For that I am more grateful than I can say.

My greatest thanks go once again to Amy Gangl. As a student of the theater (imagine how Aristophanes would mock that self-important self-description!), I have benefitted greatly from talking with her about her own creative projects. I have also learned immensely from our conversations about the television we watch together (from *The Wire* to *Battlestar Galactica*) and the movies we see (even the bad ones—*Thirty Minutes or Less* was atrocious, but think what we learned from it about plot and dialogue!). Amy has read what I have to say about Aristophanes again and again, always as an honest and gentle critic. Much more importantly, she is and always will be my best friend and my partner in everything.

INTRODUCTION

Contemporary democratic theory increasingly poses a choice between democracy as the power of the people resisting all institutionalized rule or democracy as rule by the people through carefully specified procedures and institutions. On one side is a diverse group of theorists often referred to as *agonal democrats*.[1] From various perspectives, these theorists insist that contestation, struggle, and resistance lie at the heart of politics in general and democratic politics in particular. Agonal democrats thus reject the drive for consensus that they find in theories of those on the other side, *liberal democrats* and *deliberative democrats*.[2] Consensus, according to the agonal view, amounts to the end of contestation and the squelching of resistance to dominant ways of thinking and acting. But liberal and deliberative democrats insist—again in various ways—that democracy properly understood involves the ordered, reasonable, and responsible exercise of the power of the people, which can only occur when contestation and resistance are tempered by consensus-producing practices of public reason, deliberative procedures, and institutional safeguards.

At its most basic, this book draws on Aristophanes to help move beyond any either-or choice between democracy as contestation and rebellion and democracy as ordered and responsible collective action. Instead, I take rebellion and collective action as rival impulses within democracy. On my reading, Aristophanic comedy shows ordinary people at once pulled toward resistance to all attempts to impose order or rule on democratic politics and, at the same time, pulled toward contributing to the collective action of the demos. Put differently, we can understand Aristophanic comedy as exploring what I will call the challenge of democratic citizenship, which requires citizens to navigate the perpetual tension between democracy's twin impulses. Aristophanes's surviving plays, I argue, both draw upon and seek to instill in spectators a comic disposition necessary for meeting the challenge of democratic citizenship so understood.

Aristophanes most often chooses for his protagonists recognizably ordinary Athenians. He does not portray his heroes and heroines as members of the social, political, or economic elite. His eleven surviving plays instead place at center stage men and women who see themselves as excluded from that elite or as oppressed by it. Some of Aristophanes's protagonists do suffer more profound exclusion or oppression than others. Praxagora, the intrepid heroine of *Assemblywomen*, organizes the women of Athens as

1

they act to challenge the utter dominance of Athenian politics by men. By comparison, Diceapolis, the peace-loving hero of *Acharnians*, is relatively powerful. As a full Athenian citizen, he can attend the Athenian assembly, try to speak, and, in the end, vote as he wishes. But he finds himself without an effective voice in an Athenian politics dominated by war mongering demagogues. And so, like Praxagora, he launches a clever scheme to change the status quo.

In these two plays, and in others, Aristophanes shows us ordinary Athenians embarking on extraordinary attempts to challenge those with greater political status, resources, and power. His protagonists might appear at first glance, then, as potential heroes of a rebellious, agonal democracy. But the political implications of Aristophanic comedy are more complex than this. A common reading of Aristophanes in fact casts him as an Athenian conservative worried precisely by the excesses and unruliness of the fully developed Athenian democracy of the later fifth century BCE.[3] On this reading, Aristophanes harkens back nostalgically to a more ordered, responsible Athenian politics tended by the proper elites of Athens's own greatest generation—those who fought and won the Battle of Marathon.

While I aim to move beyond this common reading of Aristophanes, I do not mean to argue that he embraces the often radical schemes of his heroes and heroines, nor do I mean to argue that Aristophanes presents his protagonists as models of good democratic citizenship. Aristophanes, on my reading, is neither an advocate of a populist democratic politics driven by the rebellious whims of ordinary citizens nor a conservative hoping for an elite-driven tempering of the popular will. Instead, again, I take his comedy as pointing toward the kind of comic disposition ordinary people would need to meet the challenge of democratic citizenship. In this way, Aristophanic comedy might help us rethink the possibilities of democracy, in his day and our own.

This argument rests on two underlying premises about Aristophanic comedy: first, that an engagement with ancient Athenian democracy can speak to contemporary democratic politics; and, second, that we can approach comedy in general and Aristophanic comedy in particular as a meaningful resource for democratic theory. By way of introducing the main themes and arguments I pursue in the remainder of this book, I turn in this introduction to consider these two basic premises. I first draw on recent work on Athenian democracy to expand upon the understanding of the basic challenge of democratic citizenship sketched above. Despite the vast differences between ancient and modern democracy, I argue that ordinary citizens today confront the same basic challenge as did citizens of ancient Athens. I then turn to consider how Aristophanic comedy might be read as offering a response to this challenge of democratic citizenship and so as casting new light on the possibilities of democratic politics. Along the way, I situate my approach to the comedies against the backdrop of common readings of Aristophanes as a nostalgic conservative or more simply as an apolitical entertainer.

The Challenge of Democratic Citizenship, Ancient and Modern

Despite the frequent pitting of liberal, deliberative, and agonal theories of democracy as antithetical to one another, we can easily enough find connections among them. Rawlsian liberalism, after all, insists that any consensus must and can only be thin, allowing for the continued presence of pluralism. That pluralism must be reasonable, but this hardly denies the possibility of significant and ongoing conflict. Likewise, deliberative democrats often enough emphasize the temporary nature of any consensus and the inevitable reemergence of disagreement. "Although a decision must stand for some period of time," Gutmann and Thompson write, "it is provisional in the sense that it must be open to challenge at some point in the future."[4]

Agonal democrats, on the other hand, hardly dismiss the idea that democratic politics might need some tempering to be rendered responsible and, in particular, to respect difference or pluralism. Chantal Mouffe, to take a prominent example, casts the agonal politics she favors as an alternative to a dangerous antagonism. Drawing on Carl Schmitt's account of the centrality of the friend-enemy distinction to politics, Mouffe argues that democracy depends upon a demos, upon a "we" that excludes a "they." For Mouffe, our task is to ensure that the "ethico-political principles" that unite the demos lead, not to hostile antagonism, but to healthy agonism. From this point of view, an appropriately agonal politics may take place in the context of liberal principles and institutions. "If we take 'liberty and equality for all' as the 'ethico-political principles' of liberal democracy," Mouffe writes, "it is clear that the problem with our societies is not their proclaimed ideals but the fact that those ideals are not put into practice."[5]

Again, I do not take these seeming points of contact as undermining the differences between the rival points of view we find in contemporary democratic theory. Rather, they suggest the potential for thinking, not about differences between incompatible conceptions of democracy, but, instead, about rival impulses within democracy itself—or, in my preferred framing, about the challenge that democracy as a tension-filled practice poses to ordinary citizens.

But if this potential is already present in contemporary political theory, why turn to ancient Athens in general and to Aristophanes in particular? Though a growing body of work in both classics and political theory aims to bring the Greeks to bear on contemporary thinking about democracy,[6] there are a variety of good reasons to be at least initially wary of turning to Athenian democracy (much less to a comic poet) for insights about contemporary democracy. I consider three such concerns here. The first focuses on the vast and important institutional differences between ancient and contemporary democracy. The second focuses on the absence of anything like contemporary pluralism in ancient Athens. A final concern emerges from my use of the language of *disposition*, which, with its Aristotelian connotations, might be seen as lacking contemporary resonance.

Democracy and Institutions

We are often rightly reminded of the institutional differences between ancient and modern democracy. Democratic Athens did of course have political institutions. The familiar list includes the assembly, the boule, the lawcourts, and a host of administrative offices, most of which were filled by lot.[7] Still, Athens had no equivalent of the modern state, did not rely upon elections and representation, and, though we sometimes speak of the "Athenian constitution," knew nothing of the principles of modern constitutional design. The details of these institutional differences do matter. More interesting for my purposes, though, is the different way in which Athenians understood the relationship between their institutions and democracy. Here we can turn first to the work of Sheldon Wolin and then to that of Josiah Ober.

Wolin's conception of *fugitive democracy* has been influential and controversial among political theorists.[8] In the contemporary world, Wolin argues, democracy is not and cannot be a lasting form of government. It instead erupts periodically as a "rebellious moment" in which a self-defining, self-constituting demos acts to end its oppression.[9] Wolin developed the idea of fugitive democracy in part from a reading of ancient Athenian politics. In an early essay, "Norm and Form: The Constitutionalizing of Democracy," Wolin suggests that we ought to embrace Plato's and Aristotle's descriptions of democracy as resistant to the stability and order that elites might impose. Where Plato and Aristotle found a cautionary tale in the turbulence of fifth-century-BCE Athenian democracy, Wolin finds a "dynamic and developing political culture" that was wary of institutions that limited democracy by enhancing elite power.[10] Athenian democracy thus consistently resisted its own constitutionalization as a "form" of government. Indeed, to the extent that Athenian democracy relied on institutions, those institutions were in Wolin's paradoxical phrasing "formless forms." As if picking up on the warnings of the Greek philosophers, liberal constitutionalism thus for Wolin works from outside or above democracy to impose ordering institutions on it. It aims to render democracy, from the liberal point of view, responsible or safe. In Athens, by contrast, random selection of officials by lot and constant rotation in office in fact kept faith with the salutary destabilizing tendency of democracy.

In contrast to Wolin's emphasis on the rebellious nature of Athenian democracy, Josiah Ober finds in the etymological roots of democracy a creative, constructive capacity. Though Ober's earlier work emphasizes tensions between elite political actors and the people in ancient Athens, he insists that democracy did not mean opposition to all forms of rule. In his recent *Democracy and Knowledge*, Ober instead argues that democracy (*demokratia*) meant that "the capacity to act in order to effect change (*kratos*) lay with a public (*demos*) composed of many choice-making individuals."[11] Following along these conceptual lines, Ober casts Athenian democracy as evolving a set of institutions well designed to aggregate the knowledge of individual citizens and to make that knowledge the basis of effective collective action. He thus presents democratic Athens as pointing toward the importance of institutions that harness the potential of democratic knowledge.

The juxtaposition of Wolin's and Ober's accounts of Athenian democracy maps in a rough way onto contemporary disputes about whether democracy is or is not a form of rule. Where Wolin sees democracy as resistant to all forms, Ober casts Athenian democracy precisely as a form of government—indeed as the most effective form. These arguments, though, are not as opposed as they might first appear. Again, Wolin means to contrast democracy's rebellious, disruptive power with attempts to curtail, order, or domesticate democracy. Ober, though, does not view the institutionalization or formalization of democracy in Athens as checking or moderating democracy; nor does he, in the manner of liberalism, cast institutionalization as first and foremost a matter of protecting individual Athenians from the majority, or, in the manner of deliberative theory, as imposing rational procedures on deliberative practices. For Ober, the institutions of Athenian democracy were, instead, tools crafted by the Athenian demos to be used as the demos exercised its capacity to effect change. They were, we might say, expressions of the desire of the demos for effective collective action.

The contrast between Wolin's and Ober's accounts of Athenian democracy thus does not reduce to pitting rebellious democracy against moderating institutions, as contemporary arguments sometimes seem to do. Instead, we can think of Wolin and Ober as emphasizing two distinct impulses *within* democracy: a rebellious impulse that resists form as a challenge to the power of the people alongside an impulse toward collective action that finds form useful as a way to exercise the power of the people. My argument will be that the tension between these two impulses defines the challenge of democratic citizenship. Exploring this notion of democratic citizenship as a tension-filled practice is, I think, more promising than rehashing arguments about whether democracy is best understood as a form of institutionalized rule or as resistance to imposed consensus or elite domination or rule in general.

It is important here to emphasize that finding tension between democracy's two impulses is not the same as finding them to be incompatible or simply opposed to one another. Along these lines, and despite their different emphases, we can note the similar way in which Ober and Wolin treat a central moment in Athenian democratic history: the so-called Cleisthenic revolution of 508/507 BCE. As the traditional label suggests, the events of 508/507 BCE have most often been described as part of an ongoing battle among Athenian elites. Competing for power with the Spartan-backed Isagoras, the Athenian Cleisthenes in Herodotus's words "brought [the Athenian people] into his own faction and increased the numbers of their tribes and gave them new names."[12] The suggestion here is of a top-down revolution or, better, of a set of elite-driven social and political reforms, albeit reforms that in the long run had democratic implications. Challenging this point of view, Ober argues that the revolution of 508/507 BCE was in fact a popular uprising, instigated by the Athenian demos constituting itself as a political actor for the first time.[13] Put differently, the first moment of Athenian democracy, understood in Ober's terms as the capacity of a public to effect change, was a moment of revolution or rebellion.

Wolin places somewhat less emphasis than does Ober on the events of 508/507 BCE, treating them as one significant episode in a "series of struggles" through which democracy developed. His understanding of those struggles, though, is quite similar to Ober's: "To be sure, many of the democratic reforms . . . were associated with notable leaders, such as Solon, Cleisthenes, Ephialtes, and Pericles, but the evidence suggests that the demos was an active force in all the reforms, exerting pressure, siding with one leader rather than another, and gradually extending its power by gaining access to existing institutions or by establishing new ones."[14] During the Cleisthenic revolution and at other key moments, the demos was a "force." It acted in Wolin's description with its own seemingly unified will: exerting, siding, extending, gaining. Wolin thus finds various moments of concerted collective action by the demos aimed at effecting democratic change.

Wolin's and Ober's similar readings of the events of 508/507 BCE thus mark more than agreement on the interpretation of a particular historical event. They also suggest that the basic understandings of democracy that they offer need not be understood as mutually exclusive. As the example of the Cleisthenic revolution suggests, Wolin's rebellious moments involve the demos using or claiming or creating what Ober calls its capacity to effect change. We might say that such moments represent the convergence of the two impulses of democracy. Democracy's rebellious impulse, emphasized by Wolin, resists all attempts to impose any form of institutionalized rule. Democracy's impulse toward collective action, emphasized by Ober, may well lead to—may even require—attempts to fashion popular power into a form of rule. The latter impulse may thus ultimately result in institutions that channel and enhance the capacity of the demos to effect change. Such institutionalization, of course, is precisely what Ober thinks happened in fifth-century-BCE Athens. But, again, the moment of the Cleisthenic revolution itself reflects both democracy's rebellious impulse and its impulse toward collective action. The Athenian people, from this point of view, came together, realizing and making effective their collective capacity to end the domination of Athenian politics by oligarchs (and Spartans).

In the case of ancient Athens, thinking of democracy as containing both an impulse toward rebellion and an impulse toward collective action by the demos can thus help us to move beyond any sort of either-or choice between the accounts of Wolin and Ober. If the Cleisthenic revolution highlights the possible convergence of the impulses of democracy, then the development of Athenian democracy through the fifth century BCE reminds us of the tension between them. Ober's own analysis of the challenge of aggregating and deploying the knowledge of the often unruly Athenians offers one way to understand this tension. Wolin's notion of Athenian democratic institutions as formless forms captures the tension in a more general way. Once the power of the people had ended the rule of tyrants and oligarchs, the challenge became finding ways to preserve the rebellious impulse of democracy by, paradoxically enough, containing it within institutionalized forms.

On a conceptual level, then, we might think of Athenian democracy in particular and democracy more generally as enacting or playing out the tension between two often conflicting impulses, and we might think of the two impulses of democracy as posing a basic challenge to the ordinary citizen. Democracy calls upon ordinary citizens to resist institutionalized rule as a potential gateway to domination by would-be elites; at the same time, it calls upon them to work toward effective and responsible collective action, which may well require institutions. A central task of democratic theory, then, is to think about this tension between democracy's twin impulses and so to face more squarely the basic challenge of democratic citizenship. A chief task of this book is to explore the ways in which Aristophanes's comedy portrays ordinary people engaging with that challenge. My argument, again, will be that Aristophanes's comic art draws upon and seeks to instill in its audience the complex *comic disposition* necessary for facing the challenge of democratic citizenship so understood. From this point of view, to the extent that the contemporary debate revolves around these competing definitions of democracy, it risks missing what is most interesting and complex about the democratic political experience.

Of course, the contemporary debate is not merely definitional. Indeed, though both sides claim the mantle of democracy, one might argue that this is a diversion from the central matter of dispute, which concerns how democracy (whatever it means) relates to pluralism. Pluralism plays a central role in contemporary democracy and contemporary democratic theory. In general terms, liberalism aims to temper democracy precisely by demanding the recognition and protection of pluralism. To the extent that it seeks to do so via institutional safeguards, we might note, it suggests the potential danger in Ober's notion of institutions as tools to make the power of the demos more effective. Making the power of the demos more effective, after all, may in practice mean empowering the majority to have its way at the expense of minority views or individual rights. A similar concern underlies the search for deliberative procedures that might yield, not simply the effective aggregation of majority support, but instead a consensus that excludes or ignores no reasonable point of view. Finally, central to agonal democrats' critique of liberal and deliberative theories is the claim that the brand of consensus they promote in fact stifles rather than respects the contestation that pluralism invites or demands.

Democracy, Pluralism, and the Ordinary

This centrality of pluralism to contemporary political life poses a second challenge to any turn to Athenian democracy for resources for contemporary theory. We might quibble about the extent of Athenian citizenship, think carefully about the role of women in Athenian culture, or ask after the place of resident foreigners in Athens. Simply put, though, nothing comparable to contemporary pluralism existed in ancient Athens. In ethnic and religious terms, the population of Athens and Attica more generally will have known little diversity in our contemporary sense, and the Athenian citizen body—adult, male, free born of Athenian parents—was even more homogonous. There remains, then, a seemingly unbridgeable chasm between the Athenian experience and our own in terms of how we think about the demos and the key divisions or cleavages within it.

This difference is marked in this book by my frequent use of the language of *ordinary* citizens. Ordinary suggests a contrast with extraordinary. Put differently, it frames a single fault line in democracy running between ordinary citizens and elites. Here, again, the language I use follows both Wolin and Ober. Each emphasizes the basic centrality of ordinary citizens to democracy, ancient or modern. Wolin describes democracy as "a project concerned with the political potentialities of ordinary citizens."[15] Ober reminds us that the ancient philosophical critics of classical Athenian democracy "assumed that democracy—the political power (*kratos*) of the mass of ordinary citizens (*demos*)—was real."[16] While Athenian democracy "was threatened (actually and potentially) by the attempts of powerful elites to dominate the political realm," he argues that the power of the demos, particularly its power over public speech, regularly frustrated such attempts.[17] For my purposes, this shared emphasis on the political lives of ordinary people fits well with Aristophanes's choice of ordinary citizens rather than political, cultural, or social elites as the heroes and heroines of his comedies.

Focusing on the dynamics of the ordinary-elite fault also, I think, holds considerable promise for bringing Aristophanes to bear on contemporary mass politics. I say this despite the vast and important differences between ancient and contemporary democracy already catalogued. Athenian institutions, again, allowed ordinary citizens to participate directly in decision-making processes. That participation was mediated neither by a powerful state nor by technologically advanced media. Consider, by contrast, the description of modern politics offered by Walter Lippmann in the mid-1920s:

> The private citizen today has come to feel rather like a deaf spectator in the back row, who ought to keep his mind on the mystery off there, but cannot quite manage to keep awake. He knows he is somehow affected by what is going on. Rules and regulations continually, taxes annually and wars occasionally remind him that he is being swept along by great drifts of circumstance. Yet these public affairs are in no convincing way his affairs.[18]

For Lippman, the category of the spectator itself suggests a largely passive detachment that seems an ill fit with the ideal of citizenship. I will in due course want to question that assessment of the spectator. But Lippman's account of the ordinary citizen in modern democracy (which I take as being broadly applicable in our own day, too) can also help to remind us of the significantly different contexts of ordinary citizenship in the ancient and contemporary worlds.

Still, the basic dynamics of mass democracy, in which a small group of elites or would-be elites must (at least periodically) seek the support of a mass of ordinary citizens who, as spectators, listen and (at least from time to time) make decisions of political consequence, were from a certain perspective not so different in Athens. In earlier work, Ober explores the ways in which the rhetoric of elite orators reflects an understanding of the ideology of the demos and so, too, reflects the power of the mass of ordinary citizens over the political fortunes of the orators themselves.[19] Ober here builds on the work of Moses Finley, who describes a central problem of political stability in ancient democracy. Finley asks why the ancient demos would have accepted—as surviving evidence suggests it did—the dominance of what he calls "spokesmen in the Assembly" drawn from a small elite of politically active citizens.[20] We might say that Athenian politics—as sources like Plato, Aristophanes, and Thucydides depict it—seems to have worked in considerable part as a process in which elites aimed to "manufacture consent" (to borrow a phrase from Lippmann) for their preferred policies.[21]

We must, again, be careful not to understate the differences. The Athenian assembly met regularly and was, at least in theory, open to all citizens (with the category of citizen of course being troublingly exclusive even when Athens was at its most radically democratic). Would-be elites thus confronted the power of the demos directly and frequently and without the intermediary of modern technology, no doubt a powerful tool for manufacturing consent. Still, the basic challenges facing both elites and ordinary citizens are familiar enough: elites, to continue as elites, had to find ways to convince or persuade or manipulate or dupe the demos, and ordinary citizens had to navigate the political world in considerable part by means of the claims made by elites.[22]

To the extent that those citizens most often took on the role of spectators in the assembly, it seems particularly possible that the comic theater, where they similarly sat as spectators, might help us to understand the basic challenge they faced. It is now possible to further refine the description of that challenge. The ordinary citizen of Athens, as an observer of the spectacle of elite political competition, was at once subject both to the rebellious democratic impulse to reject elite attempts at domination and to the democratic impulse toward effective collective action, which would almost inevitably involve elite influence in and through the institutions of (at least nominally) democratic politics. Thucydides, we might say, shows us a Pericles raised to great heights by the latter impulse (as in his speech at the outset of the war) and then brought to the point of groveling by the former impulse (as in his final speech in the *History*).[23] Aristophanes shows us matters from the point of view of the ordinary citizen and works, at the same time, to instill in citizens the kind of comic disposition they would need to navigate the challenges of democratic citizenship.

Whatever the promise of this ordinary-elite framing of democratic politics, though, we must bear in mind the challenge contemporary pluralism poses to it. Whether in Lippman or Aristophanes, thinking of the demos as a mass of ordinary citizen-spectators confronting a small elite risks collapsing the diversity of the contemporary demos into a false homogeneity and unity. One would like to think that the category of ordinary citizen is more capacious and open today than in ancient Athens. And yet there is no escaping the fact that ordinary is itself a political term of art, one subject to contestation—and so manipulation—through political argument.

Indeed, in the modern world the characterization of some sorts of citizens as ordinary marks a particular kind of populist appeal with exclusionary and oppressive potential. We thus at times hear of "ordinary" or "real" Americans who, presumably, are to be contrasted with everyone else.

This points toward the (at least) double meaning of ordinary. Ordinary can be the opposite of elite, the opposite of extraordinary. It can also be the equivalent of usual or normal and so the opposite of abnormal. As we will see in later chapters, I mean to respect this malleability—and danger—of the category of the ordinary citizen, something I think necessary to appreciating the complexity of Aristophanes. The comic disposition I aim to draw from Aristophanes in part works by complicating the very idea of the "ordinary" part of ordinary citizenship. Still, I aim to keep in mind throughout the tension between thinking about democracy as a politics of the ordinary citizen and the idea that, in the context of contemporary pluralism, no one is simply ordinary.

Democracy and the Disposition of Citizenship

In using the language of *disposition*, I have not deliberately set out to be Aristotelian, but Aristotle's use of *hexis*, or disposition, in his definition of virtue is suggestive: "The dispositions are the formed states of character in virtue of which we are well or ill disposed in respect of the emotions; for instance, we have a bad disposition in regard to anger if we are disposed to get angry too violently or not violently enough, a good disposition if we habitually feel a moderate amount of anger; and similarly in respect of the other emotions."[24] Where a proper ethical disposition for Aristotle involves a proper relationship to the emotions, I aim here to think about how ordinary citizens experience and respond to the conflicting impulses of democracy. To put the matter in Aristotelian terms, then, we might think of ordinary citizenship as involving a disposition toward the two impulses of democracy.

We might, moreover, think of better and worse dispositions in this regard. In the passage above, Aristotle points to the possibility of being well or ill disposed toward anger. In a broadly analogous way, I read Aristophanes as exploring the possibility that citizens may be well or ill disposed toward democracy's two impulses. Indeed, though I read his comedies as suggesting the need for a proper comic disposition in ordinary citizens, I do not mean to suggest that Aristophanes saw either his protagonists or his fellow Athenians as regularly achieving that proper disposition. His heroes and heroines at times seem disposed to rebel too quickly or in the wrong way. At other times, they seem disposed to seek order or form or collective action too quickly or in the wrong way. For Aristotle, virtue rests on a difficult to achieve ethical disposition to seek the mean between extremes.

For Aristophanes, on my reading, ordinary citizenship rests on a difficult to achieve comic disposition that holds democracy's impulses in continual tension, rather than simply follows one or the other.

We might well worry about the contemporary resonance of a quasi-Aristotelian notion of *hexis*. Here, in response, we can note a similar turn in certain threads of contemporary political thought. Steven White, for example, locates his own argument for an "ethos" of late modern citizenship in the context of an "ethical turn" in political theory that he traces to the late work of Michel Foucault and finds as well in the more recent work of Wendy Brown and William Connolly. White's ethos rests on his notion of weak ontology understood as a deep commitment to "certain figures of self, other, and the beyond human" that does not amount to "absoluteness of conviction."[25] Manifested in a particular sort of moral attentiveness and self-restraint, this ethos, White thinks, can help orient citizens to democracy's contemporary "predicament," in part by engaging with a type of citizenship that moves beyond a focus on rights, duties, membership, and participation.[26]

I return in the conclusion to consider the relationship of the comic disposition I draw from Aristophanes to White's notion of an ethos of citizenship. The potential links suggested by the related language of ethos and disposition are borne out by affinities between the substance of White's ethos and, in particular, the comic voyaging and comic recognition I find in Aristophanes. Still, there are important potential complications to these sorts of connections. White thus argues that ancient Athenian democracy was premised on a notion of the collective demos that simply does not apply to today's western societies, with their pluralism and their (relative to Athens) widespread affluence. Returning to White's concerns in this book's final pages and engaging with these differences will allow me to revisit and sharpen questions about whether the same sort of democratic possibilities present in Athens are available to us today, and vice versa.

Aristophanes's Politics and the Possibilities of Comedy

Over the course of a long career, Aristophanes wrote some forty plays, eleven of which survive today. The earliest of these eleven, *Acharnians*, was produced in 425 BCE; the last, *Wealth*, in 388 BCE. This time span includes nearly all of the thirty-year-long Peloponnesian War (431–404 BCE), as well as the oligarchic revolutions near the war's end. The war and the politics attending and surrounding it thus provide the context for many of the surviving comedies; the lingering aftermath of hostilities and the restoration of democracy in Athens sets the scene for Aristophanes's final plays. All the plays were staged at one of two annual Athenian civic festivals, the City Dionysia and the Lenaia, where they competed with other comedies to win first prize. As with tragedy, the cost of staging comedies was underwritten by the city or, more precisely, by the wealthy individual Athenians (*choregoi*) charged by the city with funding the comic choruses.[27]

With some important exceptions,[28] my fellow political theorists in general have paid relatively little attention to Aristophanes's surviving plays, except for *Clouds* and, to some extent, *Lysistrata*. Classicists, in contrast, have long debated the political implications of Aristophanes's work. A first question has been whether we can find any serious political comment at all in Aristophanes. He was, after all, a comic poet engaged in contests with other comic poets, seeking the rewards that came with winning first prize. The topical and satirical political references spread through his work were surely aimed in large part simply at making the audience laugh. The poet will thus have faced pressures to conform not only to prevailing political sentiment but also to the festive demands of the occasion. Indeed, early in his career, Aristophanes was brought before the Athenian lawcourts by the demagogue Cleon, and charged with disparaging the city before an audience that included foreigners. Aristophanes won the case, but the prosecution itself perhaps suggests the potentially "domesticating" influence exerted on comedy by its civic context.[29] In this vein, Malcolm Heath argues that "the plays are so nicely attuned to the prejudices and expectations of Aristophanes' audience" that we ought to hesitate reading them as expressing Aristophanes's considered political views.[30]

This sort of argument should no doubt prompt us to remain alive to how Aristophanic comedy worked in its particular context. As Heath suggests, we should perhaps be particularly wary of claiming that we can locate Aristophanes's own particular political positions and intentions in the plays. Still, the question of comedy's domestication by the city is complex. What might it mean for Aristophanic comedy to be "tuned to the expectations and prejudices" not just of Athens, but of *democratic* Athens? Drawing on the understanding of Athenian democracy and the attendant challenge of democratic citizenship sketched in the previous section, we might first expect comedy in Athens to be attuned to the tension between ordinary citizens and elites (including self-proclaimed elites). We find precisely this in the comedies, from Aristophanes's engagement with the demagogues in his earliest plays to his imagining women challenging the elite status and exclusive power of male citizens in *Assemblywomen*. Aristophanes, not surprisingly given the context, thus on some level sees Athens as divided between the political elite and everyone else. A passage from *Assemblywomen* suggests that he sees his audience as similarly divided: "I have a small suggestion for the judges: if you're intelligent [*sophois*], remember the intelligent [*sopōn*] parts and vote for me; if you've got a sense of humor [*gelōsi*], remember the jokes [*gelōn*] and vote for me. Yes, it's virtually all of you that I'm asking to vote for me" (1155–56).[31]

Aristophanes is of course having a bit of fun with his audience and particularly with the judges seated in the front row, who will determine whether *Assemblywomen* wins first prize. He mocks what we today might think of as the distinction between highbrow and lowbrow humor while at the same time suggesting that the Athenians recognize something like such a distinction among themselves. We might say that this sort of passage affirms that Aristophanic comedy is in some basic sense democratic or that it is at least open to democratic possibilities. In part this means that it aims to appeal to the sense of humor of anyone and everyone, but it also means that comedy reflects and reflects upon the political and cultural division between ordinary and elite citizens.

This is not to say that we should expect Aristophanic comedy simply to take the side of either ordinary citizens or elites. Indeed, we might expect a kind of comedy that is in tune with democracy to itself be subject to what I have called the twin impulses of democracy and to the tension between those impulses. To the extent that Aristophanic comedy plays upon the prejudices and expectations of its audience, we might, in other words, expect to find in it reflections of both the democratic impulse toward responsible collective action and the democratic impulse toward rebellion. In a sense, the impulse toward collective action is deeply implicated in the city's role in funding comedy. And, as we will see, Aristophanes at times (most often in the *parabasis* of various plays, when the chorus leader claims to speak for the poet himself) proclaims himself a defender and teacher of the city as a whole. Such claims, though, coexist with harsh criticism of current civic and political practices, with Aristophanes, we might say, casting himself and his comedies as rebellious. Beyond reflecting the ordinary-elite division, Aristophanic comedy, on my reading, is thus also democratic in the character of its stance toward the city itself, simultaneously drawn toward the city and its collective life and rebelling against it.

The complexity and tension that consequently flow through and between the plays complicate traditional readings of Aristophanes's politics. Aristophanes has often been seen as a conservative, aristocratic Athenian, distrusting radical democracy and nostalgic for the days before its advent.[32] In its simplest form, the idea that Aristophanes means to criticize rather than to celebrate Athenian democracy draws support from the complicated results of his protagonists' schemes. As we will see in later chapters, though his heroes and heroines often seem to achieve their goals, their victories also often come with disturbing consequences. In *Acharnians*, Diceapolis manages to conclude his own private peace treaty with the Spartans, but in doing so he must withdraw from Athenian civic life; and in the bargain he comes to seem rather selfish and uncivil. Similarly, though Praxagora and the women of Athens manage to take control of

Athenian politics in *Assemblywomen*, the play raises serious questions about whether the reforms they then initiate can possibly succeed. In these and other plays, though Aristophanes seems to celebrate the possibility of ordinary citizens doing extraordinary things, he also seems to undermine the possibility that their actions will lead to lasting, positive change.

At its simplest, this line of thinking would find Aristophanes subtly mocking the ambitions of ordinary citizens and so, ultimately, ridiculing their potential as democratic political actors. The idea that Aristophanic comedy works against—or at least aims to control or correct—Athenian democracy, though, has been explored in more complex and interesting ways. David Konstan, for example, presents Aristophanes as trying—more or less unconsciously—to bridge the fissures or gaps that emerge from contradictions or tensions within Athenian ideology. This bridging works not to advance or protect democracy but to temper it with a dose of Athenian conservatism. Aristophanes's *Wasps*, for example, portrays the struggle of a young man to contain his father's addiction to serving on Athenian juries. Konstan reads the play as working "to mask the popular character of the court system and valorize the upper class ideals of withdrawal and privatism."[33] Though it places at its core an ordinary Athenian struggling against an attempt to deny him access to a core activity of democratic citizenship, *Wasps* on Konstan's reading thus ultimately works to blunt such rebellious impulses. It does this not so much by providing a safety valve for popular discontent as by resolving or soothing or downplaying ideological tension in Athens. It thus aims to tame ordinary citizens and so to render democracy at least marginally less dangerous.[34]

In contrast to such arguments casting Aristophanes as more or less hostile to democracy, one might read the plays as celebrating the possibility of ordinary people upsetting existing social and political hierarchies. Much recent work emphasizes the importance of fantasy—understood broadly as the overcoming of the limits of everyday reality—in Aristophanes's plays.[35] Among other things, after all, Aristophanes imagines human beings riding dung beetles to the gods in search of an end to the Greeks' warlike ways (in *Peace*) and establishing a city in the sky to escape the litigiousness of the Athenians (in *Birds*). Such fantastic plots can be read as more evidence of the poet's basically conservative politics. Fantasy or fairy tale after all, may itself distract attention or soothe discontent or simply provide a momentary catharsis, as frustration and anger are vented without that venting leading to any sort of change. But there is also the possibility of taking the fantastic seriously. Though he accepts the idea that Aristophanes's earlier work reflects a traditional aristocratic politics, Alan Sommerstein, for example, sees in the imagined end to poverty brought about by the hero of *Wealth* a sincere Aristophanic interest in the possibility of radical change by democratic means.[36]

One need not accept the idea that Aristophanes favors such radical change to view him as on balance a friend of democracy. Ober, for example, includes a reading of Aristophanes's *Assemblywomen* in his account of intellectual dissent in democratic Athens. Ober argues that Aristophanes presents to the Athenians exaggerated visions of their most closely held political beliefs. For example, Athenian ideology, as Ober calls it, asserts the equality of all. *Assemblywomen* then tests the Athenians' commitment to equality by imagining women taking power in the Assembly. Do the Athenians really see women as equal? Or is the idea of women having an equal or even greater part to play in fact simply nonsense for an Athenian audience? Likewise, Ober argues that Athenian democratic ideology rested on a belief in the ability of democratic assemblies to make wise decisions impacting the shared life of the citizenry. Again, Aristophanes tests this commitment in *Assemblywomen* by presenting to the Athenians an Athens in which the decisions of the democratic Assembly take aim at materialism and selfishness.[37] On the one hand, this is all comic playfulness. On the other hand, comedy here works simultaneously to remind the Athenians of their core beliefs and to raise for them difficult questions about the extent to which they can actually accept the implications of their beliefs. The power of the demos is affirmed, but the playwright also situates himself as a critic, or at least an educator, of the people—aiding democracy by ensuring that it thinks more carefully about what it does.

One of the merits of Ober's approach is that it complicates the question of whether Aristophanes was a democrat. Ober's notion of Aristophanes as an internal critic of democracy by and large avoids an artificial choice between simply praising democracy and hoping for its curtailment or at least taming. Along similar lines, I work here from the basic assumption that Aristophanes need not have been a full-throated democrat or admirer of ordinary citizens to have valuable insights into democracy. In the end, though, I am less interested in thinking about Aristophanes's critique of Athenian ideology than about how he portrays ordinary people navigating the tension that lies at the heart of democracy and democratic citizenship. My approach thus involves rejecting both the idea that Aristophanes simply celebrates the rebelliousness of his heroes and the idea that he ultimately insists simply upon the need to tame or control democracy for the good of the city. Instead, I read his comedies as recognizing both democracy's rebellious impulse and its impulse toward collective action.

My claim will ultimately be that, as it both embodies and portrays the tension between these impulses, Aristophanic comedy encourages spectators to grapple with that same tension. In part, that claim depends upon the idea that spectators (or, today, mostly readers) will somehow identify with the ordinary heroes and heroines onstage. Jeffrey Henderson captures well the potential appeal of such heroes and their heroic schemes to the ordinary Athenians seated in the theater:

> But there, onstage, is a rather likeable person. Not an actual person, and in fact not the sort of person who would be prominent at all: a farmer, a seller from the markets, the debt-ridden victim of a socialite wife and a social-climbing son, a juror, the target of too many lawsuits who has decided to try his luck elsewhere, a housewife. This person is in the same fix as most of us and it is pleasant to see someone like that in the spotlight for once.[38]

That it is "pleasant" to see such heroes and heroines suggests, rightly I think, that Aristophanes calls us to cheer on his protagonists as they struggle against elites and the structures of power they dominate. But that, again, is only part of the story. For just as the plays call us to identify with those protagonists, they also (as readings of Aristophanes as a conservative rightly emphasize) call spectators to stand at a critical distance from them. And so while our heroes and heroines are celebrated, they are also ridiculed; while their schemes speak to democratic fantasies of rebellion, they at the same time have troubling consequences that suggest the appeal of institutions and forms that preserve the possibility of less idiosyncratic action by the demos.

This complex portrayal of ordinary citizens and their schemes follows from what I take to be the basic disposition of Aristophanic comedy. Aristophanes stands always ready to satirize the powerful and the powerless, to present fantastic schemes of political, civic, and human change and rejuvenation, and then to puncture those fantasies with sometimes bitter irony. I read his comedy as simultaneously seeking to engage and nurture a similarly complex comic disposition in its audience. And I take this comic disposition—appreciative of satire, fantasy, and irony, open to possibilities, cognizant of limits—as akin to the kind of disposition needed for meeting the challenge of democratic citizenship as I have defined it here. In this sense, I work toward an understanding of Aristophanic comedy as neither conservative nor radical. Instead, I see Aristophanes's appeal to diverse senses of humor, his focus on ordinary citizens, and his sense of the conflicting demands those citizens face as indications of his deep concern with the possibilities and problems of democracy.

Plan of the Book

My arguments in this introduction and throughout this book emphasize the idea of tension. I find tension in and between democracy's basic impulses. I describe the challenge of ordinary citizenship as a matter of navigating while preserving this tension. Finally, I see Aristophanic comedy as resting upon a comic disposition that embraces tension, particularly the tension between fantasy and irony. Accordingly, I approach Aristophanes in a manner that tries to remain alive to tensions within and between his eleven surviving plays. Each of the following chapters considers two (or, in the case of chapter 2, three) plays. I have found this approach helpful in preserving the complexity of Aristophanes's comic art and in looking for the ways in which the juxtapositions I create might reveal more about the comic disposition of ordinary citizenship.

Each chapter further situates its argument against the backdrop of a contemporary political phenomenon or a contemporary controversy in political theory. In doing so, I have tried to avoid the danger of forcing Aristophanes into direct but false contemporary relevance. My aim, rather, is to bring Aristophanes's concerns into contact with our own and to explore both the continuities and discontinuities between them. My broad approach, then, is thematic. I do not claim to offer a comprehensive reading of any individual play nor, for that matter, of Aristophanes's surviving corpus as a whole. Nor do I here make any sort of chronological or developmental claims about Aristophanes's work (though his comedy quite obviously changed over time in various ways); indeed, though I end with Aristophanes's last surviving works, and though I tend to juxtapose earlier plays with other earlier plays and later plays with other later plays, my argument here does not follow the order of the plays' production. My aim, instead, has been to develop thematic threads that I think both central to Aristophanes's comic art and relevant to our ongoing attempt to understand the challenges of democracy and democratic citizenship.

My argument about the comic disposition of ordinary citizenship unfolds in three broad stages. The first involves working to understand how Aristophanic comedy engages with its audience and, in particular, to explore the sort of appeal it makes to ordinary citizens. My suggestion is that Aristophanes invites his spectators to engage in what I call a kind of *comic voyaging*. I next turn to the very idea of the ordinary citizen. Though this idea lies at the heart of my argument, I draw on Aristophanes's plays to complicate and problematize it. Finally, I turn to think about how the comic voyaging of ordinary citizens as spectators might lead to the kind of comic disposition appropriate to the challenge of democratic citizenship. I here develop an understanding of what I call *cleverness* and *comic recognition* as further manifestations of the comic disposition of ordinary citizenship.

Chapter 1 begins by reflecting on the contemporary popularity of *Lysistrata* and the relative contemporary obscurity of *Peace*. I use this as a way to begin to consider just how Aristophanic comedy works as a way of reflecting on politics. Drawing on the image of the hero of *Peace*, an ordinary

Athenian farmer named Trygaeus, flying to the gods on the back of a dung beetle and on Jacques Rancière's work on the emancipatory potential of art, I introduce the idea of comic voyaging. The idea of a comic voyage not only points to a way of understanding the political relevance of comic poetry but also begins to introduce complications into the very idea of the ordinary citizen.

Chapter 2 continues to explore the idea of the ordinary citizen by thinking about the relationship of Aristophanes's heroes to the main intellectual and cultural currents of fifth-century Athens. While in *Clouds* Aristophanes imagines an ordinary Athenian challenging cultural elites, in *Frogs* and *Women at the Thesmophoria*, he puts the god Dionysus and the tragic poet Euripides at center stage. I emphasize these choices of protagonists as a means of exploring the role Aristophanes sees for ordinary citizens in culture and the role of culture in saving the beleaguered, war-weary city. But I also use the juxtaposition of ordinary citizens, gods, poets, and philosopher-sophists as a way to continue to think more critically about the idea of the ordinary itself.

Chapters 3 and 4 turn to plays in which Aristophanes engages more directly with the dynamics of Athenian democratic politics. In chapter 3, I consider the portrayal of ordinary citizens as jurors in *Wasps* and the escape from the whirl of Athenian life—including the law courts—in *Birds*. As others have noted, *Wasps* centers the role of the (often indiscriminate) anger of the ordinary citizen in the courts and in Athenian political life more generally. In *Birds*, an ordinary Athenian founds a city in the sky that aims to transcend the turmoil of Athens, but in the end anger finds its way back into this utopia. I explore the ways in which the anger and rebelliousness of the ordinary citizen (sometimes called "populist rage" in our day and seen sometimes as a threat to democracy, sometimes as its very essence) relates to the nature of rule or *archē* in Aristophanes's comic Athens and in Cloudcuckooland, the city among the birds.

Chapter 4 considers a potential Aristophanic alternative to the anger ordinary citizens might feel toward elites who aim to rule them. Drawing on *Acharnians* and *Knights*, I consider the possibility that ordinary citizens might meet elites not with anger but with a particular kind of cleverness. In these plays, cleverness can refer to verbal dexterity on the part of political speakers. Aristophanes, though, also attributes to the theater audience a kind of cleverness that, were it brought to the political realm, might make ordinary citizens a more savvy and critical audience for political elites. But just as he opens the possibility of a democratic politics rejuvenated by a clever citizenry, he raises questions both about the likely side effects of such cleverness and about the role of elites in transforming ordinary citizens. I consider these questions of cleverness in the context of democracy's rebellious impulse and recent calls for agonal democracy.

Chapters 1 and 2 together introduce the idea of the ordinary citizen and open up the possibility of an emancipatory kind of voyaging. Chapters 3 and 4 more directly consider Aristophanes's complex presentation of the characteristics of ordinary citizens acting to challenge the existing political order. Chapter 5 works to bring these themes together through a consideration of *Assemblywomen* and *Wealth*. Written near the end of Aristophanes's artistic career and in the wake of the destruction wrought by the Peloponnesian War, these two plays imagine radical economic change in Athens. Chapter 5 considers the comic disposition with which Aristophanes's ordinary citizens approach the possibility of making social and economic justice present in human life. Working against the backdrop of contemporary debates about recognition and redistribution as goals of social theory and action, I here develop a notion of comic recognition that draws not only on *Assemblywomen* and *Wealth* but also on the complex portraits of ordinary citizens and their voyages developed in the preceding chapters. Finally, I turn in the conclusion to consider at more length how this notion of comic recognition and the comic disposition which it manifests might bear upon the challenge of democratic citizenship and the possibilities of democratic politics in Aristophanes's Athens and in our own day.

Chapter 1

PEACEFUL VOYAGES

PEACE AND LYSISTRATA

March 3, 2003, was a banner day for the contemporary popularity of Aristophanes. On that day, according to an organizer, participants in *The Lysistrata Project* staged "over 1,000 readings" of *Lysistrata* "in 59 countries and all 50 states," reaching "over 200,000 people."[1] Reflecting on the project in a later interview, organizer Kathryn Blume said that "in an ideal world the project would change the relevance of the voice of ordinary citizens and it would make war on Iraq impossible."[2] As a way of stopping the Iraq War, of course, the project failed. That failure no doubt reflects the difficulty of making the voices of ordinary citizens more relevant in contemporary politics, particularly in the political environment during the inexorable run-up to the invasion. But the *Lysistrata Project* seemed to aim as much at building a sense of efficacy as at effecting policy change. Here again is one of the organizers: "We told participants: 'we are just here to help. You tell this story as you think best. You create this world as you want it to be.'"[3] Whatever the prospect for stopping the war, the project on this understanding had the salutary goal of opening creative space for ordinary citizens to offer, if not their own story, then their own version of "this story."

Lysistrata is no doubt the most read and performed of Aristophanes's surviving plays. As the play opens, the title character calls the women of Greece to join in her two-part plan to end the Peloponnesian War. The younger women will deny sex to their husbands until peace is concluded. Meanwhile, the older women will seize the Athenian treasury on the Acropolis to cut off funding for the war. Much of the humor of the play comes as the success of the sex strike unfolds. A considerable amount of the conflict of the play, though, attends the seizure of the Acropolis. Unusually for an Aristophanic comedy, the chorus divides in two. One semichorus consists of the older women on the Acropolis, the other of older men who try to break their occupation by setting fire to the gates. In the course of the conflict of the choruses, we also witness an *agon* between Lysistrata herself and an Athenian magistrate over the causes of the war and women's role in ending it. By play's end, both aspects of Lysistrata's plot succeed, Sparta and Athens negotiate peace, and the two semichoruses reconcile and celebrate. It is, then, not particularly surprising that antiwar activists inclined to turn to ancient comedy (though that may be a relatively small group) would seize upon *Lysistrata.*

Still, a basic tension seems to attend the stated goal of the *Lysistrata Project*—or, rather the *two* stated goals of the project: first, to stop the Iraq War; and, second, "to change the relevance of the voice of ordinary citizens." Put simply, the coupling of these two goals rests upon the assumption that ordinary citizens wanted in 2003 to stop the Iraq War. Given that the war initially enjoyed a certain level of public support, that assumption is at the very least open to serious question. An analogous potential tension emerges from the instruction to "tell this story as you think best." Given the "ideal world" in which the Iraq War might become "impossible," the invitation to "tell this story" rests upon both an assessment of the political message of the play and an expectation about the performances that will occur. The organizers, that is, took the play as telling an antiwar story. They expected the performances to "tell this story," to project the antiwar message at the core of the play. What, then, of the second part of the instruction, "as you think best"? This gesture of openness was clearly reflected in the wide variety of performances, from full theatrical productions with celebrity casts to children's storytelling to radio documentaries.[4] But what of performances that differed not in artistic style but in political import? Given the complexity of Aristophanes's comic spirit, it is not impossible to read *Lysistrata* ironically and so, if not as pro-war, then at least as calling into question the possibility or desirability of ending (or preventing) war by the means the play envisions.[5] Could *The Lysistrata Project*'s instruction to "tell this story" bear with an ordinary citizen who "thought it best" to use *Lysistrata* to tell something other than a straightforward *antiwar* story?[6]

This sort of question can best be approached, I argue here, by juxtaposing *Lysistrata* with Aristophanes's *Peace*. *Peace* revolves around a fantastic attempt by a hero named Trygaeus to bring an end to the Peloponnesian War. By all signs an ordinary Athenian citizen, Trygaeus has hit upon an extraordinary idea. He has domesticated a giant dung beetle. Parodying Euripides's *Bellerophon*,[7] he calls the beetle "my little Pegasus" (76), and he rides it to the realm of the gods. He finds that all the gods have left save Hermes, who tells Trygaeus that War has entombed Peace (here represented by a giant statue) in a cave. The hero frees Peace with the help of the chorus, argues with Hermes about the origins of the war, then returns to Athens. There ensue typical Aristophanic complications, with various Athenians complaining that the return of peace will destroy their livelihoods, but the play ends with an equally typical Aristophanic celebration, attended by Peace's servants Cornucopia and Holiday.

In this chapter I consider what we can learn from the juxtaposition of *Lysistrata* and *Peace* about the relationships among ordinary citizens as Aristophanic characters, ordinary citizens as spectators of comedy, and

ordinary citizens as political actors. More broadly put, I here offer a preliminary account of how Aristophanic comedy works politically. I argue that
we ought not to read Aristophanes as offering a particular political teaching that his spectators might take to heart and act upon. Instead, against
the backdrop of Jacques Rancière's understanding of the emancipatory
potential of art and with Trygaeus' fantastic voyage to the gods in mind, I
suggest that Aristophanic comedy encourages spectators to engage in what
I call comic voyaging. In the language of the organizers of the *Lysistrata
Project*, rather than offering a particular "story" to be told and believed and
retold, the plays invite spectators to embark on uncertain voyages in search
of their own stories about war and peace, about democracy and demagoguery, and about what it means to be ordinary. Comic voyaging, from this
point of view, is more than a way of understanding the political work of
Aristophanes's comic art. It also appears as a manifestation of the comic
disposition of ordinary citizenship that might meet the challenge democracy poses.

Aristophanes's Plea for Peace

In her reading of *Lysistrata*, Martha Nussbaum distinguishes between
readings of Aristophanes that have him offering "serious specific advice
in comic form" and those that locate his serious teaching at "a more general level than that of specific policy-prescriptions."[8] At least on their surface, *Lysistrata* and *Peace* offer the same basic advice or "specific policy
prescription" to the Athenians: make peace with the Spartans. They do so
in rather different political contexts. *Peace* was produced in 421 BCE. The
negotiations that would lead to the Peace of Nicias were already underway, following the death of the Athenian demagogue Cleon and the Spartan general Brasidas at the battle of Amphipolis in 422 BCE.[9] *Lysistrata*,
by contrast, was produced in 411 BCE, with the Spartan army in Attica
and with the Athenians still trying to recover from the disaster met by
their expedition to Sicily two years before. Coupled with the imagining of
peace in *Acharnians*, produced near the outset of the Peloponnesian War,
Lysistrata and *Peace* suggest the constancy of this aspect of Aristophanes's
"serious specific advice" to Athens, even as the strategic and tactical context of the war changed.

What is more, *Lysistrata* and *Peace* make the case against—or tell a story
about—war in basically similar ways. Both plays suggest a link between war
and a kind of madness (*mania*) among the Athenians. That link is drawn
most explicitly by the women's semichorus in *Lysistrata*. After the women
have seized the Athenian treasury and barricaded themselves on the
Acropolis, the men's semichorus threatens to burn the gates and so, too,

the women themselves. In response to this threat, the women's semichorus proclaims, "Goddess, may I never see these women aflame, but rather
see them rescue from war and madness [*maniôn*] Greece and their fellow
countrymen" (343–44). Later, Lysistrata tells the Athenian magistrate with
whom she tangles that she and her coconspirators will one day be hailed by
all Greece "if to begin with we can stop people from going to the market
fully armed and acting crazy [*mainomenous*]" (555–56). These suggestions
that madness attends war provide some context for the claim made at the
outset of *Peace* by one of Trygaeus's slaves. "My master's mad [*maínetai*] in
a novel way," he says, "not the way you all are, but another, quite novel
way" (53–55). The slave here addresses the audience, which does not share
Trygaeus's mad desire to fly to the gods and find peace. The suggestion
seems to be that the Athenians are still caught up in the same sort of mania
that attends war, a mania which the (also manic, albeit in a different way)
hero has escaped.

We can further read the two plays as suggesting that the madness of war
is linked, unsurprisingly, to both money and politics. Though it is sometimes overshadowed by the sex strike, Lysistrata makes the seizure of the
treasury on the Acropolis central to her plan for peace. The older women
thus aim "to keep the money safe, and to keep [the men of Athens] from
using it to finance the war" (488). Likewise, the latter part of *Peace* makes
clear not only that money allows for war in this way but also that for many
Athenians, war means profit. Trygaeus is thus delighted when an arms
dealer appears and complains that peace has "destroyed my business and
my livelihood" (1212–13) a fate shared in the play by a helmet maker, a
spear maker, and an oracle monger.

As for politics, we find in *Peace* and *Lysistrata* a claim familiar from many
of Aristophanes's plays. Wily and manipulative elites have duped the Athenians into seemingly perpetual war. In *Peace*, Aristophanes has the god
Hermes first blame Pericles, who "blew up so great a war" (610) and then
the Athenian orators who "took to driving this goddess [Peace] away with
double-pronged bellowing" (635). The Athenian people were complicit in
both instances, since Pericles acted out of fear of the Athenians' "inherently mordant behavior" (607) while the orators found the demos "quite
happy to swallow whatever slanders anyone tossed its way" (644).[10] Similarly, Lysistrata says that "many a time [the Athenian women] would hear
in our homes about a bad decision [the men] had made on some great
issue of state" (512). And elsewhere she claims that "Pisander and the others who aimed to hold high office" looked "for opportunities to steal" and
so "were always fomenting some kind of commotion [*korkorugên*] (491–93).

That idea of war's "commotion"—an idea that appears in *Peace* as
well—will be significant later in this chapter. For now I simply note that
we can on one level draw from both *Peace* and *Lysistrata* a fairly straight-

forward sort of political advice. The Athenians have gone mad, and this madness stems from and is manifested through the dysfunction of Athenian democratic politics, understood as the interaction of dishonest and manipulative elites with an irresponsible and inconstant people. Athenian madness also appears in a willingness on the part of some to drain the city's finances while they profit from the war. Peace offers the only cure for these maladies. All this we might say works at what Nussbaum describes as the level of "serious specific advice." And, again, we can see from this sort of reading why *Lysistrata* seemed in 2003 to be an excellent vehicle for the expression of antiwar sentiment. Its story is, on this level, one in which the madness of war, fed by greed and elite demagoguery, meets its match in the sanity of a few brave dissidents. "This story" thus sounded all too familiar in the early 2000s.

But part of the appeal of *Lysistrata* involves, to borrow from Nussbaum, the sort of "reflection at a more general level" that its plot provokes. For help in thinking about the more general reflections of *Lysistrata*—and to prepare the way for the argument about *Peace* that I make in the following section—I turn to the work of Rancière. Drawing on his idea of the partition, or distribution, (*partage*) of the sensible, Rancière unfolds an understanding of the experience of art and drama as a kind of emancipatory voyage. Here I move from this idea of emancipatory voyaging to an Aristophanic notion of comic voyaging.

In *The Politics of Aesthetics*, Rancière describes the distribution of the sensible as "the system of self-evident facts of sense perception that simultaneously discloses the existence of something in common and the delimitations that define the respective parts and positions within it."[11] A particular distribution of the sensible thus defines or reveals the community by establishing that which is common and similarly defines or reveals the relationship of the community's component parts. It includes some and excludes others, casting those excluded as nonsensible, as unable to be heard or seen. Among those included as partaking in the "something in common," a distribution of the sensible establishes an order which is inevitably, or at least always has been, hierarchical.

This understanding of any particular distribution of the sensible as drawing the line between inclusion and exclusion and as rank ordering the included underlies Rancière's account of the relationship of philosophy to democracy. Particularly in *On the Shores of Politics* and *Disagreement*, Rancière foregrounds a particular reading of Plato's and Aristotle's treatments of democracy.[12] Rancière describes democracy as the emergence on the scene of "the part that has no part." Democratic politics, that is, involves those whose voices have been silenced claiming for themselves an equal share. Insofar as the excluded claim the mantle of democracy, they pose not as a part but, rather, as the demos or the whole of the people.[13]

From this point of view, Plato and Aristotle for Rancière offer two philosophical responses to democracy. In Rancière's (rather too literal) reading
of *The Republic*, Plato aims to silence the demos, to relegate it or return
it to the realm of those who do not speak.[14] Aristotle, by contrast, comes
especially in the *Politics* to practice what Rancière calls "democracy corrected—democracy governed by the judicious use of its own ungovernabil-
ity."[15] Here, rather than being silenced, the people are brought into the
political realm, where their supposed power is rendered visible but also
made safe insofar as it is hedged, directed, managed, limited.[16] Plato and
Aristotle, then, stand as paradigmatic instances of the tendency of philosophers, diagnosed in depth by Rancière in *The Philosopher and His Poor*, to
craft images of ordinary people that serve in one way or another to put and
keep them in their proper place—and to ensure the continued privilege of
philosophers, namely the privilege of thinking.[17]

Rancière does not discuss Aristophanes at any length. Drawing on Rancière's idea of the distribution of the sensible, though, we might sharpen
Nussbaum's distinction between "serious specific advice" and a "more general level" of reflection in Aristophanes, at least in the cases of *Lysistrata*
and *Peace*. Caution is in order here, of course. I mean to use Rancière to
suggest a particular way of thinking about how Aristophanic comedy works,
and I want to avoid forcing Aristophanes into Rancière's categories (or
those of any other contemporary theorist). Provisionally, though, we might
replace the distinction between "specific advice" and "general reflection"
with a distinction between working within a particular distribution of the
sensible and exploring challenges to a particular distribution of the sensible. Put most bluntly, we might understand the analysis of war as the result
of a kind of manic dysfunction of Athenian politics—the sort of analysis
we find in both *Lysistrata* and *Peace*—as working within the prevailing way
of describing the Athenian political community and ordering its parts.
And we might think about *Lysistrata* as quite obviously going beyond this
to explore challenges to the prevailing Athenian distribution of the sensible. *Lysistrata*, that is, directs our attention to the ways in which some are
counted as part of the Athenian community while others are, to borrow
from Rancière's description of Plato's treatment of the demos, "doomed to
the night of silence," rendered insensible or, more precisely, inaudible to
proper Athenians.[18]

The theme of silence in fact stands out in Lysistrata's agon with the
Athenian magistrate. We have seen that Lysistrata indicts Athenian men
for their poor decision making. Significantly, the Athenian women have
witnessed this decision making *silently*: "Before now, and for quite some
time, we maintained our decorum and suffered in silence whatever you
men did, because you wouldn't let us make a sound" (507–8). The women
of Greece will put things "back on the right track" if the men are "ready

to listen in your turn . . . and to shut up as we had to" (526–28). From this point of view, the sex strike is not first and foremost about getting the men to end the war. It is, rather, about getting men to listen to women or, perhaps more accurately, to *hear* women in the first place. The refusal to have sex is, in this sense, a countertactic, a way to neutralize the force with which men have imposed silence on women. "If you hadn't shut up," the magistrate tells Lysistrata, "you'd have gotten a beating," and Lysistrata replies, "well, that's why I did shut up" (516–17). The sex strike itself is not for Lysistrata a matter of force, but of persuasion. She assures her Spartan counterpart that "we'll handle the persuasion [*peisomen*] on our side" and has the women swear an oath to "Mistress Persuasion [*Peithoi*]" (203).

We might be led by this emphasis on persuasion to understate the radical nature of Lysistrata's plan. Persuasion, after all, surely sits at the center of the dominant Athenian way of understanding and practicing politics. But Lysistrata means both to introduce a new means of persuasion and to make heard new actors in the play of persuasion. Her plan is not simply to meet force with force nor only to marshal novel persuasive arguments. She aims to alter who and what counts as sensible in Athens, to change the relationship of Athens to what it considers exterior to it.[19] In Rancière's terms, she suggests a new distribution of the sensible in which, among other things, women are heard rather than silenced and in which the body and its desires and demands occupy a place of prominence instead of being denied. Consider along these lines the words of the oracle she produces to rally the women when their patience for the plot flags: "high-thundering Zeus shall reverse what's up and what's down" (770). There is a sexual double entendre here ("You mean *we'll* be lying on top?" one of the women asks archly). But there is also an indication that the prevailing order of things in Athens will be overturned as women, literally, speak for themselves.

No wonder, then, the reaction of the magistrate: "it's shocking, you know, that they're lecturing the citizens—mere women!" (626). Lysistrata means precisely to challenge this distinction between citizens and "mere women." No wonder, too, the ongoing appeal of *Lysistrata*, particularly in the context of the march to a deeply controversial war and especially for a project determined "to change the relevance of the voice of ordinary citizens." *Lysistrata* remains relevant, from this perspective, not so much because of the sex strike, but because of the way in which the sex strike and the seizure of the Acropolis together bring about a radical change in who counts and who can be heard.

By contrast, *Peace* appears at first glance to offer no such challenge to "the distribution of the sensible" in Athenian politics or our own. In 421 BCE, with peace at hand, the play simply flowed with the prevailing political sentiment, as Dover suggests in comparing the hero of *Peace* with

Diceapolis in *Acharnians*: "Trygaeus is not the mouthpiece of a far-sighted minority lamenting the continuation of an apparently unending war, but a man who performs on a level of comic fantasy a task to which the Athenian people had already addressed itself on the mundane level of negotiations."[20] In place of *Lysistrata's* radical repositioning of the previously excluded, *Peace* offers the ridiculous idea of flying on a dung beetle to complain to the gods. Again, though, I mean to find something more inspiring in this sort of comic voyage.

A Ride on the Back of a Dung Beetle

After he has returned to earth with Peace, Trygaeus declares that his voyage to the gods has been a (successful) quest for a sort of liberation, saying to the chorus,

> You do owe me a lot,
> Trygaeus of Athmonum,
> For freeing (*apallaxas*) the commons (*dēmotēn*)
> And the country folk (*geôrkikon leôn*).
>   (917–21)

He goes on to say here that he has freed his fellow Athenians "from terrible hardships." But he also claims a more direct political impact for his voyage, since he has "put a stop to Hyperbolus." Earlier in the play, Hermes has derided this same demagogue—whom Thucydides describes as "a lout and a total disgrace to the city"[21]—as a "sleazy champion" for the Athenians to choose (684). To this charge Trygaeus had responded with a play on Hyperbolus's supposed occupation of lamp maker. Sleazy though he may be, the Athenians will "become better deliberators" under Hyperbolus's influence because "now we'll be planning everything by lamplight" (691–92). If we take this as anything other than an opportunistic joke, then we might say that Trygaeus's trip to the gods and back has freed the Athenians not only from terrible hardships but also from their dependence on the sleazy Hyperbolus for illumination. Following along these lines, we might also think that his liberation of the Athenians has something to do with the madness with which they have been afflicted, which, as we saw in the last section, has something to do with the dysfunctional relationship between ordinary citizens and elites. Part of freeing the Athenians from the "terrible hardships" of the war, then, is freeing them from themselves.

All this, of course, is to find in *Peace* a political argument that goes beyond advocating peace to suggest the need for a transformation of Athenian politics and, indeed, of the Athenians themselves. On this score,

Trygaeus's voyage on the dung beetle carries the promise of emancipation because it carries a particular political message for the audience to absorb. Again, though, I want to think about another possible political effect of *Peace*. Is it possible that *Peace*, like *Lysistrata*, moves beyond the "serious specific advice" that both plays offer (i.e., ignore the demagogues and make peace) to a level of more "general reflection"? Trygaeus does in an obvious, ludicrous way go beyond the confines of common Athenian understandings of political actors and action. After all, he flies a dung beetle to the gods. Might something about this trip "free" the Athenians or at least those in the theater in a way that, like the recounting of bodies in *Lysistrata*, goes beyond the play's advocating peace? To think more about the sort of freedom Trygaeus brings to Athens, or at least to the comic theater, I first turn again to Rancière and the notion of emancipation he develops.

In *The Ignorant Schoolmaster*, Rancière contrasts a truly emancipatory type of education with what he describes as the "explicatory" pedagogy of the prototypical "Old Master." In *The Emancipated Spectator*, he applies the same distinction to the theater. An understanding of education or art as explication concerns itself with closing the imagined distance between knowledgeable teacher and ignorant pupil or, in the theater, between artist and spectator. Explication claims to close this distance by transmitting the knowledge of teacher or artist to pupil or spectator. In the traditional schoolroom or theater, though, we can see this distance as given by the dominant distribution of the sensible, which is to say the distribution offered by the teacher or artist. This distance, Rancière writes in *The Emancipated Spectator*, "is based on the privilege the schoolmaster grants to himself—the knowledge of the 'right' distance and ways to abolish it."[22] In reality the Old Master of education or art never allows the closing of the distance, never allows pupil or spectator to achieve equality. Rather, "at each stage the abyss of ignorance is dug again; the professor fills it in before digging another."[23] Instead of emancipating, explicatory education or art, in Rancière's formulation, produces only "stultification."

In both *The Emancipated Spectator* and *The Ignorant Schoolmaster*, Rancière's response is to reject the very idea of closing the distance between performer and spectator or master and student. "Distance," he writes, "is not an evil that should be abolished," but "the normal condition of any communication." The performance or spectacle in the theater maintains the distance that is the "condition" for communication between performer and spectator as equals. It thus plays the same role as the book *Télémaque* played in Rancière's account of the French schoolmaster Jacotot's "teaching" his Flemish-speaking students to read French: "The materiality of the book keeps two minds at an equal distance, whereas explication is the annihilation of one mind by another."[24] In place of performance or text as a conduit for the transmission of the master's or performer's "knowledge," the performance or text creates the gap whereby two intelligences might meet. In that gap, the two discover or enact their equality as they each search for meaning or understanding or knowledge or feeling or action (all terms Rancière uses in writing of the emancipatory potential of texts and performances). Performances or texts thus "put to test" what Rancière calls "the capacity which makes anybody equal to everybody," a capacity that "works through unpredictable and irreducible distances" and through "an unpredictable and irreducible play of associations and dissociations."[25]

Alongside the way in which the distances inscribed in particular distributions of the sensible impose hierarchy, distance in this alternative sense—the irreducible distance that performances or texts create and maintain—thus has emancipatory potential. The traversing of "unpredictable and irreducible distances" and the "associating and disassociating" that occurs when performer and spectator or master and student face one another across such distances Rancière says "could be the principle of an 'emancipation of the spectator.'" And these metaphors of traversing distances and associating and disassociating point toward another metaphor Rancière offers for emancipation, that of the *voyage*. This idea of emancipation as the voyage of an intelligence equal to all other intelligences, an unpredictable voyage across an unknown distance with an unknown destination, also suggests the context for Rancière's description of Platonism as "anti-maritime" and of politics as involving sailing on uncertain seas. Philosophy's "claims in respect to politics," Rancière writes in *On the Shores of Politics*, "can be readily summed up as an imperative: to shield politics from the perils that are immanent to it, it has to be hauled on to dry land, set down on terra firma."[26] Like (Rancière's) Plato, the Old Master and certain students of the theater seek a transmission of learning that might find firm ground; in doing so, they mean to close the very distance upon which the voyaging of emancipation depends.

Rancière's readings of Plato are polemical and at times overdrawn,[27] but the distinction he draws between the pedagogy of the Old Master and the possibilities of emancipation are suggestive. In a sense, the readings of *Lysistrata* and *Peace* that I have offered so far take the approach of the Old Master. That is, they find in the plays a teaching or teachings ready for presentation to the spectator. I have thus noted that both plays appear to counsel the advantages of peace and that both link continuing war to dysfunction in Athenian democratic politics. These are bold enough positions for the playwright to take (if they *are* his positions, about which more momentarily). But from Rancière's point of view, the offering of such advice is not really emancipatory. It amounts instead to an attempt by the master to close the distance with his pupils, an attempt to awaken them to the master's truth. This is true even of the more radical redistribution of the sensible in *Lysistrata*. If we take Aristophanes as commending that redistribution to the audience, this amounts to finding in the text a teaching that the poet aims at the spectators. And for Rancière this is not emancipation, but "stultification." We might here recall the injunction from the organizers of the *Lysistrata Project* to "tell *this* story." Emancipation for Rancière lies in the way a text allows for the telling of the pupil's story or, perhaps, a voyage in search of a story to tell.

Rancière, that is, locates the emancipatory possibilities of a text not in its teaching (what it advocates, rejects, suggests, explores) but in the way it mediates the distance or distances between author or performer and reader or spectator. Aristophanic comedy in its own way brings to the fore an interlocking set of distances between spectators, characters, and the playwright (with the latter doubled by the parabasis).[28] All of the surviving plays work with these distances. Sometimes, they do so by exaggerating the gap between Aristophanes and Athens or between a protagonist and the spectators. Sometimes, by contrast, the plays rather paradoxically point out these distances by ignoring them, particularly by puncturing the (admittedly always thin) pretense of dramatic illusion. *Peace* is, on this score, no exception. Take, for example, a scene from the play's opening. As in other plays, a minor character—one of Trygaeus's slaves—turns to the spectators early on to offer a bit of exposition. "I'm going to explain the plot to the children, to the teenagers, to the high and mighty gentlemen, and above all to these supermen here," he says (50–51). And so he does. This line reflects the complex way in which Aristophanes has his characters address the audience: part mockery, part rank flattery (especially of the "supermen," the judges seated in the front row). Such things at once confirm and yet playfully close the distance between audience and playwright. Again, this is familiar stuff from a variety of Aristophanic comedies.

Peace stands out, though, in the extent to which it not only has the actors address the audience but also makes the spectators part of the action of the play itself. Trygaeus, for example, suggests that the spectators are in effect his collaborators, declaring that he is "performing these labors," that is, flying to the gods, for their sake and begging them not to distract the dung beetle during the voyage with their own excretory functions (93–101). Similarly, once he has brought Peace and her attendants back to Athens, he searches the audience itself for a proper "guardian" for Holiday, who is to be presented to the Athenian *boulē* (877–905). Alongside the continuing mix of barbs and flattery thrown at the spectators, all this has the effect of emphasizing that the audience—whose members might be expected to some extent to identify with the hero—is itself part of the show. Put differently, Aristophanes works throughout *Peace* to decrease the distances between himself, his characters, and the spectators and, more generally, between the comic portrayal of Athenian democracy and the Athenian demos gathered as theater audience.

All of which throws into sharper relief the ways in which *Peace* reasserts or reaffirms that complex set of distances. Consider on this score the way the play works with the distance between Trygaeus himself and the Athenians in general or, more particularly, the spectators as Athenians. On the one hand, the hero of *Peace*, like so many Aristophanic heroes, is presented as a typical Athenian. And yet as he tells us of the play's plot, Trygaeus's slave suggests that his master is different: "My master's mad," he says, still addressing the spectators directly, "not in the way you all are, but in another, quite novel way" (52–54). His madness has to do not simply with his wild scheme to domesticate a dung beetle but with the basic belief that fuels that scheme: "All day long he gazes at the sky with his mouth open like this, railing at Zeus. 'Zeus,' he says, 'what on earth do you plan to do? Lay down your broom; don't sweep Greece away!'" (57–60). Trygaeus's madness, then, lies not so much in thinking he can bring peace by flying to the gods as in his blaming the gods for the war in the first place. Though he appears at first as an ordinary Athenian, and though he claims the spectators as coconspirators, the hero stands apart from them in his peculiar form of madness.

This is comedy, and so we shouldn't really take these diagnoses of the madness of Trygaeus or the Athenians at face value. Indeed, as Trygaeus's voyage unfolds, he gets conflicting signals about whether he is in fact mad about the origins of the war. On the one hand, he does discover that the gods have, as he thought, had a hand in visiting war upon the Greeks. Hermes tells him that the gods "grew angry with the Greeks. That's why they've ensconced War here, where they used to live, turning you over to him to treat exactly as he pleases, while they themselves have set up house as far above it all as they could get; that way they won't see any more of your fighting or hear any more of your prayers" (204–9). On the other hand, Hermes makes clear that, though the gods have allowed War to lock Peace away in a cave, the *origins* of the war are to be found in the actions of the Greeks themselves. When Trygaeus asks why the gods are so angry, Hermes says simply "because you all kept choosing war, though they often tried to arrange a truce" (211–12). Later he offers a lengthy explanation of how Peace first "disappeared" (604), focusing upon political elites who "took to driving this goddess away with double-pronged bellowing" (635) but who, from Pericles on, did so in large part because of their fear of the Athenian demos, "dreading your inherently mordant behavior" (608). As we have already seen, Aristophanes often makes these sorts of claims about Athenian democratic politics, about the unhealthy interaction of ambitious elites with an irresponsible demos. Here in *Peace*, though, he juxtaposes this sort of explanation of Athens's plight with a claim that the gods have intervened to ensure that War keeps punishing all the Greeks. In the end we might say that Trygaeus is not entirely mad to blame Zeus, though he perhaps only sees part of the story before he meets Hermes.

The slave's exposition of course suggests that the audience of Athenians is mad, too: Trygaeus is not mad "in the way you are." Again, a gap or distance opens between spectators and Trygaeus on this score. Neither the slave nor the rest of the play indicates exactly how we ought to understand this distance. But we do get telling hints of how Trygaeus differs—or at least sees himself differing—from his fellow citizens. He refers to himself as "Trygaeus of Athmonum, an accomplished vintage, no informer and no lover of litigation (*pragmatôn*)" (191). Aristophanes's plays often enough include jabs at Athenian litigiousness; the entire play *Wasps* revolves around one old man's love of serving as a juror. But the Greek here translated as litigation can suggest something beyond a fondness for legal proceedings—namely the general Athenian love of action, of engagement in the affairs of the world, of busy-ness.[29] In this context, consider the following passage, in which the chorus of *Peace* imagines how it will be transformed when the war ends:

> And you'll no longer find me a severe and colicky juror.
> Nor such a hard case as I was before;
> No, a gentle me you'll see
> And far more youthful
> With trouble (*pragmatôn*) off my back.
> For long enough we've been
> Destroying ourselves . . .
> (350–55)

The suggestion is, I think, that the hero of *Peace*, unlike his fellow Athenians, already feels the weighty consequences of the immersion in worldly affairs upon which the Athenians often pride themselves. Under the influence of Trygaeus and his fantastic voyage, the chorus has only just begun to see the relief that will come fully with peace and the quiet it brings. This helps to clarify the distance between Trygaeus and the ordinary people who constitute the chorus (and the theater audience). We might say that he seeks only peace and, at least initially, sees the war as a plague sent by the gods. The Athenians, on the other hand, tend to see war as an extension of their general engagement with the world; troublesome, yes, but inevitable for those who are active. War in this sense has little to do with the gods; it is the result of the action of humans.

Peace in this way offers up two visions of the ordinary citizen: one who seeks relief from the gods for the trials of war, another so immersed in the flow of events that he cannot see the broader picture.[30] We might well ask what Aristophanes thinks of the gap between these two perspectives, each of which is enmeshed in a different presentation of the ordinary Athenian. We have already seen enough to say that *Peace* endorses neither view without reservation. Aristophanes has Hermes both acknowledge the role of the gods and locate the origin of the war in the interaction of elite demagogues and the Athenian *demos*. Like nearly all of Aristophanes's comedies, *Peace* does dwell on the latter explanation.[31] And a passage in the parabasis suggests that Aristophanes aims especially at the role of political elites, while leaving ordinary citizens alone: "By getting rid of such poor, lowbrow buffoonery, he's [i.e., Aristophanes has] made our art great and built it up to towering size with impressive verses, conceptions, and uncommon jokes. He didn't satirize ordinary little men and women, but in the very spirit of Heracles he came to grips with the greatest monsters, braving terrible smells of raw leather and mudslinging threats" (745–49). From this passage, and others like it, it looks as if Aristophanes would have us focus once again on Cleon to understand the ongoing war (the "smells of raw leather" is a common Aristophanic reference to Cleon).

Yet we can hardly credit the description of the comedies here. Beyond being obviously rank flattery, the claim that Aristophanes does not satirize the "little" people is just not credible. While Aristophanes often likes in this manner to portray himself as a champion of the Athenians against elites like Cleon, his plays in fact regularly mock everyone. Even if spectators could be expected to identify with Trygaeus and his wild scheme, his portrayal is also surely meant to provoke laughter. *Peace* opens, after all, with Trygaeus's slaves calling him "mad" as they follow his orders to prepare snacks for his giant dung beetle. Put differently, Aristophanes's claim in the parabasis of *Peace* that he would never "satirize" ordinary citizens opens a distance between the Aristophanes whom the chorus leader claims to represent and the Aristophanes who wrote the rest of the play.

This distance in turn reinforces the sense that *Peace* does not settle on any particular account of the causes of the war (whether Cleon or ordinary Athenians or the gods). Together with the set of distances the play enacts between the hero Trygaeus, the chorus of ordinary citizens, and the audience of Athenians, this distance between two different accounts of where Aristophanes stands might be said to invite spectators to navigate all these distances without being directed to settle upon one or the other understanding of the war. The play invites us to tack back and forth between an understanding of the war that focuses upon the dynamics of Athenian politics and an understanding of the war that locates its causes beyond human action, in the anger of the gods. I mean here, that is, to suggest the ways in which *Peace* calls upon readers to engage in the kind of emancipatory voyaging that Rancière has in mind.

The lead character, of course, takes a voyage of his own, one that is fitting both to the spirit of Aristophanic comedy and to his own perspective on war and peace. Trygaeus believes the gods are to blame and so thinks that he must travel to find them as he seeks relief. And yet we should note that the dung beetle provides only a one-way ride. Trygaeus, having learned that both the gods and the Greeks had a hand in starting and then prolonging the war, must return to earth. And he must do so without his mount, which has fled to Zeus. He walks home, announcing upon his return that he has "sore legs" (827). A voyage on the back of a dung beetle takes one to the gods to learn what eludes humans; a trip on sore legs brings one back to the realm of human action.[32]

This idea of tacking back and forth between divine and human explanations of war and peace—between soaring in the clouds and wearing out one's feet here on the ground—points finally toward a way of reading another peculiarity of *Peace*: the changing nature of its chorus. Once Hermes tells Trygaeus of the entombment of Peace in a cave, the hero turns to the chorus for help in freeing her. At this point, the chorus is composed of Greeks, emphasizing what appears at first to be the play's general message of panhellenism. But, in fact, we learn the identity of the chorus in part because Trygaeus immediately begins to upbraid some of its members for not working hard enough to help pull Peace from her cave: "Well, isn't it awfully absurd that some of you are going all out, while others are pulling the opposite way? You're looking to get hacked, you Argives" (491–93)! And it is not just the Argives who are not fully engaged with the struggle to free peace; the Megarians and Athenians are singled out as well. Making little progress, Trygaeus calls out, "let us farmers take hold, all by ourselves" (508). Peace is finally freed, then, by a chorus that seems to have taken on the identity of Greek farmers, with the leader proclaiming that he is "ready to greet my vines" (557). Finally, after Trygaeus returns victorious to Athens, the chorus appears to be composed not of Greeks, but of Athenians, calling the hero "a man . . . who by braving many hardships has rescued our sacred city" (1034–36).[33] In this context, Trygaeus's sore feet suggest not just a return to earth, but a return to a more narrowly Athenian identity, too. He begins as a human trying to reach the gods, becomes one of many Greeks trying to free peace, and ends up as an Athenian liberating his home city from its own worst inclinations. We might see Peace as inviting spectators to explore their own identities in a similar way.

Comic Voyaging

As we saw at the beginning of the previous section, Trygaeus himself presents his voyage as an emancipatory one. The "terrible hardships" from which he says he has in particular freed the commoners and the country folk clearly points toward the war. But as I have tried to suggest, the kind of emancipatory voyaging which Trygaeus's flight enables is not simply about war or its causes. It is also about the nature of the ordinary human being. The spectators are invited, encouraged, prompted to consider themselves alternately as humans, as Greeks, and as Athenians (and even, as the chorus transforms into a group of farmers, particular sorts of Athenians). The play itself offers no final privileging of any of these potential self-understandings. Again, the visions that underlie the two main explanations for the war—Trygaeus's embrace of a broad humanity suffering the whims of the gods and, alternatively, an emphasis on the uniquely Athenian love of commotion—both are mocked in turn. We might think that the play then points to panhellenism as an intermediary term, a sense of identity that provides a resting place both from the general struggle of human life and the particularistic battles that differing civic characters in Greece engender. But the inability of the chorus-as-all-Greeks to rescue Peace seems to mock panhellenism as ineffectual. It is a typical Aristophanic outcome: everything is mocked, yet we end with a celebration of liberation. Again, the possibility toward which I here mean to point is that *Peace* aims to celebrate a kind of freedom from the stultification of political identities that normal political argument involves.

I have argued that *Lysistrata* explores what, borrowing from Rancière, we might call a kind of possible redistribution of the sensible, a different way of counting parts and of conceiving the whole. The play suggests both that the body matters more than Athenians may have thought and, too, that different bodies matter. But the reading of *Peace* I have offered should put us on guard against thinking that Aristophanes means to endorse a particular recounting of Athens and its parts. Might we instead read *Lysistrata* as encouraging the kind of unpredictable voyaging that we find in *Peace*?

The appearance of the language of flight in the play hints that this might indeed be the case. The action of the play opens with Lysistrata and her neighbor Calonice awaiting the arrival of the rest of the women. Lysistrata tells Calonice little of her plan, only that it will involve all the women of Greece and that it promises an end to war. Excited, Calonice joins Lysistrata in wondering why no one has yet arrived in response to Lysistrata's call:

> Calonice: My god, they should have taken wing and flown [*petomenas*] here ages ago!
> Lysistrata: Well, my friend, you'll find they're typically Athenian: everything they do, they do too late. (55–56)

This brief passage recalls to mind the contrast between Trygaeus's flight to the gods and his return to earth on sore feet. In this exchange between Calonice and Lysistrata, flight is associated with the panhellenic movement of women for peace. That movement here remains only a potentiality—but the expectation is that they would indeed fly to the opportunity to end the war. Lysistrata's suggestion is that what holds the Athenians in particular back is a typical tardiness. Though we would not normally associate slowness with Athenians, *Peace* again suggests a similar contrast between the fantastic possibilities of panhellenic flight and the slow, painful trodding that returns the hero to his Athenian life.

This same contrast appears later in *Lysistrata* in the differing movements of the men's and women's semichorus as they race to the Acropolis. Following Lysistrata's instructions, the older women of Athens have seized the treasury and barricaded themselves on the Acropolis. Their success in this task is marked by a loud hurrah heard offstage, but Calonice raises the possibility that "the men will soon launch a concerted counterattack" (246–47). A counterattack indeed follows, but "soon" is an overstatement. In keeping with their plan to set fire to the Acropolis and so force the women to give up their occupation, the men's chorus must first carry logs and torches up the hill. The dialogue emphasizes the difficulty of the task. The men's chorus leader speaks of a "heavy load of olivewood," and the chorus itself upon reaching "the steep stretch up to the Acropolis" wonders "how in the world are we going to haul these loads up there without a donkey" (288–89). The load "utterly crushing [their] shoulder[s]," the men thus arrive at the Acropolis after great struggle and strain. But before they can fully fire the gates, the women's chorus arrives at a run, calling to one another to "fly, fly [*petou, petou*]" (321) to the rescue of their fellow plotters.

The suggestion, again, is of a contrast between the soaring possibilities of a panhellenic movement for peace and the trudging, painful, obstructionist reality of Athenianism. That contrast is familiar in its broad outlines from *Peace*. In the previous section I argued that in *Peace* Aristophanes, rather than siding with either panhellenism or Athenianism, invites the spectator to "voyage" amongst identities. Something similar can be said of *Lysistrata*, where it is not clear that Aristophanes means us to identify simply and completely with the title character and her coconspirators. But *Lysistrata* also puts a different twist on the voyage. Panhellenic flight in *Peace* is associated with the loftiness of a human seeking the gods. It moves beyond particularized identities and their embodiment in particularized human beings. Put differently, panhellenism in *Peace* appears as a sharing of the human: it links humans as a group of beings standing in a (tortured) relationship to the gods. Panhellenic flight in *Lysistrata*, though, is linked not to an appeal to the gods but to the sex strike. It is forwarded as part of a strategy that includes making bodily desire central to political struggle and the struggle for peace.[34] Here panhellenism, in other words, puts at center stage the physicality of being human rather than the relationship of the human to that which is beyond human, something represented by the appearance of Reconciliation as a beautiful, naked young woman whose body is divided up by the combatants. In this way, the juxtaposition of *Lysistrata* and *Peace* puts into play a new sort of distance for spectators to navigate: that between different understandings of what it means to share in a common humanity.

Lysistrata also focuses our attention on a second unexpected twist. It is unusual, to put it mildly, to associate Athenian masculinity with slow trudging and the bearing of heavy weight. As *Peace* reminds us, the Athenian men (and *Peace* really only speaks of Athenian men) see themselves as always on the move, and they understand the war as being about commotion. Here we might recall the description of the Athenians offered by Thucydides's Corinthian envoys, as they warn the Spartans of the enemies they face: "The Athenians are addicted to innovation, and their designs are characterized by swiftness, alike in conception and execution. . . . They are daring beyond their judgment, and in danger they are sanguine. . . . There is promptitude on their side against procrastination on yours."[35] Thucydides has Pericles say something of the same sort in his Funeral Oration when he describes the typical Athenian as fit for the widest variety of actions. This is hardly a portrait of slowness or tardiness.

Aristophanes has his characters, though, draw a link between the Athenians and slowness not only in *Lysistrata* but in *Peace* as well. In the latter play, Trygaeus returns to Athens—and, with the chorus, becomes Athenian again instead of Greek or more generally a human representative to the gods—complains not of aching shoulders, but of "sore feet" from all his slow trekking. What to make of these portraits of slow, pained Athenian men? Perhaps the point is that the vision of active, vigorous, quick Athenians applies only in the narrow sphere of vision that sees Athens but not all of Greece or all of humanity. More generally, as I have tried to suggest here, the point is that Aristophanes's plays offer spectators the opportunity to free themselves from preconceptions about who they are, what Athens is, what it means to be Greek, and what it means to be human.

Peaceful Voyages and Democratic Citizenship

Peace and *Lysistrata* make clear Aristophanes's focus upon the plight of the ordinary citizen of mass democracy in the midst of seemingly endless war. As we have seen, these two plays on their surfaces seem to point to the comic poet's consistent commitment to peace and to his concern with the distorting role of manipulative or deceptive demagogues. His surviving plays thus frequently revolve around the possibility that ordinary citizens might in one way or another escape the perversities of Athenian politics, often enough in attempts to bring peace to the city. His similarly frequent claims that his work is of great benefit to the Athenians appear from this perspective to revolve around the idea that his comedies might help the Athenians save themselves from their politics before it is too late. From this point of view, it is not at all surprising that the antiwar activists of *The Lysistrata Project* should turn to Aristophanes. The retelling of "this story"— of *Lysistrata* in particular and, we might say, of Aristophanes's broader story of the link between dysfunctional democratic politics and war—indeed appears promising as a way to promote a message of peace. In the words quoted at the outset of this chapter, an appreciation of Aristophanic comedy might help to "change the relevance of the voice of ordinary citizens and it would make war . . . impossible."

It is important that the organizers of *The Lysistrata Project* qualified their statement of purpose, saying that that sort of outcome might occur "in an ideal world." They perhaps had in mind the limitations of any such project, given the numbing complexity of what political psychologists sometimes call the information environment. Today's ordinary citizens are bombarded with so much (mis)information from so many sources that, if they do not tune out altogether, they are still perhaps unlikely to be moved by the revival of a 2,500-year-old comedy. I have tried here to complicate the political possibilities of Aristophanic comedy in a different way, by suggesting the difficulty of saying that any Aristophanic comedy can be reduced to "this story," to a single story, to a particular, politically clear teaching from the comic poet. This is emphatically not to say that Aristophanes's comedies are "mere" entertainment. Rather, it is to claim, first, that whatever teaching emerges from the plays often works at a level other than that of "serious specific advice" and, second, that rather than offering a single teaching, the plays examined here work in the end to raise questions and generate uncertainty. I have, borrowing from Rancière, and with the image of Trygaeus on his dung beetle in mind, turned to the metaphor of voyaging. Rather than being vehicles for the political views of the poet, Aristophanes's plays encourage spectators to embark on fantastic voyages on unknown seas and toward unknown destinations—of course, laughing and enjoying themselves all along.

We might think of the willingness to embark on such voyages as a first step toward a comic disposition necessary for responding to the challenge of democratic citizenship. In the introduction, I described that challenge as demanding that citizens hold democracy's often conflicting impulses in tension with one another. What I have in this chapter called comic voyaging invites spectators in an analogous way to appreciate and preserve the multiple meanings toward which Aristophanes's plays point. This is more than a matter of appreciating the complexity of Aristophanes's plots or the complexity of politics they reflect. Fully engaging with *Peace* or *Lysistrata* requires allowing, even welcoming, the possibility that any "story" one finds in them inevitably runs up against another, simultaneously plausible story.

On my reading, *Peace* and *Lysistrata* begin in particular to point to the con-flicting democratic impulses that constitute the challenge of democratic citizenship. Both plays present rebellious individual heroes with whom spectators might be expected to identify. At the same time, both plays can be read as suggesting the necessity of concerted and well-organized col-lective action if the status quo is to change. Then, too, both can be read as suggesting that neither rebellion nor the organized action of ordinary people can successfully bring about change.

In *Peace* and *Lysistrata* the tension between rebellion and collective action intertwines with Aristophanic complications in what we would today think of as matters of identity. Together, the two plays examined here pres-ent the normal course of Athenian affairs as bound to a vision of what it means to be a gendered, embodied Athenian or Greek or human being. Each play complicates or challenges this vision in its own way. But both invite spectators to reconsider just who they are. In my terms, this means calling spectators to think about what it means to be ordinary—an ordi-nary Athenian, an ordinary Greek, an ordinary human being, and, more-over, what it means to be ordinary in extraordinary times. Before turning to think more carefully about the (extra)ordinary citizen in Athenian poli-tics and having opened up the question of how we understand our ordi-nariness, I turn more directly to the question of the relationship between the poet and the spectator. For that very way of putting it—poet and spec-tator—raises the specter of what Rancière, in his reading of emancipatory pedagogy and theater, calls stultification. It seems to suggests a cultural elite that writes and acts and so perhaps teaches the mass of ordinary, inert spectators. As we will see in the next chapter, Aristophanes seems to have been determined to invite the Athenians to call into question, or at least think very carefully about, this notion of a cultural elite.

Chapter 2

Ordinary Citizens, High Culture, and the Salvation of the City

Clouds, Women at the Thesmophoria, and Frogs

In the *Poetics*, Aristotle insists that the characters of tragic poetry must be "good [*chrēsta*]." He immediately goes on to say that this goodness is "relative to each class of people" (1454a). By this he means, for example, that women in tragedy must only be good as women, not good according to the standards of goodness for men.[1] Later, he indicates a second sense in which the goodness of tragic characters is relative. They must be "better [*beltiōn*] than ourselves" (1454b). We are left, then, with the conclusion that, though they need not be good in any absolute sense, men in tragedies must be better than the men we see around us, women in tragedies must be better than the women we see around us, and so on. All this, for Aristotle, is necessary if tragic characters are to engage in the "serious [*spoudaious*]" sort of action proper to tragedy.

In describing the characters of comedy, Aristotle likewise chooses a term that suggests something relative rather than absolute. Comedy, he tells us, "is a representation of inferior people [*phauloterôn*]." The Greek word rendered here as "inferior," a comparative form of *phaulos*, can hint at a potentially more generous evaluation. In reference to either people or things, *phaulos* often does mean "inferior" or, more strongly, "mean" or even "bad." It can also, though, suggest "easy" or "slight" or "indifferent." At times it takes on a more positive sense, particularly in regard to people who are "simple" or "unaffected" or simply—in the language I use in this book—"ordinary." Aristotle himself evidently does not mean with this language entirely to condemn the characters of comedy. Those characters are laughable, and "the laughable [*geloion*] is a species of the base or ugly [*aischrou*]; but the people of comedy, Aristotle allows, are not inferior "in the full sense of the word bad [*kakian*]."[2]

Whether we describe the people of comedy as inferior or simply, as I prefer, particularly ordinary, this way of thinking about comedy suggests, again, that their status is, like that of tragic heroes, a relative matter. Comic heroes in Aristotle's account are inferior as compared to their better or superior tragic counterparts. Comic heroes understood as ordinary stand contrasted most obviously to those who are or who claim to be extraordi-

41

nary or elite. Comedy, on this way of thinking, depends upon a distinction between elites and ordinary people. This in turn suggests the possibility that comedy might be a vehicle for some sort of cultural populism. In the early 1990s, Jim McGuigan, diagnosing what he called "an uncritical populist drift" in his field of cultural studies, offered the following definition of cultural populism: "Cultural populism is the intellectual assumption, made by some students of popular culture, that the symbolic experiences and practices of ordinary people are more important analytically and politically than Culture with a capital C."[3] Cultural populism on this definition works in large part by celebrating the cultural and political lives of ordinary people because they are ordinary. The kind of *uncritical* cultural populism that worries McGuigan brings no other standard than ordinariness to the evaluation of popular culture.

McGuigan's definition already suggests that questions about cultural populism intertwine with questions about political populism: cultural populism, he says, assumes the greater *political* importance of "the experiences and practices of ordinary people." If cultural populism becomes uncritical—if the sole standard of judgment it deploys is ordinariness—there follow potentially troubling political consequences. On one level, an uncritical populism paves the way to elite manipulation—from George H. W. Bush's clumsy work with pork rinds to the more insidious rhetoric of Americanism in recent years.[4]

More broadly, an uncritical populism ends up being politically self-defeating. Drawing on the discussion of the challenge of democratic citizenship I offered in the introduction, we might provisionally think of populism as a force akin to the rebellious impulse of democracy.[5] So understood, populism—cultural or political—reflects a basic resistance to or rebellion against the assumption of elite superiority. When the ordinary as a category of evaluation moves beyond criticism, though, populism risks stifling the very rebellious impulse to which it at first seems so closely related. The ordinary, which begins as a position from which to challenge elitism, itself moves beyond challenge. Uncritical populism, then, might be seen as a kind of perversion of democracy's rebellious impulse and so as a potentially dangerous departure from the kind of comic disposition of the ordinary citizen which I aim to develop.

Against the backdrop of these issues of cultural and political populism, I turn in this chapter to consider Aristophanes's portrayal of ordinary citizens interacting with cultural elites. I am particularly concerned with the implications of Aristophanes's focus on ordinary people for the self-understandings of the ordinary people among his spectators. As I argue throughout this book, Aristophanes invites spectators to recognize something of themselves in the characters he puts on stage. His comedy rests upon the possibility that those in the audience will identify with the ordinariness of his heroes and heroines and with their struggles against those who position themselves as extraordinary, as elites of one sort or another. We might see precisely in this moment of identification, though, the possibility of an uncritical celebration of the ordinary and so an uncritical self-satisfaction on the part of spectators. Is it possible, then, that Aristophanes's choice of protagonists opens the space for an uncritical cultural populism with potentially troubling consequences for democracy's rebellious side?

The last chapter already began to offer some reassurance on this score. I there introduced a notion of comic voyaging that itself might be the beginnings of a check on uncritical populism. As an account of how spectators might experience Aristophanic comedy, the idea of comic voyaging calls upon a disposition that resists the drawing of a single meaning or clear political message—including a simplistic populist message—from any particular play. More broadly, as I began to suggest at the end of chapter 1, comic voyaging extends to matters of identity. I thus suggested that both *Lysistrata* and *Peace* invite spectators not simply to identify with their ordinary protagonists but to ask just what it means to be ordinary.

This chapter pursues that line of thought further. I turn to three plays in which Aristophanes explores the relationship of ordinary heroes and cultural elites: *Clouds, Women at the Thesmophoria*, and *Frogs*. I avoid the temptation to read the plays as either straightforward populist celebrations or simple elitist warnings about ordinary citizens. I instead read them as working—separately and together—to destabilize the category of the ordinary. They thus work as well to destabilize the identification (or self-identification) of spectators as ordinary heroes or heroines. The end result is to locate an appreciation of the fluidity of the idea of elite and ordinary as a central part of the comic disposition necessary for the comic voyage of ordinary citizenship.

Ordinary Citizens and Cultural Populism: *Clouds*

The ending of *Clouds* (or at least the revised version of the play we have) is unusual among Aristophanes's surviving comedies. Rather than the usual joyous dancing, *Clouds'* final scene finds the play's hero Strepsiades maniacally celebrating the burning of Socrates's school the Thinkery. To the extent that spectators are meant to identify with Strepsiades, his act of arson might be read as suggestive of the dangers of a kind of uncritical cultural populism. We seem to find here an ordinary citizen turning to destruction as a means of revenge against a cultural elite whose teachings he has tried but failed to appropriate for his own ends. Little wonder from this point of view that Plato's Socrates would in the *Apology* lay a portion of the blame for his fate on a "playwright" who, among nameless others, "stir[red] up convictions against me out of envy and love of slander."[6]

If *Clouds* did in fact help to shape the context in which Socrates was eventually executed, we might find in the Athenians' response to the play two basic errors, one concerning Socrates, the other concerning Strepsiades. We might think of each error as a matter of mistaken identity that (again if we take Socrates's claim in the *Apology* seriously) might have helped to fuel an uncritical populist response to Socrates's presence in the city. A first mistake will have involved taking the Socrates of *Clouds* as, in fact, a reflection of the actual Socrates and so taking the actual Socrates as a threatening cultural elite. The Socrates of *Clouds*, after all, little resembles the Socrates we know from Plato or Xenophon. The comic character is at best a parody of a young Socrates, before his turn to moral and political concerns.[7] Beyond this, whatever the substance of his philosophy, Socrates in *Clouds* is hardly presented as a key player in Athenian cultural or political life. Though the Thinkery claims to house a kind of learning beyond the grasp of the ordinary Athenian, it seems to exist on the margins of the city. Michael Zuckert thus describes Aristophanes's Socrates as "a rather isolated figure, unknown and of little interest to most of the city."[8] If the Athenians took this Socrates for a powerful, and so potentially dangerous, figure, they perhaps succumbed to a certain populist paranoia.

My purposes here do not require working out the relationship between Aristophanes's Socrates and the "real" Socrates. I am more concerned with the second possible case of mistaken identity, which concerns the ordinary figure at the center of *Clouds* and the way in which spectators might have and identified *with* him. Just who is Strepsiades, then, and what might we make of his relationship to the ordinary Athenian spectator?

Strepsiades comes to Socrates's Thinkery hoping for help in avoiding the debts amassed by his profligate son, Phidippides. Strepsiades in many ways appears, like so many of Aristophanes's protagonists, as a quite ordinary sort. By this I mean not so much that he possesses a set of characteristics that are somehow essentially ordinary as that—in line with Aristotle's account of the characters of comedy—his relative standing marks him in various ways as non-elite.

Along these lines, consider Strepsiades's account of his upbringing and subsequent marriage: "Mine was a pleasant country life, moldy, unswept, aimlessly leisured, abounding in honey bees, sheep, and live cakes. Then I married the niece of Megacles son of Megacles, I a rustic, she from town, haughty, spoiled, thoroughly Coesyrized" (41–45). Strepsiades's social status is in a sense on the cusp, indeterminate, but he clearly does not fit in the bounds of the Athenian social or political elite.[9] Reinforcing the story of his life, Strepsiades's account of his current predicament reflects his lack of great wealth and, too, his lack of the kind of political or social standing that might provide an easier route from debt: "I'm being eaten alive by my bills and stable fees and debts, on account of this son of mine. He wears his hair long and rides horses and races chariots, and he even dreams about horses, while I go to pieces as I watch the moon in her twenties, because my interest payment looms just ahead" (14–17). Unable to convince his son to take up Socratic learning, Strepsiades himself appears at the door of the Thinkery, seeking the assistance of Socrates and his students: "I'll say a prayer to the gods and go to the Thinkery to be trained myself. But then again, how is an old man like me, forgetful and dense, to learn the hairsplitting of precise arguments? I've to go" (128–31). In its simple, indebted, forgetful, dense protagonist, *Clouds* thus appears at first glance to offer spectators a hero with whom they might well identify. Are spectators, though, meant as well to identify with what Strepsiades does?

Strepsiades aims to solve his problems as Aristophanes's heroes and heroines tend to do: by rising above his very ordinariness to do something extraordinary. If not his son, then he himself will learn the ways of Socrates and his students. The plot takes comic twists and turns: Strepsiades has difficulty following Socrates's teaching (see especially Socrates's frustration at lines 782–84) and so must ultimately force his son to the Thinkery to learn in particular from the Worse Argument the ways of sophistic argumentation (877–85). But in the most basic sense, his scheme proves a success, for his creditors appear later in the play to be defeated; at the least, they flee from the stage in fear (1215–1300).

In typical Aristophanic fashion, *Clouds* complicates this apparent victory by suggesting that it has unexpected consequences. It turns out that the new learning can be used for most any end, and so its value may turn on the one who seeks to use it. Thus Strepsiades finds himself on the losing side of an argument with his son on the subject of filial piety, as Phidippides deploys the cleverness he had used on his father's creditors to justify beating his father (1321–44). In this outcome some see the deeper message of the play about the new sophistic learning. As Dover has it, "Phidippides learns from Wrong a nonchalant, selfish nihilism" that can only merit the sternest condemnation given the "moral framework" of *Clouds*, which Dover describes as being "as stark as that of an evangelical tract."[10] Because it in this way gives us reason to wonder about Strepsiades's triumph, *Clouds* ultimately refuses simply to replace a potential hierarchy of the intellect with the simple celebration of the ordinary person that marks uncritical cultural populism. On this level, *Clouds* leaves open the question of the ultimate relationship of the ordinary spectator to Strepsiades and so, too, of the ordinary citizen to the philosopher.

In thus complicating any effort to draw from it a straightforward message about intellectuals and ordinary citizens, *Clouds* calls upon spectators to join—or at least endure—the kind of uncertain comic voyaging I found in *Peace* and *Lysistrata* in the last chapter. If the Athenians, identifying with Strepsiades, nonetheless found the play simply endorsing ordinary citizens taking vengeance upon philosophers, then we can safely say they were mistaken. But there is another potential aspect to the Athenians mistaking the identity of Strepsiades and so mistakenly identifying with him. Where *Peace* and *Lysistrata* on my reading point toward questions about what it means to be ordinary, *Clouds* leaves us with questions about whether the apparently ordinary hero is really the protagonist at all.

We can in this context note a structural difference between *Clouds* and Aristophanes's more explicitly political plays. We have seen that in *Lysistrata* the formal agon involves an extended rhetorical contest between Lysistrata and an Athenian magistrate who means to foil her plot. We can find in other plays a similar use of the agon as a pivotal moment in the ordinary citizen's struggle to overcome existing limits or boundaries. In the agon of *Acharnians*, Diceapolis battles the chorus of Acharnians, who are determined to stymie his effort to enjoy a private peace. In *Knights* the agon consists of the rhetorical battle between the heroic sausage-seller and the villainous Cleon.

In *Clouds*, though, the agon involves the famous argument between the Better Argument and the Worse Argument or, alternatively, the old and the new education. Strepsiades is, of course, an interested audience for this argument, since it will determine which type of learning his son undergoes. But he is not a participant. While the particular form his assault on his creditors will take depends upon the agon, his basic strategy of using higher learning to fend them off does not. Here consider Strepsiades's admonition to Socrates just as the agon begins: "Just see that he [Phidippides] learns that pair of arguments, the Better, whatever that may be, and the Worse, the one that pleads what's wrong and overturns the Better. And if not both, by all means teach him at least the Worst" (881–85). And note that at the end of the agon, Strepsiades does not determine a winner. Instead, the Better Argument seemingly concedes the contest as he exits the stage: "Uncle! You buggers, for heaven's sake take my cloak; I'm deserting to your side!" (1102–4). In the end, the play's ordinary hero stands one step removed from the intricacies of the higher learning that he nonetheless aims to use for his own purposes.

On the one hand, this structural oddity of *Clouds* simply adds to the play's overall complexity. That complexity alerts us to the error of seeing the burning of the Thinkery either as a celebration of the victory of the ordinary citizen or as a straightforward warning of the dangers of putting too much faith in people like Strepsiades. Ultimately, the play does not simply endorse nor does it simply reject the sort of faith in the rebelliousness of the ordinary citizen that marks cultural and political populism. Rather, *Clouds* puts such faith in tension with abiding concerns about the limitations of ordinary people as cultural actors. And by at a pivotal moment supplanting the ordinary person as protagonist with the abstractions of the

Better and the Worse Argument, the play begins to decenter the idea of the ordinary person as hero. From the perspective of Socrates's claims in the *Apology*, we can say from this final perspective that the Athenians, if they identified with Strepsiades as the hero of Aristophanes's *Clouds*, mistook his identity and so their own. More broadly, we can see *Clouds* as pointing the way toward Aristophanes's own doubts about the distinction between ordinary citizens and cultural elites. Those doubts become more apparent in *Women at the Thesmophoria* and *Frogs*.

Who is Ordinary? *Women at the Thesmophoria*

Women at the Thesmophoria begins with even more explicit conflict between elites and non-elites than does *Clouds*, but it ends with a seemingly happier conclusion. The central conflict of *Women at the Thesmophoria* concerns Euripides's portrayal of the women of Athens as, in the words of one of the women's leaders, "lover-keepers, man-chasers, wine-oglers, traitors, chatterboxes, utter sickies, the bane of men's lives" (392–94). Gathered for the annual festival of the Thesmophoria, the women hold what Dover calls a "quasi-political assembly" at which they consider how they will punish Euripides.[11] While he begins the play in fear of his life, Euripides ends up suffering neither death nor anything analogous to the burning of Socrates's Thinkery at the end of *Clouds*. After his plan to infiltrate the Thesmophoria festival is foiled, he saves himself (and his captured kinsman) by compromise: he agrees "that in the future none of you women will ever again be slandered in any way by me" (1162–63). We might see this "permanent peace treaty" (1160–61) as an indication that ordinary citizens (if we can describe the women as such given their exclusion from Athenian politics, about which more in a moment) might exert some control over cultural elites.[12] From this perspective, *Women at the Thesmophoria* affirms a kind of cultural populism. But, more fully developing what *Clouds* only began, *Women at the Thesmophoria* complicates matters by calling into question the very distinction between the elite and the ordinary.

Women at the Thesmophoria opens with an exchange between Euripides and his otherwise unnamed kinsman:

> Kinsman: Ah, Zeus, will the spring swallow ever show up? This guy will be the death of me, plodding around since daybreak. Might it be possible, before I puke out my guts, to find out from you, Euripides, just where you're taking me?
> Euripides: You needn't hear it all, since you're going to see it for yourself.
> (1–6)

We find this sort of exchange at the beginnings of other surviving Aristophanic comedies, with a complaining character raising for the audience the question of just what is going on and so opening the door to a basic exposition of the play's plot. *Acharnians* thus opens with its hero Diceapolis complaining about his "umpteen million loads" of pains and his "scant, quite scant" pleasures (1–3) and waiting for the Assembly to begin so that he might make one last plea for peace. At the start of *Wealth*, we hear from Cario, who describes himself as "the slave of a fool" (1). The fool in question is Cario's master Chremylus, who soon explains to his slave and the audience just why he has insisted upon bringing home an old blind man—who turns out to be the god Wealth himself.

It does take longer for the moment of exposition to arrive in *Women at the Thesmophoria* than it does in these other plays. Aristophanes first treats us to some sharp repartee between Euripides, the kinsman, and the slave of Agathon, to whose house the protagonists have been walking. But a more striking difference between the opening of other plays and the opening of *Women at the Thesmophoria* lies in the identity of the protagonists. The complaining figures at the opening of other plays are, again, either markedly ordinary Athenians (as in *Acharnians*) or their slaves (as in *Wealth*), with the complaints preparing the way for extraordinary schemes meant to relieve the suffering of the protagonists. Here, though, the complaints come from the kinsman of Euripides and the scheme is meant to relieve the suffering of the tragic poet—or at least the potential suffering threatened by the women of Athens. Euripides reveals his plan in the sort of expository exchange that, again, we find in various other plays:

> Kinsman: But what's your strategy [*mēchanēn*] against these women?
> Euripides: To persuade Agathon, the tragic producer, to go to the Thesmophorium.
> Kinsman: And do what? Tell me.
> Euripides: To attend the women's assembly and say whatever's necessary on my behalf.
> Kinsman: Openly or in disguise?
> Euripides: In disguise, dressed up like a woman. (86–92)

In *Women at the Thesmophoria*, then, Euripides finds himself threatened by the powerful and so launches a plan for personal salvation. As the play's initial protagonist, Euripides, that is, appears to occupy the space of the ordinary citizen.

Except of course that he is not an ordinary Athenian, he is the famous tragic poet Euripides. If we needed more proof of his extraordinary place in Athens, the very fact that Aristophanes has devoted a play to him and his work reflects his prominence. Euripides also differs from the more ordinary Aristophanic hero in his eagerness to let others carry out his plans for him. His attempt to persuade his fellow poet to infiltrate the Thesmophoria on his behalf allows Aristophanes to score some comic points about Agathon's sexuality and looks. "I'm an old graybeard," Euripides says to Agathon in explaining his thinking. "You, by contrast, are good-looking, pale, clean shaven, soft, presentable, and you sound like a woman" (190–92). Euripides's turn to another character (or characters, since when Agathon refuses, he prevails upon the kinsman to take over), though, also differentiates him from, for example, Lysistrata, who herself oversees the enactment of her plans; or Diceapolis, who in *Acharnians* strikes out to make his own peace treaty with the Spartans; or Peisetaerus of *Birds*, who leaves Athens and himself founds a city in the sky. Unlike these characters, who take matters into their own hands, Euripides—though he suggests his very life is at stake—lets others do the dirty work for him. Though he finds himself in the same kind of position as the typical Aristophanic hero, his approach, like his stature, mark him as something other than the ordinary protagonist.

We might say something analogous about those who threaten Euripides, the women of Athens. If Euripides is hardly the typical Aristophanic hero, then the women of Athens are hardly the typical Aristophanic villain. Aristophanes's comic heroes typically confront powerful foes whom they must persuade or trick or otherwise defeat. In *Knights*, for example, the sausage-seller must defeat the Paphlagonian, who is clearly a stand-in for the powerful Cleon, while in *Peace*, as we saw in the last chapter, Trygaeus must tangle with the gods themselves. Euripides's foes in *Women at the Thesmophoria* are not powerful politicians or gods, of course, but the women of Athens. On this score, a comparison to *Assemblywomen* is to the point. In that play, discussed in chapter 5, the powerless women of Athens must disguise themselves as men to enter into and gain control of the Assembly.

Here in *Women at the Thesmophoria*, the roles are of course reversed, with the kinsman disguising himself as a woman to gain entry into the meeting at which Euripides's fate will be decided, but when the disguised kinsman arrives at the Thesmophoria, Aristophanes reminds us that the assembly held there stands at some distance from the Athenian assembly itself. The kinsman arrives just in time to hear the women of Athens led by Critylla in praying that

> this assembly [*ecclēsian*] and today's convocation [*sunodon*] be conducted in the finest and most excellent manner, to the great benefit of the city of the Athenians and with good fortune for you yourselves. And may she have the victory whose actions and whose counsel best serve the Athenian Commonwealth [*ton dēmon ton Athēnaiōn*] and the Women's Commonwealth [*tōn gunaikōn*]. (302–7)

The ambiguous status of this gathering of women is well-captured in Critylla's reference to both "the Athenian Commonwealth [*ton dēmon ton Athēnaiōn*]" and "the Women's Commonwealth [*tōn gunaikōn*]." More literally, she refers to the people or demos of Athens and the women, perhaps in the process catching something of the basic ambiguity of demos. Are *tōn gunaikōn* part of *ton dēmon ton Athēnaiōn*, or are the women distinct from the Athenian people? Does Critylla envision "the good fortune of you yourselves" as distinct from "the great benefit of the city of Athens"? Or does she mean the women of Athens to understand their good fortune as inseparable from the city's well-being? When she uses the language of assembly (*ecclesia*), just what does this suggest about the relationship of this convocation of women to the assembly of Athenian citizens?

We get something closer to an answer to these questions when Critylla explains just how the present assembly came about and delineates its purpose: "The Women's Assembly [*boule*] . . . has passed [*edoxe*] the following motion: an Assembly [*ecclesia*] will be held at dawn of the middle day of the Thesmophoria, when we have the most free time, its principal agendum being deliberation about the punishment of Euripides" (372–77). As the Greek indicates, Critylla here describes the decision to take up the punishment of Euripides in ways that suggest the procedures of Athenian democracy: a smaller council calls the assembly into session and sets its agenda. But her words also reinforce the distance of this assembly from the assembly of Athenian men on the Pnyx. This is an assembly scheduled for free time during the regular activities of the Thesmophoria. In this sense, we might say that the assembly which is to consider the fate of Euripides is situated between the "real" Athenian Assembly and the Thesmophoria. Its status and its power and so the nature of its threat to Euripides are all uncertain, much as the status of Euripides himself is uncertain.[13]

Euripides both is and is not an ordinary Athenian, and the women of Athens both are and are not a typical threat to the ordinary Athenian. Put differently, in the first half of the play—where the conflict is structured as occurring between Euripides and the women of Athens—we do not find in any straightforward way the more typical Aristophanic pattern of ordinary citizen confronting powerful elites. More sharply, we cannot really find the ordinary Athenian at all here. There is instead a gap or distance between Euripides and the women of Athens, an empty comic space where we might otherwise expect the ordinary citizen to be.

In a sense that gap is filled in the second half of the play by the kinsman, but only imperfectly. Arriving at the Thesmophoria still disguised as a woman, the kinsman gamely tries to speak on Euripides's behalf, saying that the poet is guilty only of "mentioning two or three of our misdeeds, out of the thousands of others he knows we've committed" (473–75). Though the chorus is briefly swayed by this argument (531–32), their leaders are not;

and once Cleisthenes arrives to warn the women that Euripides has placed a male spy among them, they turn with suspicion on the kinsman, who is placed under guard. Our attention had for the first half of the play been focused upon Euripides's attempt to save himself; now the action focuses on the kinsman's predicament. "What's my plan for saving myself now?" he wails. "What move [*mechane*]? What idea? The man who tumbled me into this mess in the first place is nowhere to be seen" (795). Euripides's original strategy, announced early in the play using the same language of *mechane*, has left his kinsman in need of a clever strategy of his own.

Jeffrey Henderson, in his introduction to *Women at the Thesmophoria*, suggests that in these developments Aristophanes offers the kinsman as the "on-stage representative" of comedy, describing him as "earthy and irrepressible," like comedy itself. Aristophanes also, Henderson suggests, presents the kinsman as offering in his pseudodefense of Euripides a more comprehensive account of women's supposed misdeeds than does the tragic poet himself. By embodying Aristophanic comedy, the kinsman thus allows comedy to "reveal its own superiority at depicting the real world." Finally, Henderson sees this superiority of comedy as reflected in Euripides's need "to resort to a comic ruse to rescue himself and the Kinsman."[14] He has in mind on this last point the contrast between Euripides's failure to save the kinsman by disguising himself as characters from his own tragedies and his success when he reappears as a comic figure and proves able to distract the Scythian archer guarding the kinsman by means of an attractive dancing girl.

No doubt these final scenes imagine a sort of victory of comedy over tragedy. But it is still the case that the kinsman, standing as the sort of ordinary person who is the standard comic hero, cannot save himself. That takes Euripides, and even if the poet must stoop to disguise himself in comic garb, he remains something other than an ordinary comic hero. In a sense, the captured kinsman remains caught in between the poet who will save him, on the one hand, and, on the other hand, the women of Athens and the Scythian archer who guards their prisoner. Euripides at one point refers to the archer as a "savage [*barbarous*] lout" (1024). Put more sharply, the kinsman as the representative of comedy stands in the space between the barbarian and the cultural elite. If we are to take him as another of comedy's ordinary heroes, then the ordinary is in this sense, again, a matter of one's relative position. We might say that *Women at the Thesmophoria*, by first leaving empty the cultural space where we might expect to find the ordinary citizen and then only tentatively placing the unnamed kinsman there, problematizes the idea of the ordinary that enables cultural and political populism. In the language I used in chapter 1, we might say that the play invites spectators to embark on an uncertain voyage in the empty space signified by the idea of the ordinary.

The Ordinary Citizen and the Cultural Politics of *Frogs*

Like *Clouds* and *Women at the Thesmophoria, Frogs* puts particular cultural elites on stage and uses their presence to complicate our thinking about the relationship between elites and ordinary citizens. *Frogs* embarks on a comic search for a kind of cultural politics that might save Athens from the woes it suffered as the long Peloponnesian War drew near its end, in the process complicating the idea of ordinary citizen as cultural savior of the city. On its surface, the play has as its political goal restoring the unity of Athens, as the overt appeal of the play's parabasis suggests: "First, then, we think that all the citizens should be made equal, and their fears removed. . . . Next I say that no one in the city should be disenfranchised. . . . Now relax your anger, you people most naturally sage, and let's readily accept as kinsmen and as citizens in good standing everyone who fights on our ships" (686–700). The chorus leader here speaks directly on behalf of those suspected of offenses during the oligarchy of 411 BCE and, more generally, issues a plea for civic unity and good leadership. He goes on to offer a familiar Aristophanic complaint about the Athenians—they routinely pick as leaders "bad people with bad ancestors"—and admonishes them, "you fools, do change your ways and once again choose the good people" (730–35). But unlike the earlier political plays such as *Knights* or *Wasps*, *Frogs* does not dwell on the dangers of demagoguery or on the need for the Athenian people to find better political leaders. Rather than focus on political division itself, *Frogs* calls for an all-encompassing unity, one meant to save the city from threats to its very existence. In keeping with this, the plot of the play does not explore conflict between different parts of Athens. Indeed, rather than doing direct battle with the "bad people with bad ancestors" who lead Athens, the hero of *Frogs*—the god Dionysus—must escape troubled Athens to find the source of its salvation, so that "our city might survive and continue her choral festivals" (1419).

The promised source of cultural unity, and thus of civic salvation and survival, comes in the person of the dead poet Aeschylus, who defeats the more recently deceased Euripides and so is chosen to return to his native city. Near the play's end the chorus, in praising the victory of Aeschylus, suggests a connection between the outcome of *Frogs* and the outcomes of both *Clouds* and *Women at the Thesmophoria*:

> So what's stylish is not to sit
> Beside Socrates and chatter,
> Casting the arts aside and ignoring the best of the tragedian's craft.
> To hang around killing time
> In pretentious conversation
> And hairsplitting twaddle
> Is the mark of a man who's lost his mind. (1491–99)

To the extent that Aristophanes sees some connection between Euripides and Socrates (a connection Nietzsche will later make much of),[15] we might say that *Clouds, Women at the Thesmophoria,* and *Frogs* all produce a similar result: rebellion against the new learning, against elite cultural innovation.[16]

In this context, though, one aspect of *Frogs'* basic plot stands out. As I argued above, *Clouds* in various ways complicates the success of the ordinary citizen appropriating Socrates's new-fangled philosophy: by making Strepsiades unable to grasp Socrates's teaching, by making his attempt to use that teaching backfire, and by locating the ultimate defeat of Socrates in the startling image of the burning Thinkery. *Frogs,* by contrast, is relatively untroubled by such complications to its basic plot. Indeed, Aeschylus's victory over Euripides comes almost at the end of the play, and we are not made witness to his actual return to Athens. If this means that we do not, in fact, see the fantastical rebirth of civic unity driven by an Aeschylean rebirth in Athens of the old ways, it also means that we do not see the hope of such rebirth challenged by the sort of unrealized or unexpected consequences we find following the victories of the ordinary heroes of other plays.

These complications instead arise from the identity of *Frogs'* hero. Where *Clouds* places a recognizably ordinary Athenians front and center, *Frogs,* following *Women at the Thesmophoria,* does not. Rather than an ordinary person, *Frogs* takes as its protagonist the god Dionysus. We must be careful in framing our approach to this difference. It is not quite right to ask *why* Aristophanes chooses Dionysus, as if that choice is unusual or inappropriate. Far too few plays have survived for us to say that the choice of a god as comic hero for *Frogs* is unique or unusual for Aristophanes. What is more, as the god of the theater, Dionysus seems an entirely appropriate choice to judge a contest between tragic poets, even a contest between *dead* tragic poets.[17] These points aside, if we indulge in the tempting counterfactual for a moment, we might well imagine Aristophanes's comic spirit producing a different *Frogs,* one in which a Strepsiades-like character makes the journey in place of Dionysus, deciding the contest between Aeschylus and Euripides. Such a plot would give us a more direct—and no doubt complex—Aristophanic vision of the ordinary citizen as judge of tragedy and would-be savior of the city. But, in the end, rather than ask why Aristophanes did not write such a play, we can ask after the character of Dionysus in *Frogs* and the relationship of that character to the ordinary heroes of other plays.

Frogs, in fact, points us toward the possibility that something lurks in the character of Dionysus: that he is something more or something other than he appears. Disguise and shifting identity are central to the play. Dionysus begins his trip disguised as Heracles, and Aristophanes derives great comic effect from Dionysus and the slave Xanthias exchanging and fighting over their identities. On some level, the play thus asks us repeatedly to question just who Dionysus is.[18] But for my purposes here, the most significant aspect of Aristophanes's Dionysus is his place as a *comic* character, as a subject of ridicule. In this sense, the hero of *Frogs*, in fact, shares traits with other Aristophanic heroes.

Dionysus is, first, funny to look at. The mere sight of Dionysus at his door sends Heracles over the edge: "By Demeter!" he exclaims, "I just can't stop laughing! Even though I'm biting my lip, I can't help laughing" (43–44). Furthermore, like other Aristophanic heroes Dionysus's determination to reach his goal commingles with fear, even cowardice.[19] Though he proclaims himself a "fighter," he hides behind his slave Xanthias for fear of the "awful beasts" of the underworld (280–90). And in a riotous scene at Pluto's door, he is torn between an overriding fear that leads him to exchange roles with Xanthias and his lust for the dancing girls that might be inside. Indeed, Dionysus most resembles Aristophanes's other heroes in his comic combination of base fear and desire.[20] Just after the chorus leader has called for the Athenians to turn again to the "well-born, well-behaved, just, fine and outstanding men" among them—to the proper gentlemen of Athens—Xanthias declares that his master himself is "a gentleman: all he knows is boozing and balling" (740–41).[21] But, at least for the first half of the play, Dionysus is driven by a different sort of desire, one which he describes as a "longing for Euripides" so strong that "nobody on earth can persuade me not to go after him" (69). Like Strepsiades's desire for relief from debt, this desire drives Dionysus to overcome great obstacles.[22]

Though a god, the Dionysus of *Frogs* thus shares much with Aristophanes's ordinary heroes. We might even expect Aristophanes's audience to have felt some identification with Dionysus as they laughed at him, just as they felt some identification with all the other Aristophanic heroes in whom they saw something of themselves.[23] And yet, however much the comic Dionysus resembles the ordinary citizen, he remains Dionysus; he remains a god. He cannot in this sense simply stand in for the average Athenian. Bowie makes this point in thinking about Dionysus's relationship with his slave Xanthias. Put simply, it is often unclear in *Frogs* precisely who is master and who is slave. Aristophanes makes great fun of this confusion, beginning with Xanthias's opening complaints about the burden he carries even though he rides a donkey while Dionysus walks and continuing through a scene in which the two repeatedly switch roles as Dionysus (still disguised as Heracles) alternately tries to avoid being beaten by Aeacus by posing as a lowly slave (465–90) and to enjoy the dancing girls inside by insisting that Xanthias is the slave and he the immortal (505–30).

Pointing to this sort of "confusion between master and slave," Bowie considers a parallel to the civic confusion brought about when some citizens lost their status for their failures at Arginusae while some slaves were granted freedom for their role in the battle: "the relationship between Dionysus and Xanthias in the play thus provides an articulation of the relations between citizens and non-citizens in the state, though any obvious one-on-one allegorical reading is prevented by the fact that Xanthias did *not* fight in the battle [Arginusae] and Dionysus the god has no meaningful counterpart among the citizenry."[24] The point here, as Bowie indicates, is not that the characterization of Dionysus and Xanthias lacks *all* allegorical significance. In bringing these characters together, Aristophanes prompts his audience to think about the relative status of citizens and noncitizens. But he simultaneously undermines the parallel, for Xanthias, unlike those freed after Arginusae, remains a slave, while Dionysus remains a god. In this sense, despite intriguing potential links to issues of status in Athens, *Frogs* in the end leaves empty the civic space between Dionysus and Xanthias, between god and slave—the space, that is, where we might find Athenian citizens, ordinary or not. If *Frogs* like *Women at the Thesmophoria* offers no obvious or precise counterpart to the ordinary citizen, then we might sharpen our statement of the basic question posed by the ambiguity of Dionysus as comic hero: what are we to make of the civic space the play from one perspective leaves empty or, more particularly, of the gap between the ordinary citizen as comic hero and the comic Dionysus?

Dionysus as comic hero thus carries multiple potential meanings, for Dionysus is both like and unlike the ordinary Athenians upon whom the salvation of the city will ultimately depend. Or, we might say, the ordinary Athenian is both like and unlike Dionysus. The path Dionysus takes to choosing Aeschylus further sharpens the question of his simultaneously ordinary and extraordinary status as comic hero. Just as Dionysus might be something other than he seems, so his ultimate selection of Aeschylus is something other than the straightforward fulfillment of the play's plot.

We have already said that Dionysus sets off for the underworld not for Aeschylus, but for Euripides. He tells Heracles, again, that he has "eating away" at him a "longing" (*pothos*) for Euripides (66), to whom he refers as a "potent poet" for his "adventuresome" turns of phrase (99–100). Only after he has reached the underworld and shed his disguise does he change his purpose to judging the contest between Aeschylus and Euripides. That contest, though, is not the result of Dionysus's visit, but had been looming since Euripides's death. Once he arrives, Dionysus is chosen to judge it for two reasons, according to Pluto's slave. There is, of course, the fact that he is "familiar with the art" (811). But that qualification is presented by the slave as secondary to another consideration, namely that "Aeschylus wouldn't agree to use Athenians" (805). Dionysus, that is, is chosen precisely because he is something other than an ordinary Athenian.

Even after he is fully ensconced as judge of the tragic agon, it is not Dionysus but Pluto who links his new role to his initial desire to bring a god back to the world of the living. Well into the contest, Dionysus confides to Pluto his reluctance to make a decision: "These men are my friends, and I'll not judge between them. I don't want to get on the bad side of either of them. One I consider a master, the other I enjoy" (1411–13). When Pluto responds that Dionysus must choose if he hopes to "accomplish [his] mission," we might well wonder just what that mission now is. Pluto soon explains that "the one you choose you may take back with you, that way you won't have come for nothing" (1415). Dionysus, though, had not come for an unspecified poet to be chosen later, but for Euripides, the object of his longing. Still, he immediately repeats Pluto's explanation to Euripides and Aeschylus, adding that he aims by retrieving a poet to save the city: "Now listen to me. I came down here for a poet. Why? So our city could survive and continue her choral festivals. So whichever one of you is prepared to offer the city some good advice, he's the one I've decided to take back with me" (1417–20). The twofold reshaping of Dionysus's mission—from longing for Euripides to judging who would take the chair of tragedy in the underworld to choosing which poet to bring back—thus comes at the impetus of others.

Dionysus goes on to tap Aeschylus as "the one that my soul wishes to choose" (1468), apparently because of his advice about Alcibiades (1421–22). The changes in Dionysus's purpose and in Dionysus himself that lead to this conclusion can give the play a disjointed feel. Some have seen in Dionysus's change both a unifying theme for the play and, particularly given the role of the play's chorus of Eleusinian initiates, an Aristophanic metaphor for a hoped-for transformation in the Athenians themselves.[25] If the comic figure at the center of *Frogs* can overcome his intense longing for Euripides, why not the ordinary Athenian who, after all, faces some similar obstacles and distractions—fear, desire, and the like? No doubt this latter reading fits well with what seems to be the play's overall concern with promoting better judgment amongst the Athenians about whose advice to follow and how to save the city. *Frogs* ends with Pluto wishing Aeschylus well on his return to Athens, admonishing him to "save our city with your fine counsels, and educate the thoughtless people; there are many of them" (1500–1503).

Clearly, though, the disjunctures in Dionysus's path to choosing Aeschylus complicate this reading. Here we can move beyond the straightforward observation that in *Frogs* it takes a god, not just an ordinary Athenian, to overcome the lure of Euripides. From a certain point of view, Dionysus's coming to be a proper judge of tragedy depends not so much on a transformation in his character as on the set of happy coincidences just reviewed. When he arrives in Hades, Euripides and Aeschylus are already about to spar. No other suitable judge is to be found, particularly since Aeschylus will not abide an Athenian judge. Pluto dictates that the winner of the contest will be the one to return to Athens. Are we to see Dionysus as moving from ordinary to extraordinary and to find therein hope that the Athenians might, in a sense, become enough like the god of the theater to find an Aeschylean path to salvation? Or are we to see a set of comic twists and turns that reminds us, again, of the gap between the fortuitous path that Dionysus takes and the real possibilities open to (or real limits placed upon) ordinary citizens in the struggling city?[26]

An Aristophanic comedy engendering multiple possible meanings is familiar enough by now. But the particular complications *Frogs* enacts move us farther along. *Clouds* prompts us first and foremost to worry about cases in which the ordinary is mistakenly identified and uncritical populist outrage and rebellion against elites enabled. *Women at the Thesmophoria* takes the additional step of calling into question the very notion of the ordinary citizen. On the reading advanced here, *Frogs* leaves us less doubt about the proper relationship of ordinary citizens and political-cultural elites; a poet—the right kind of poet—can save the city if only the Athenians will recognize and embrace him. Instead, in its choice and description of its hero and his adventure, *Frogs* raises the question of the capability of ordinary citizens to a grander level. The city's salvation in *Frogs* depends upon the Athenians becoming like Dionysus, who both does and does not seem like an ordinary sort and whose transformation both does and does not seem like a model for a kind of cultural and political education of the Athenians. In a sense, the play asks us to think about whether ordinary citizens are or can become godlike enough for the task they face.

The Complexity of the Ordinary

I have tried throughout the previous section to avoid suggesting that the *presence* of Dionysus as the comic hero of *Frogs* reflects the simple *absence* from the play of the ordinary citizen. Indeed, in the end it is not at all clear that the ordinary citizen is absent from *Frogs*. Precisely by suggesting a gap between its hero and its audience, *Frogs* points toward a set of reflections on the possible conflation of ordinary citizens and gods. On the one hand, Aristophanes's Dionysus in *Frogs* does what Aristophanes's heroes so often do: he embarks on a fantastic scheme that promises on some level to get the city on the right track again. What is more, in his desires and fears as well as his appearance and manners, Dionysus seems like an ordinary Athenian. On the other hand, he remains a god. Indeed, the action by which he would save the city—choosing Aeschylus over Euripides—comes only after he has resumed his proper place in the (under)world of the theater, only after the gap between god and ordinary citizen has been firmly reasserted.

An appreciation of this complexity of Dionysus as comic hero, especially taken in the context of *Clouds* and *Women at the Thesmophoria*, points in the end toward a consistent insistence on Aristophanes's part that we appreciate as well the complexity of ordinary people. This insistence is, I think, enough to acquit Aristophanes of any charge of uncritical cultural populism. It also suggests an Aristophanic complication for the appeal of political populism (and any sort of democratic theory that edges toward such populism). Appreciation of the complexity of ordinary people means not looking to them as godlike bringers of political salvation, though it also means holding on to the hope that ordinary citizens may from time to time rise up to reclaim the promise of democracy.

But appreciating the complexity of ordinary people goes beyond maintaining a proper sense of both their possibilities and limitations. Taking the three plays I have discussed together, Aristophanes also points toward the inherent fluidity of the category of the ordinary. The relevant danger here is not unreasonably deifying the ordinary citizen but, rather, needlessly reifying the idea of ordinary people. This is the risk run by both political and cultural populism. Both treat "the people" as an undifferentiated referent in order to draw on the abstract notion of "ordinary people" as the locus of political or cultural authenticity. Aristophanes suggests that ordinary people are too complex to bear the weight of such generalization. Just as we recognize Strepsiades as ordinary even though we cannot precisely pigeonhole his status in Athens, and just as we must continue to wonder whether the Euripides of *Frogs* or the women gathered for the Thesmophoria or the kinsman are truly ordinary citizens, so we can maintain a notion of the ordinary citizen without forcing ordinary citizens into a single mold. Aristophanes's heroes are united not so much by shared characteristics as by a sense of struggle—against existing elites, against the imposition of political, social, and cultural forms, and against their own faults and foibles. Even a god, for Aristophanes, can in this sense be altogether ordinary.

Aristophanes puts this complexity of the ordinary person continually before our eyes and in doing so undermines any simplistic or uncritical populist celebration of the rebelliousness of ordinary people. His comedy in turn demands a comic disposition in its spectators that can navigate— or embark on comic voyages in the midst of—this complexity. Spectators must at once identify with the ordinary citizens they see on stage and avoid slipping into an uncritical populist identification of and with the ordinary itself. The ability to do stands closely related, I think, to the more directly political ability to hold democracy's quasi-populist impulse toward rebellion in perpetual tension with its impulse toward ordered collective action. Along these lines, we might consider once more the multifaceted prescription for the salvation of the city *Frogs* offers.

Frogs appeals, no doubt sincerely, to the potential for tragedy, particularly Aeschylean tragedy, to produce a kind of cultural unity. In the blunt advice offered by the chorus leader in the parabasis (686–705), this cultural unity would play out politically in a renewed emphasis on equality ("all the citizens should be made equal") and kinship ("let's readily accept as kinsmen and as citizens in good standing everyone who fights on our ships"). But along with equality and kinship, the Athenians must also "once again choose the good people" to lead them, must recognize some of their kin as somehow more than equal (735). *Frogs* thus calls Athenians to recognize their equality and kinship—to appreciate the complicated sense in which we are all ordinary even as the ordinary has no stable meaning—and to resist arguments that render Athenians unequal and so divide them. At the same time, though, the play calls Athenians to acknowledge that some in the city have a more prominent political role to play. The relationship between elites and ordinary citizens, then, cannot consist either in bowing to elites or, importantly, in simply rebelling against any role for elites at all. The complicated sense of the ordinary that emerges from *Clouds*, *Women at the Thesmophoria* and *Frogs* thus demands not only that spectators embark on the kind of comic voyaging I have discussed in this and the last chapter. It also points toward the need for a particular attitude toward political elites or, put differently, to the claims some will make to positions of authority or rule or *archē* even in the democratic city. Drawing on Aristophanes's *Wasps* and *Birds*, the next chapter considers one way in which ordinary citizens may well respond to such claims: with anger.

Chapter 3

ARCHĒ AND THE ANGER OF
THE ORDINARY CITIZEN

WASPS AND BIRDS

In chapter 2, I sought to complicate the idea of ordinary citizenship chiefly by emphasizing the fluidity of the ordinary. Though Aristophanes's plays revolve around the relationship between ordinary citizens and cultural or political elites, they at the same time resist the reification (or deification) of ordinary citizens. This, I suggested, is one way in which Aristophanes avoids what today we might think of as uncritical populism, cultural or political. Insofar as they allow the meaning of ordinary to shift, the plays render problematic any simplistic celebration of the ordinary.

I return to these arguments about the identity of the ordinary citizen in chapter 5. In the present chapter (and in chapter 4), I focus more intently on a different set of issues raised at the end of chapter 2. I there briefly highlighted *Frogs'* simultaneous emphasis on equality and kinship among the Athenians and on the necessity of elevating some citizens above the rest as "the right leaders." In this we might see another aspect of Aristophanes's distance from uncritical populism. Though his plays take ordinary citizens as their heroes and heroines, they do not simply reject any role for elites, thereby endorsing popular rebellion against all claims of political authority. Indeed, Aristophanes most often seems to assume the presence of elites in democratic politics and to focus his attention instead on how ordinary citizens might act in this context. In the present chapter, I focus on a seemingly common response of the ordinary citizen to the perceived dominance of elites: anger.

This sort of anger is hardly limited to Aristophanes's plays or to ancient Athens. From time to time in contemporary American politics, we are warned of the dangerous anger of the mass of ordinary citizens. Such was the case in the wake of the financial meltdown of late 2008 and early 2009. In the midst of the February 2009 battle over Barack Obama's $787 billion stimulus package, *New York Times* columnist Frank Rich diagnosed a "tsunami of populist rage coursing through America." Rich argued that this rage ran deeper than mere public annoyance with the failure of several of Obama's cabinet nominees to pay their taxes, and he argued that it did not amount to "blind class hatred." Rather, Rich described a basic sense on the part of ordinary citizens that "the system has been fixed for too long." He even found in this widespread populist sensibility an explanation for the popularity of the film *Slumdog Millionaire*.[1]

Not long after, *Newsweek* placed on its April 1 cover a grainy black and white photo of angry citizens carrying torches, with the promise that inside the magazine readers would find "The Thinking Man's Guide to Populist Rage." We might well ask whether most Americans were really enraged—as opposed to, say, afraid or anxious or confused—in the spring of 2008. But of equal interest is the suggested contrast between the enraged populist and the "thinking man" (the enraged populists of *Newsweek*'s cover are indeed all men, each dressed in the garb of the 1920s). The idea seems to be that populists don't think or perhaps are not capable of thought. Something similar seems to underlie Rich's description of the challenge facing Obama in early 2009: populist rage is a "tsunami" that "could maim the president's best-laid plans and what remains of our economy if he doesn't get in front of the mounting public anger."[2] "Getting in front of" means leading, working to "inspire confidence and stave off panic" while "building public support" for particular policies. For Rich, because Obama is not "tone deaf to this [populist] rage," and because, no doubt, he is more thoughtful than the angry masses, he might yet be able to direct it. A year later, though, media outlets and the blogosphere continued to warn of the danger to the political elite of an enraged citizenry—and with some reason, given, for example, the crowds gathered outside the Capitol during the final votes on health care reform in late March, 2010.

Such diagnoses of populist anger are hardly novel in the American context. As one particularly prominent example, consider the historian Richard Hofstadter's account of America's late-nineteenth-century populists and of the lingering echoes of their rage. In *The Age of Reform*, Hofstadter offers a great deal of evidence from the rhetoric and writings of American populists that suggest that they were indeed angry. That anger was most focused upon Eastern elites and in particular on politicians, bankers, and financiers who would constrict the money supply and deny the populist demand for the free coinage of silver which, or so the populists thought, would relieve the burden of debt, particularly in the rural areas of the Midwest, West, and South where populism flourished. More diffusely, Hofstadter argued, populist anger was directed at "everyone remote and alien." Such people were "distrusted and hated—even Americans, if they happened to be city people."[3] Writing in 1955, Hofstadter concluded that "populist thinking has survived in our own time, partly as an undercurrent of provincial resentments, popular and 'democratic' rebelliousness and suspiciousness and nativism."[4]

Without denying that Hofstadter (and many others) are correct in locating anger as central to populist sentiment, we can note the gap between the language of "provincial resentments" and the self-descriptions of (at least some of) the nineteenth-century populists. In the documents by which they as an organized movement sought entrée into the mainstream of American national politics, the populists did not tend openly to describe themselves as "angry." The National People's Party Platform of 1892, for example, declares that "the people are demoralized," having been "plundered," and it is full of the language of condemnation and demand, complaining of the "prolific womb of governmental injustice" from which have emerged the "grievous wrongs [that] have been committed on the suffering people."[5] And yet, the populists declare that, particularly having gathered on July 4, they are "filled with the spirit of the grand general and chief who established our independence." Now the spirit of Washington might well fit with the People's Party's call for unity among "all who hate tyranny and oppression," but Washington as American icon tends to conjure images of gentlemanly restraint rather than popular anger. Four years later, the National People's Party Platform of 1896 is, if anything, less prone to the rhetoric of anger.[6] It declares that "the country has reached a crisis," laments the "defeat of the will of the people," and proceeds to "denounce" and "demand" in ways familiar from the 1892 document. But it speaks not of hatred or anger or even indignation.[7]

In book 4 of the *Nicomachean Ethics*, Aristotle famously writes that, while it is easy to get angry, "it is hard to define how, against whom, about what, and how long we should be angry, and up to what point someone is acting correctly or in error."[8] It would appear that on an even more basic level, knowing *whether* someone—the typical populist in the cases just reviewed— is angry can be difficult as well. Whether ordinary citizens are angry, it would appear, is not a matter for straightforward psychological diagnosis; it is in considerable part a subject of political rhetoric. I will return in the conclusion of this chapter to this fundamental question of whether populist sentiment is properly understood as anger. But let us posit for now that it is. If so, we might note that as a subject of political rhetoric and as an actual emotive response to political events, anger in these cases is intertwined with the relationship between leaders and followers, elites and ordinary citizens. More broadly, it is intertwined with perceptions that the "system" is "fixed," that "grievous wrongs" have been inflicted, that "the will of the people" has been stymied. Politically motivated attributions of anger and actual anger itself, that is, attend basic issues of elite (mis)rule.

In this chapter, drawing on *Wasps* and *Birds*, I argue that Aristophanes appreciates this intertwining of issues of political temperament with the relationship between elites and ordinary citizens. I do so against the backdrop of the challenge of democratic citizenship and my broad claim that Aristophanes points to a comic disposition that might enable ordinary citizens to meet that challenge. My arguments here to a large extent focus on the rebellious impulse of democracy. In this chapter, I think about the relationship of that impulse to anger at elites or, more generally, anger at the very idea of being ruled. At the same time, I read *Wasps* and, in particular, *Birds* as pointing to the inevitability of rule of some sort and so toward the other impulse of democracy: its call for citizens to engage in ordered collective action that forms of rule seem to promise. I argue that the anger of the ordinary citizen for Aristophanes flows both from the tension between rebellion and rule and from the contingency that adheres in the logic of rule itself. Anger, that is, threatens to attend the challenge of democratic citizenship in deep and complex ways. Borrowing from and tweaking Aristotle, we might, then, say that locating the kind of disposition needed for meeting that challenge necessarily requires thinking "how, against whom, about what, and how long" ordinary citizens "should be angry, and up to what point" they "are acting correctly or in error." The comic disposition of ordinary citizenship, that is, demands an appropriate attitude toward the anger that seems inevitably to follow the very idea of rule.

Wasps and the Contingency of Rule

The plot of *Wasps* revolves around the conflict between Philocleon, an older, relatively well-off Athenian who simply loves serving as a juror in the lawcourts[9] and his son Bdelycleon, who desperately wishes to cure his father of this bizarre "sickness [*noson*]" (87). The play opens with Philocleon working ingeniously to escape from the family home, where Bdelycleon has tried to no avail to confine him. Father and son eventually settle on a kind of compromise. Philocleon agrees to stay out of the Athenian lawcourts. Bdelycleon, in turn, helps the old man recreate the experience of being a juror at home, setting up a mock court whose first defendant is the family dog, which stands accused of stealing cheese from the kitchen.

Meanwhile, Bdelycleon launches a plan to broaden his father's social horizons, sending him off to an aristocratic symposium for which he proves entirely ill prepared. Indeed, the play ends with the possibility that Philocleon will himself face prosecution for abducting a slave girl and assaulting fellow citizens on his way home from the party. Like so many of Aristophanes's comedies, then, *Wasps* ends with the apparent resolution of its fundamental conflict rendered problematic by emerging complications. Bdelycleon has found a way to keep his father from being a juror, but it is unclear whether he can keep his father out of court.

A key question concerns how this complex ending bears upon a central theme of the play: anger in Athenian politics. The centrality of anger is suggested by the chorus of wasps who give the play its name. Bdelycleon early on warns of the danger they pose: "You sorry fool, whoever riles that tribe of oldsters riles a wasps' nest. They've got stingers, extremely sharp, sticking out from their rumps, that they stab with, and they leap and attack, crackling like sparks" (223–27). Later, the chorus leader describes the wasps as "men who are sharp spirited and righteous, and look mustard at you" (454–55).

Though he differs from the wasps in important respects—most significantly, he is not poor and so not as dependent on jury pay as they are[10]—Philocleon shares their love of harshly judging defendants. Confined to the house but shouting to his friends from a window he declares, "I'm ever ready to go with you to the voting urns and cause some pain" (321–22). As his name suggests, he also shares with them "love" of the demagogue Cleon who, he says, "puts his arm around us and swats away the flies" (596). A key issue in the conflict between Philocleon and his father in fact concerns whether Cleon's fawning treatment of the jurors represents the power they wield due to their waspish anger or, alternatively, their being duped by a masterful manipulator.

Surveying all this, Danielle Allen argues that *Wasps* explores two possible solutions to the problem of anger in Athenian democratic politics. The first is that pursued by Bdelycleon, who aims to "cure" his father of the disease of anger by locking him up at home. Thinking of Philocleon's behavior at the end of the play, Allen suggests that this strategy serves only to turn the old man into "something of a manic tragic monster." Domesticating anger, in other words, simply does not work. Allen finds in the criticisms Bdelycleon offers of the behavior of his father and the other jurors hints of the second solution. She contends that "two of Bdelycleon's criticisms are not refuted by the end of the play: [first,] the demagogues have the citizens under their thumb and are thereby gutting the power of the judicial system to sustain the democracy; [second,] the anger of the jurors should be preventing this but it is not"[11] For Allen, *Wasps* ultimately points not just to the inevitability of anger in democratic politics but toward the value of what she terms "straightforward democratic anger." Working through "institutionalized processes"—including the jury system in the lawcourts—this sort of anger allows "the *demos* [to] keep reasonable control over the competitions between men in the city," ensuring "the maintenance of equality" and "reasonable distributions of honor" among citizens. What *Wasps* points to, then, is the need for a proper (re)direction of the anger of citizens like Bdelycleon.

That idea of properly directing the anger of the *demos* at first calls to mind Rich's sense of the need to "get out in front" of populist rage. Allen, however, does not seem to have in mind the elite direction (or manipulation) of anger. We might thus cast Allen's call for straightforward *democratic* anger in terms of the two impulses of democracy. In a sense, Philocleon as manic tragic monster seems driven by the indiscriminate impulse of rebellion. His anger falls on whoever aims to hold him back, whoever tries to rule him. Allen's emphasis on institutionalized processes that might domesticate anger calls forth democracy's impulse toward responsible collective action. Put this way, straightforward democratic anger seems akin to Sheldon Wolin's paradoxical formless forms or to the kind of emergent institutions Josiah Ober argues made Athenian democracy so effective. Institutionalized processes preserve the angry impulse of rebellion but by rendering it straightforward make it constructive rather than merely destructive. Whether this idea of containing while preserving the anger of the ordinary citizen is in fact plausible or desirable, though, will depend in considerable part on the origins and character of that anger. Is Philocleon's anger a matter in fact driven by his rebellion against the imposition of rule?

Here it helps to think about how well the two responses to anger Allen finds in *Wasps* map onto the two philosophical responses to democracy that Rancière attributes to Plato and Aristotle.[12] As discussed in chapter 1, Rancière argues that by establishing the sensible borders (or shores) of a community, a distribution of the sensible necessarily excludes from the community those whose expressions it renders insensible or nonsensical. This is the basic strategy marked by the deployment of the sort of archipolitics Rancière finds in Plato: "'The people' is the name, the form of subjectification, of this immemorial and perennial wrong through which the social order is symbolized by dooming the majority of speaking beings to the night of silence or to the animal noise of voices expressing pleasure or pain."[13] A distribution of the sensible also establishes a hierarchy among the recognized parts of the community. This hierarchy underlies the strategy marked by the deployment of Aristotelian "parapolitics" or "democracy corrected." It allows for the inclusion of "the people" as a part of the community but simultaneously positions them as a subordinate part. Recognizing the duality of the people (as the whole community and as the common people) but using this "constitutive self division [of the people] for and/or against it," democracy corrected renders the people visible but safe. Practically, this strategy works "to institute the constitutional rules and customs of government that would allow the people to enjoy the visibility of their power through the dispersal and even delegation of their qualities and prerogatives."[14] Democracy corrected, that is, depends upon and constitutionalizes the complex distances between the people and themselves and the people and their "power."

Both of these strategies rest on what Rancière calls "the logic of archē," on the idea that certain qualities or dispositions qualify one to rule—and, conversely, that some qualities or dispositions mean that one is inherently unfit to rule. Applied to *Wasps*, this logic is most obvious in Bdelycleon's domestication of his father. Philocleon's anger, understood as a "sickness," marks him as dangerous both to the city and to himself, and so Philocleon and his anger are to be safely locked away in the *oikos*.

The same logic, though, might be seen as running through Allen's reading of the play as advocating a place in Athens for straightforward democratic rule. Anger here is not in itself disqualifying. A particular sort of anger, that which drives rebellion against the prevailing distribution of the sensible that would otherwise impose silence on the excluded, is in fact an important qualification for taking part. Provided it is channeled through institutionalized processes which work to keep the struggle for honor under control, anger need not be domesticated; it should be welcomed into the public realm. To the extent that Aristophanes does, as Allen argues, advocate the deployment of straightforward democratic anger, he engages in what Rancière calls democracy corrected. Institutionalized processes at once make the rebellious anger of the people, and so their power, visible and at the same time render it safe, guiding and directing it in a way that, by tempering the excesses of elite struggles, works in the end to ensure the continued place of elites in Athens. In Rancière's words, we might say that the idea of straightforward democratic anger in fact uses the constitutive self-division of the people for and/or against democracy.

From the point of view of the logic of *archē*, then, we might understand *Wasps* as either advocating eliminating anger from democratic politics or else using it to make democratic politics safe. This presumes, of course, that the political import of *Wasps* lies in its forwarding or at least favoring a particular ordering of Athens, complete with a particular understanding of who takes part in ruling, who is ruled, and who is simply excluded. It is to find Aristophanes engaged in a direct sort of political pedagogy that the arguments of the preceding chapters (especially chapter 1) should lead us to doubt. Rancière's understanding of politics in general and democracy in particular as "a specific rupture in the logic of *archē*," though, suggests an alternative way to understand the relationships between anger and rebellion and ruling and so a different set of interpretive possibilities for *Wasps*.

For Rancière, democracy ruptures the logic of *archē* insofar as it demands the recognition of a qualification for ruling that is, from the point of view of democracy's opponents, in fact the absence of any qualification: the presumed equal citizenship of all free-born Athenian males based solely on that free birth. Any logic of *archē*, again, rests on an assertion about the presence of some sort of qualifications in those designated fit to rule. From the vantage point of any such configuration, the *demos* "simply designates the category of peoples who do not count, those who have no qualifications to part-take in *archē*, no qualification for being taken into account."[15] The moment of democracy evokes the claim that this part that has no part is in fact the whole community—the demos in its wider sense not of "the common people" or "the poor," but simply "the people"—and so should rule. For the opponent of democracy, this amounts to a claim that those with no qualification to rule *are* qualified to rule and hence is illogical. From another point of view, this rupture in the logic of *archē* in fact reveals that any claim about qualifications to rule may be illogical, may be as much a matter of chance as Athens's use of the lot to select officials.

As Rancière puts it, "the logic of *archē* presupposes a determinate superiority exercised upon an equally determinate inferiority." But the emergence of the part that has no part calls into question this idea of deter- minate superiority and inferiority. Conversely, any particular logic of *archē* in this sense "miscounts" the parts of the whole, dividing them according to a sense of qualifications that may itself be nonsensical. This "miscount" marks a kind of "political wrong" that Rancière says "cannot be settled," only "processed."[16] This processing is not a matter of suppression or direc- tion of grievance but, rather, the giving of "substance" to the wrong as "an alterable relationship between the parties, indeed as a shift in the playing field." The wrong, which is inevitable insofar as it attends any logic of *archē*, marks and finds substance in politics as conflict between different (mis) counts of the community and its parts. As Rancière puts it in "Ten Theses on Politics," "political struggle is not a conflict between well defined inter- est groups; it is an opposition of logics that count the parties and parts of the community in different ways."[17] In all this there may be another angle from which to view the anger that flows through *Wasps*. Rather than see- ing Aristophanes as suggesting either that anger be domesticated or else brought into politics to be managed, we might read *Wasps* as exploring the inevitability of anger as a reflection of the irreducible wrong promoted by the imposition of a logic of *archē*. Anger and rebellion, that is, are directed not at *archē* per se, but at the illogic *archē* imposes.

Much of the conflict of *Wasps* in fact revolves around the problematic logic of *archē*. Enraged by the confinement of Philocleon in his home, the chorus of old jurors attacks Bdelycleon. When he and his slave Xanthias successfully drive them off (using smoke, as one does with wasps), the chorus plaintively asks of the audience, "don't the poor folk [*dēma*] see it plainly, how tyranny [*tyrannis*] has sneaked up on me?" Bdelycleon has, they say, tried to take away their "established legal rights" not by "dexterous argument, but autocratically [*achrôs monos*]" (463–70). As the play's agon begins, father and son pick up this language, contrasting *archē* as mastery with slavery:

Bdelycleon: You're unaware that you've been enslaved [*douleuôn*].
Philocleon: Stop talking about slavery [*douleian*]. I'm master [*archo*] of everyone.
Bdelycleon: Not you. You're just a slave who thinks he's a master [*archēin*]. (517–19)

The central issue in the agon of *Wasps* thus concerns the relationship between ordinary citizens and demagogues or, more particularly, the relationship between Cleon and jurors like Philocleon. As he does in *Knights* (which I discuss in chapter 4), Aristophanes diagnoses confusion in Athens over just who is the political master. Do jurors like Philocleon wield the kind of power they think they claim? Or, as Bdelycleon argues, are they simply being manipulated by clever elites like Cleon? *Wasps* in the end leaves this question open, a point to which I return below.

First, though, let us attend more closely to the connection between Philocleon's love of judging and the question of his *archē* or mastery in Athens. As evidence of his claim that the jurors' "sovereignty [*archēs*] is as strong as any king's [*basileias*]" (548–49), Philocleon begins by describing how "fortunate and felicitated" he is as a juror. As he makes his way to the lawcourts, he enjoys defendants "begging" and "groveling" before him. This is part of a broader set of claims Philocleon makes about the respect and deference shown to jurors, not only by defendants but by the "Council [*boulē*] and People [*dēmos*]" (590) and even by "Cleon, the scream champion" (595–96). At this simplest of levels, the juror loves judging because it brings him the kind of benefits—including deference—that only kings usually enjoy.

But these sorts of rewards do not fully explain why Philocleon so loves to judge. He goes on to tell us what happens after he makes his way through the cordon of favor seekers outside the court: "then after I've been supplicated and had my anger [*orgēn*] wiped away, I go inside and act on none of those promises I made" (560–61). If Philocleon loved judging only for the good things he could collect from those he is about to judge, then why would he not be content to make deals with defendants and to keep those deals? Indeed, it might well be that acting on his promises would, by establishing that he was a corrupt juror but faithful to his corruption, enable more such deals in the future. But Philocleon delights precisely in breaking his promises. It reinforces his sense of *archē*, of control or mastery. His love of judging flows from his sense of control. And, so he claims here, it ultimately has nothing to do with anger. His loves to exert control even when his anger has been "wiped away."

Of course, on Philocleon's telling his anger is wiped away by the supplicants who gather every time he proceeds to court, which is to say every day. His anger, then, is stubborn, resilient. It is wiped away repeatedly, and so only momentarily. We might say that it disappears whenever Philocleon's control is confirmed in a most immediate way: defendants whom he is about to judge begging and pleading with him. There then opens a space (literally speaking, it is the space of the lawcourts) within which the juror can exert, perhaps, a purer form of control, dictating the fate of defendants regardless of what he has promised.[18] All of this points to the possibility that Philocleon's anger flows from some challenge to his *archē*, or at least from a perceived threat to his sense of control. Philocleon (and the other jurors) are angry because, while they love being in control, they often feel as though they are not.[19]

All of this is compatible with Allen's understanding of Aristophanes's preferred solution: straightforward democratic anger. If Philocleon and his peers can be assured of their control—through institutionalized processes—then their rebellious anger or their angry rebellion can be soothed, contained. From Rancière's point of view, though, this presumes that *archē* and the love of control that attends its exercise can be institutionalized without residue or remainder. As I suggested above, the basic conflict of the agon of *Wasps* calls precisely this into question. To Philocleon's claim that he exercises mastery over his fellow Athenians, Bdelycleon replies, "You, master [*archōn*] of a multitude of cities from the Black Sea to Sardinia, enjoy absolutely no reward, except for this jury pay, and they drip that into you like droplets of oil from a tuft of wood, always a little at a time, just enough to keep you alive" (698–701). The response here is rooted in the same idea that benefits flow from and so indicate the presence of *archē*. On this score, one can imagine a tallying up of benefits showing whether father or son has the better account of who rules Athens.

Elsewhere in the agon, though, Bdelycleon points toward the deeper contingency that attends any logic of *archē*, as he explains to Philocleon where all the money that flows from the Athenian empire goes: "[It goes] to the 'I won't betray the Athenian rabble and I'll fight for the masses' bunch! You choose them to rule [*archēin*] you, father, because you've been buttered up by these slogans" (666–67). Who, then, actually controls the interaction of elites and demos in Athens? Do Cleon and his ilk manipulate the demos? Or do ordinary citizens, because they have the ultimate say in the Assembly, in fact control the demagogues?

Bdelycleon's arguments—and these fundamental questions they raise about the relationship of Cleon and his followers—eventually have their impact on Philocleon. "You're shaking me to my very depths," he says, "pulling me closer to your viewpoint, doing I don't know what to me!" (696–97). The mysterious nature of persuasion for the ordinary citizen will make another appearance in the discussion of *Wealth* in chapter 5. But whatever unknown thing is happening to Philocleon here, it is evidently not simply a matter of changing his mind about Cleon or about judging. His plaintive cry that he is deeply shaken might be played for great comic effect by a good actor, perhaps with a touch of ironic overstatement. But hyperbolic or not, Philocleon might well feel shaken. Bdelycleon's arguments aim to dissolve his comfortable certainty about his place in Athenian political life. I have here suggested the possibility that Philocleon's anger earlier in the play already reflects his unease on this score, his need to have his control, his *archē*, constantly affirmed and reaffirmed. Along these lines, we might read the passage at hand as marking the transformation in the agon of that anger into a dawning, fuller awareness that things are not what they have seemed. Soon after he proclaims that he is shaken in this way, in any event, the chorus leader announces, "I've slackened my anger and now throw in the towel" (727–28).

It seems as though Philocleon, who says that a kind of "paralysis" has crept over his sword hand, has slackened his anger as well (713). He has not, however, lost the love of judging that, I have suggested, is so closely connected to his love of control. His son hits upon the idea of trying the family dog at home because Philocleon, though he has agreed not to return to the Athenian lawcourts, says he would rather die—or kill—than "stop being a juror" altogether.[20] "Before I do that," he warns his son, "death will decide between us!" (762–63). His anger, it would seem, lurks just beneath the surface, ready to return whenever he is denied the opportunity to judge, to punish—to exercise mastery, control, *archē*. This may, too, be why Bdelycleon's plan to rehabilitate his father socially ends with Philocleon being "far the most drunk and disorderly man at the party" (1300).[21] Such is the description offered by the slave Xanthias, who has accompanied Philocleon to the party. He further reports that Philocleon, after gorging himself at dinner, "jumped up and started to prance about, fart, and make fun of people" (1305–6). He shouted at one disapproving dinner companion, "Say, why do you act the bigwig and pretend to be stylish, when you're only a clown sucking up to anyone who's doing well at the moment?" (1315–16). The charge here sounds rather similar to the arguments Bdelycleon uses to shake his father to his depths. Like his son, Philocleon intends to puncture the pretensions of one who thinks he has a position of prominence but in fact is a toady for those momentarily in a commanding place.[22]

My point here, then, is that Philocleon's anger flows from and later is directed at the contingency of *archē*. The bigwig is in fact a clown, just as the powerful juror is in fact a pawn of Cleon. In Rancière's terminology, the logic of *archē* is always based on an illogic, on an inevitably and inherently faulty claim about the bases of any hierarchical arrangement of rule. What Rancière calls the grievance attends this inevitable miscount. But we should carefully note here that the grievance is not simply the anger of the excluded. For Philocleon, it is the anger of one who appears to rule but does not, or does rule but not with any certainty of the real basis of that rule. The grievance involved does not seek the absence of rule but, rather, seeks a firmer basis for rule. As the play's closing scenes suggest, Philocleon cannot be cured of his desire for mastery. His anger is, in the end, an outgrowth of this more fundamental desire. It can be assuaged momentarily, but will return when his sense of control comes into question or when another—like the bigwig at the party—presumes to act the part of master.

Leaving Rancière's terminology aside, we might return to the language I have used in discussing democratic citizenship. In the end, we find that Philocleon's anger is not simply a product of democracy's rebellious impulse. No doubt he is angry in part because his son aims to impose a form of rule upon him. But as we have seen, he is also angry because he wants a firm basis for his own mastery or rule that he cannot, in the end, secure. The inevitable illogic of rule, in other words, means that the stable, ordered, institutionalized collective action toward which democracy also impels ordinary citizens will prove maddeningly elusive as well. In a sense, Philocleon's anger itself flows from or reflects the basic challenge of democratic citizenship. He both rebels against being ruled and seeks a basis for the rule of himself and his fellow jurors. The inevitable frustration of both impulses and the ultimate impossibility of finding a secure and stable reconciliation of the two (as might happen if either he or his son clearly "wins" the agon) infuriates him. These complex links between rebellion, rule and anger appear in *Birds*, as well.

Archē and *Logos* in *Birds*

In part, *Birds* simply celebrates birds. The gathering of the chorus gives any producer of the play an opportunity to present in vivid costumes the diversity of avian species, and the play's parabasis unfolds an elaborate cosmogony with birds playing a central role.[23] Throughout the play, the flight of birds carries with it awe-inspiring (which is not to say altogether positive) possibilities. Still, the play begins not with wondrous birds in flight, but with humans "trekking back and forth . . . rambling aimlessly every which way" (3–4). This suggests a basic thematic connection with *Peace*, whose hero experiences both the possibilities of flight and the realities of the earthly trek.

In *Peace*, Trygaeus flies to the gods and returns afoot to Athens. I suggested in chapter 1 that we might think of this contrast between flight and trekking as tied to the contrast between escaping the whirling *pragmata* of the Athenians and remaining connected to or perhaps mired in that very frenzied activity. It is interesting that when Euelpides, one of the two human heroes of *Birds*, turns to the audience to explain why he and his fellow traveler Peisetaerus are fleeing Athens (and thereby to set up the plot), he employs what from the standpoint of *Peace* seems a mixed metaphor: "You see, gentlemen of the audience, we're sick with the opposite of Sacas's sickness: he's a non-citizen trying to force his way in, while we, being of good standing in tribe and clan, solid citizens, with no one trying to shoo us away, have up and left our country with both feet flying [*anep-tomesth*]" (30–35). The mixed metaphor of flying feet hints at what turns out to be a significant difference between Trygaeus on the one hand and Peisetaerus and Euelpides on the other. Both plays begin with heroes leaving Athens, but we might say that Trygaeus, flying away on his dung beetle, aims at a more fantastic and decisive break with Athens than do the two heroes of *Birds* who, though they later will grow wings, can at the start of the play fly only with their feet. Though it is Trygaeus who by the end of *Peace* finds himself back in Athens, we will see that Peisetaerus and Euelpides in a sense remain more anchored in Athenian—or, for Aristophanes, more broadly human—ways throughout.[24]

Like Philocleon in *Wasps*, the heroes of *Birds* suffer from a sickness (*nosos*), but their sickness is unlike Philocleon's (and in a different way than it is unlike Sacas's). Philocleon's sickness—his love of jury service—compels him to be in Athens; indeed, it enmeshes him in the public life of Athens. By contrast, Peisetaerus and Euelpides aim to leave Athens for "a peaceable place [*topon apragmona*] where we can settle down and pass our lives" (44–45). Indeed, the heroes are sick precisely of Philocleon and his sort. Upon meeting Tereus—once a human, now a bird—who will be their guide to the birds, they describe themselves as *apēliastai*:

> Tereus: . . . tell me who you two are.
> Peisetaerus: We two? Humans.
> Tereus: What nationality?
> Peisetaerus: Where the fine triremes come from.
> Tereus: Not a couple of jurors [*ēliastai*], I hope!
> Euelpides: Oh no, the other kind: a couple of jurorphobes [*apēliastai*].
>   (107–9)

Henderson's translation of *apēliastai* as "jurorphobes" in a way understates the contrast between the heroes of *Birds* and Philocleon. It is true that Peisetaerus and Euelpides are afraid of the power of Athenian jurors. They thus cannot simply settle on a sea coast, for the Athenians will send a ship with a summons for them to appear in the lawcourts (145–46). But they leave Athens not only seeking to avoid the prosecution they fear but also and more generally to distance themselves from what the lawcourts represent. They seek, again, "a peaceable [*apragmona*] place" (44–45). More than just jurorphobes, they are or wish to be the opposite of jurors. Unlike Philocleon, who likes nothing more than to meddle in the affairs of fellow citizens, these two Athenians present themselves as simply wanting to be done with the public business—and busy-ness—of Athens.

For Philocleon, the lawcourts, and we might say more broadly the *pragmata* of Athens, offered an arena for the exercise of control. We might, then, think that the peaceable and very *un*-Athenian place that Peisetaerus and Euelpides seek would be free of the struggles of *archē*. More generally, if being caught up in the complexities of ruling and rebelling prove so maddening, why not find an an-*archic* place? In this context, Peisetaerus in fact turns out to be surprisingly quick to (re)embrace the struggle for *archē*. Cloudcuckooland, the fabulous city of the birds he helps establish, thus originates in a flash of insight on the part of the comic hero: "Aha, aha [*Pheu, pheu*]! Oh what a grand scheme [*bouleum*] I see in the race of birds, and power [*dynamin*] that could be yours if you take my advice!" (162–63). Peisetaerus's advice to the birds, of course, is to "settle and fortify" their place in the sky, so that it might "be called a city [*polis*]" (184). The birds will then be able to prevent humans' sacrifices from reaching the gods: "And then you'll rule [*arxet*] over humans as you do over locusts; and as for the gods, you'll destroy them by Melian famine" (185–86). Whether he has thought his plan through or not, this return to matters of rule and mastery—to the language and logic of *archē*—will by the conclusion of the play end up enmeshing Peisetaerus in precisely the sort of *pragmata* he had sought to escape upon leaving Athens.

Why would Peisetaerus, in search of an escape from the public life of Athens, so quickly seize upon the establishment of *archē*, with all its maddening consequences, in the realm of the birds? The answer seems complex in ways bound up with the complex relationship of Peisetaerus and his companion to Athens. As I noted above, where Trygaeus's flight in *Peace* suggests an attempt to break altogether from Athens, Peisetaerus and Euelpides's departure from the city leaves them—with that mixed metaphor again in mind—with a foot still in the city. They are bound to the earth and to Athens in a way that Trygaeus as he mounts his trusty steed is not. Euelpides emphasizes that they are "of good standing in tribe and clan, solid citizens"; however much they wish to flee, they are after all Athenians. Euelpides further explains that it is "not that we hate [Athens] per se, as if it weren't essentially great and blest and open to everybody to come and watch their wealth fly away in fines" (136–38).

That last line, with its sarcasm, nicely catches the complexity of the heroes' view of Athens. Again, they do not really disassociate themselves entirely from the city, but they do want a (perhaps permanent) break from it. With this complexity in mind, it is not altogether surprising that Peisetaerus—an Athenian "of good standing"—seizes upon the opportunity to found a great city, but we ought also to be wary of saying that Aristophanes presents his return to *archē* simply as a matter of an Athenian in the end being an Athenian.

It might be more accurate to say that the return to *archē* is a matter of humans being humans.[25] By contrast with the two heroes, the birds—who in Peisetaerus's scheme will in fact do the ruling—appear to have no prior understanding of the concept of rule. The language of *archē* only enters the play with Peisetaerus's scheme to create a city among the birds. We soon find that prior to the founding of Cloudcuckooland the birds themselves have had neither a polis nor anything like the concept of the polis. More generally, they appear to have had no system or logic of *archē* amongst themselves. Likewise, the idea of a system or logic of *archē* structuring interaction between humans and birds and gods seems entirely novel to them. They accordingly describe their relationship with humans in other terms. When the chorus at Tereus's bidding gathers to hear Peisetaerus's plan, they angrily warn that humans are "an unholy race, that since its very creation has been groomed to be my foe [*polemion*]" (333–35), and they describe human nature as "a treacherous thing always and in every way" (451–52). Tereus himself uses the same sort of language, referring to humans as "enemies [*exchroi*] by nature, yet friends [*philoi*] by intention" (371–72). There is here no notion of rule or mastery. The natural relationship of birds and humans is that of enemies, and it might be transformed into one of friendship.

Peisetaerus aims quite explicitly to replace this way of thinking rooted in notions of enmity and friendship with a relationship structured by and understood in the terms of *archē*. He does this, significantly, by means of what he calls a "special speech [*logos*]" (462), a "big juicy utterance [*legein*]" that he struggles to put "into words [*epos*]" (465). The key point of this speech, or *logos*, for support of which Peisetaerus cites Aesop (471), is that the birds "once were kings [*basilēs*]" (467). "In olden days," he concludes, "it wasn't gods who ruled [*erchon*] mankind and were kings, but birds" (481). He later again refers to the time when "the kite was the ruler [*ērchen*] and king [*kabasileuen*] over the Greeks" (499), and he explains why humans who call themselves kings turn to birds as symbols of their authority: "And so dominant [*ērchon*] was [the birds'] dominance [*archēn*] that in the Greek cities if some Agamemnon or Menelaus ever *was* king [*basileuoi*], a bird would be perched on his scepter, getting a share of any presents he received" (508–10). Such are the "arguments" or "signs" [*tekmēria*] by which Peisetaerus says he can "prove" that his plan will simply return birds to their proper place (482). His proof rests ultimately on the idea of *archē* and its previous unacknowledged embodiment in the kingship of the birds.

In the last section, I drew on Rancière for an understanding of *archē* as resting upon a logic—a *logos*—that in every case is illogical. At this point, setting aside the illogical nature of the logic of *archē*, we might say that the unfolding plot of *Birds* similarly suggests that *archē* is a *logos* and, more specifically, a *logos* told by humans and drawing its persuasiveness from *tekmēria*.[26] That *logos* works to justify a new regime by supplanting a prior *logos* that works in terms of the friends-enemies dichotomy. The new *logos* of *archē* proves persuasive to the birds, and Peisetaerus advises them on how to "reclaim your rulership [*archēn*] from Zeus."

Soon the city is established and the chorus turns to the parabasis. In a sense, the cosmogony the birds offer there might be read as a confirmation of and elaboration upon Peisetaerus's tale. The chorus thus echoes the claim that the birds are older than humans or gods. They are "the immortals, the everlasting, the ethereal, the ageless, whose counsels are imperishable" (687–89). Therein lies the basis for a new scheme of benevolent avian rule. "Mortals get all their greatest blessings" from birds, who will prove to be more accessible, attentive rulers, ones who "won't run off and sit up there preening among the clouds, like Zeus" (726–28). As an added attraction of the birds' new *archē*, if any humans join the birds in the sky, they will find a place—unlike the human world—that is "uncontrolled by custom [*nomō*]" (1755). That final promise figures in the complications that ensue in the second half of the play, when more and more humans come seeking the advantages of Cloudcuckooland.

First, though, let us attend to a different set of complications, deriving not from humans but from the gods. Cut off from humans by the birds' new city, the gods first send Iris to the birds to demand a resumption of sacrifices (1230–33). Peisetaerus mocks her, calls her names, says that she is breaking the law [*adikeis*] (1221), and declares that she should be sentenced to death (in a particularly funny line, Iris replies in confusion, "But I'm deathless!"). Later, first Prometheus and then Poseidon, Heracles, and a Triballian god arrive. Peisetaerus engages the latter three in argument, asking, "Won't you gods actually have greater power if birds are sovereign [*arxōsin*] down below?" (1606–7). His claim is that as the gods' allies the birds can help keep an eye on humans. This proves persuasive, and the three consent to the rule of the birds. In part this is a negotiation in which, as Heracles puts it, "Zeus surrenders [*paradous*] his tyranny [*tyrannida*] (1644–45)" to the birds. But it is also, again, the telling of a tale, the offering and acceptance of a *logos* in which tyranny is replaced by *archē* as the proper interpretation of the relationship between gods and birds—just as *archē* had earlier been accepted as replacing the friend-enemy dichotomy between humans and birds.

In *Birds*, then, *archē* appears as a *logos* told by humans to the birds, to the gods, and eventually to other humans. The acceptance of the *logos* of *archē* carries with it consequences—baggage might in fact be an appropriate word. We have already seen that this includes the potential overturning of custom, since human *nomoi* are not enforced among the birds. Among the customs visitors to Cloudcuckooland might be able to shed is, the chorus promises, punishments for runaway slaves and the prohibition on children hitting their fathers (755–65). Right on cue, one of the human visitors in the second half of the play is indeed a "father-beater" (1350). Perhaps more to the point for Peisetaerus and Euelpides and their earlier desire to find an *apragmon* place is the arrival in Cloudcuckooland of a series of characters associated with the day-to-day (mal)functioning of politics in Athens: not only a priest and a poet and a herald and two messengers, but also less savory characters, including an informer, an oracle collector, and a decree seller.

Once the birds accept the *logos* of *archē*, then, their new city soon enough comes to look more and more like Athens itself. If Peisetaerus fled precisely these things when he left Athens, his grand scheme for the birds in a sense brings him right back to where he started. No doubt that is why Peisetaerus gets so angry in the second half of the play. In scenes reminiscent of the ending of *Acharnians*, he greets the arriving humans with yells and kicks and punches. He drives them out of Cloudcuckooland. We might read this as a victory for Peisetaerus's dream of finding find a *topon apragmaton*. Alternatively, we might read it as a denial of that dream, a suggestion that no human can escape the lures and the consequences of *archē*.[27] And one of those consequences, it would seem, is anger directed at least in part at the tendency of other humans to complicate one's enjoyment of rule.

Birds, though, does not associate anger solely with *archē*. Anger in fact appears in the play even before Peisetaerus tells his tale of the birds' rule. The birds respond to the arrival of the heroes with outrage. When Tereus tells them that humans have arrived, they respond: "We are betrayed, we are impiously defiled!" (328). They call for "a hostile bloody charge" (344–45), and Peisetaerus and Euelpides are rightly terrified. Only when Tereus convinces them to hear Peisetaerus out do they "slacken their anger [*orgēs*]" (383) and "ground [their] temper alongside [their] anger [*orgēn*]" (401–2). *Archē*, or at least the promise of a compelling tale of *archē*, works here to calm anger. But later, as we have just seen, the successful *logos* of *archē* works to produce anger.

Together, then, the two plays examined in this chapter suggest the complexity of the relationship between *archē* and anger. Generally speaking, anger appears in *Wasps* and *Birds* as a consequence of ordinary citizens' response to the contingency of any regime of *archē*. That contingency is inevitable because rule is always a more or less clever tale told by humans to whoever will listen. Rule is always a *logos* but is also always, at least from the perspective of the ruled or the excluded, illogical. Anger will, then, often seem to be associated with democracy's rebellious impulse against a particular sort of rule. But because it flows more generally from *archē*'s illogic, from the absence of any sure foundation for rule, anger may also attend democracy's institutionalizing impulse or any tenuous balance between rebellion and institutionalization. Indeed, as *Birds* suggests, a certain kind of anger flourishes in the complete absence of *archē*. It appears that for

Aristophanes humans are driven by the anger that attends the absence of rule to seek the security of rule, to tell tales of *arché*, and they are driven simultaneously to rebel against the very contingency of those tales. They are driven, that is, to make themselves quite mad.

Arché and Anger

The reading of *Wasps* and *Birds* I have developed here might, first, suggest a reorientation of contemporary analyses of populist "rage." Aristophanes would have us understand that rage as directed not at a particular set of elites or even, in a sense, at elites in general. Rich's description of ordinary citizens as angry that "the system has been fixed for too long" comes somewhat closer to the mark. On my reading, though, *Wasps* and *Birds* suggest that we look beyond the way in which any scheme of *arché* creates a hierarchy fixed to benefit some and hold others down. The plays suggest as well that the anger of ordinary citizens flows from a kind of anxiety rooted in the inherent contingency of any form of rule.

In the contemporary context—and particularly in a time of widespread and deep economic suffering—we might see populist "rage" as emerging from two aspects of that contingency. To the extent that they do indeed see that the system has been fixed, ordinary citizens in a democratic polity will wonder whether they do in fact rule, whether they are, in the language Aristophanes deploys in *Wasps*, really masters or, in fact, slaves. Alternately, to the extent that they have come to accept the rule of existing elites and merely nominal democracy as tolerable, ordinary citizens might, again particularly in the context of widespread economic suffering, come to worry that the rule of those elites is uncertain. Put differently, *Wasps* and *Birds* point to the possibility that populist rage flows both from the sense that elites dominate and the simultaneous and somewhat contradictory sense that the elites in fact have no control and so their rule is ineffective. The ordinary citizen, from this point of view, experiences his or her own powerlessness but also comes to see those who occupy elite positions as similarly powerless. The resulting sense that no one is in control might well produce anxiety, anger, even rage.

Francisco Panizza describes populism as "a mirror in which democracy can contemplate itself, warts and all, and find out what it is about and what it is lacking."[28] The outpouring of populist sentiment in contemporary American politics, replete with the exclusionary rhetoric of real Americans and bizarre conspiracy theories of "foreign" influence at the highest levels, surely shows the warts of some ordinary citizens. The anger and anxiety on display, though, can also, in Panizza's words, help us to find out what democracy is about. As I have already suggested, *Wasps* and *Birds* point to the relationship between popular anger and the basic challenge of democratic citizenship. Ordinary citizens are subject both to the rebellious impulse of democracy and to its impulse toward effective collective action. We might hope for a logic of *archē* that could soothe the tension between these impulses—something like Wolin's formless forms or Allen's straightforward democratic anger. But that hope will always be disappointed, for every logic of *archē* is illogical, every claim to rule is a tale told by humans. The ordinary citizen is left, then, to negotiate the tension democracy enacts, and, again, that can be maddening.

The comic disposition that emerges from Aristophanes's plays holds the promise of meeting the challenge of ordinary citizenship in a sense because it engages fully with contingency and tension. Most broadly, as I argued in chapter 1, Aristophanes calls his spectators to embark on comic voyages that allow his plays to point in multiple possible directions at once rather than settling upon a particular meaning, message, or teaching. This comic voyage extends, as I argued in chapter 2, to the very idea of the ordinary itself. Aristophanes thus simultaneously places ordinary citizens at the center of his comedy but then asks that we call into question the distinction between elites and ordinary citizens. All this points, again, toward the need for—and the possibility of—a comic disposition that abides and perhaps even delights in contingency, multiple meanings, tension.

In this context, *Wasps* and *Birds* bring us up short. The comic disposition we might hope for in ordinary citizens promises a willingness to live with, even welcome, the tension inherent in democracy's relationship to rule. *Wasps* and *Birds*, though, suggest that that tension or contingency is deeply intertwined with anger. And while that anger might well be productive at times of democratic rebellion against elite domination, it may also be destructive. On this score, beyond the anger that flows through *Wasps* and *Birds*, we might also recall the angry Strepsiades burning Socrates's Thinkery. The argument of this chapter, then, leads to a basic question about the comic disposition of ordinary citizenship: how might we nurture a comic disposition that can abide the inherent contingency of *archē* without falling into unbridled anger at that contingency?

We can begin to frame an approach to that question by recalling that *Birds* in particular does not simply stress the anger that attends *archē*. It also, after all, celebrates new possibilities. In this context, I want to close this chapter by briefly considering another perspective on the relationship of *archē* and democracy that can help us toward a perhaps even more complex assessment of what Aristophanes suggests in the two plays under consideration. Patchen Markell has argued that in describing democracy as rebellious or disruptive, as resisting the imposition of form, Rancière, Wolin, and others nonetheless maintain the notion that *archē* inherently involves the imposition of order. For Markell, this choice between *archē* as order and democracy as disorder is a false or at least unnecessary. Markell turns to Hannah Arendt for an alternative understanding of *archē*. For Arendt, on Markell's reading, we can recover from the original meaning of *archein* an idea not of imposed rule but of beginning. In place of *archē* as rule demanding obedience, we can think of *archein* as a sort of beginning that requires completion. In place of closure and order, beginning-completion demands openness, an "attunement" to the possibility of new beginnings coupled with a willingness to relinquish control over where those beginnings will lead. For Markell, Arendt points to a world in which "there never ceases to be a fund of doings and happenings—beginnings . . . to which we might respond." From this point of view, "the most fundamental threat to democratic political activity lies in the loss of responsiveness to events."[29]

We might view *Birds* as in accord in two ways with the vision of *archē* Markell finds in Arendt. First, the play clearly takes as its focus the start of something altogether new. There is, of course, the founding of Cloudcuckooland, but there is also the growing of wings by the two human heroes. Each of these two new beginnings has questionable consequences, of course: Cloudcuckooland aims at empire, and the granting of wings soon extends to a would-be father beater. But as the dancing at play's end reminds us, the play does on one level simply celebrate Peisetaerus and Euelpides's successful escape from Athens and the (mis)rule of the lawcourts and the exhaustion of Athenian *pragmata*.

This points toward the second affinity with the idea of *archē* as beginning. It is not just Peisetaerus and Euelpides who make a new beginning, but the birds as well. The arrival of the two humans—and Peisetaerus's scheme of *archē*—offers to the birds not only the opportunity to rule but also the chance to move beyond enmity to a new relationship with human beings. Whatever satirical or allegorical aspects run through the play, part of its undeniable appeal is certainly to be found in its vision of escape—from Athens, from busy-ness, from anger, from the old—and of the start of something brand new and surprising. There is for the two ordinary Athenians who stand at the play's center an undeniable element of empowerment, empowerment not just over others, but empowerment to begin again.

Of course, alongside this sort of empowerment is the omnipresent contingency of *archē*. On the one hand, this contingency fits with Markell's reading of *archē* as a beginning open to a multiplicity of possible completions. On the other hand, for Aristophanes this contingency is deeply intertwined with potentially destructive anxiety and anger, and so new beginnings may bring distressingly familiar results.[30] Certainly this accords with the elements of *Wasps* and *Birds* that suggest that human beings cannot, godlike, rise above the lure of *pragmata* and *archē* in human life, even by joining the life of the birds. But, drawing on Markell's alternative vision of *archein*, we might say, too, that *Birds* calls upon spectators to recognize, to remain attuned and responsive to, the enduring appeal and the enduring possibility of new beginnings. As always, the comic playwright is concerned with both the possibilities and the limitations of the human beings. I turn in chapter 5 to address more directly Aristophanes's engagement with the fantasy of transcending the limitations of the ordinary political world. In the next chapter, though, I turn to *Acharnians* and *Knights* to consider in more depth how Aristophanes's comic heroes negotiate the contingent and maddening real world of elite-dominated Athenian democracy.

Chapter 4

Elite Domination and the Clever Citizen

Acharnians and *Knights*

Though it ended with a gesture toward the idea of new beginnings, the previous chapter emphasized the seeming inevitability of what appears in *Wasps* and *Birds* as an old and familiar problem: the inevitable contingency and illogic of any scheme of rule, of any claim by some to be better fit for positions of power. As I there suggested, this illogic or contingency stands closely related to the challenge of democratic citizenship as I have understood it in this book. Ordinary citizens are called both by democracy's rebellious impulse and by democracy's impulse toward organized collective action. The former impulse suggests that ordinary citizens (in whatever sense they are "ordinary") ought to resist the rise of any elite. The latter impulse may well allow and perhaps even calls for ordinary citizens to identify and follow "the right leaders," understood as those who can help the demos pursue its collective ends (including, as *Frogs* has it, the "salvation" of the city itself). The frequent recurrence of political populism, with its tendency toward the rhetoric of rebellion and its susceptibility to demagoguery—and its apparent anger, even rage—might be seen as evidence of the difficulty of balancing these two impulses or, put differently, of how often ordinary citizens fail to fully meet that challenge of democratic citizenship.

In this chapter, I consider the beginnings of an alternative Aristophanic response to the realities of elite rule in democracy. In doing so, I take as my contemporary point of contact theories of agonal democracy. Like many strands of populist argument, the idea of agonal democracy emphasizes what I have called democracy's rebellious impulse. With this emphasis in mind, I turn here to Aristophanes's *Acharnians* and *Knights* to consider how they portray the rebellion of ordinary citizens against political elites. In a sense, I mean to ask whether we might see the protagonists of *Acharnians* and *Knights* as heroes of agonal democracy. In the process, though, I find in the plays more evidence of Aristophanes's concerns about rebelliousness as the sole marker of ordinary citizenship. And I locate his possible response in a particular kind of cleverness. Rather than a precursor to simple rebelliousness, this cleverness maintains a wariness about elites even as it accepts their inevitability. In thus balancing the competing impulses of democracy (or, put differently, in abiding the uncertainty that attends the meaning of democracy), cleverness thus appears as a manifestation of the comic disposition of ordinary citizenship.

Dana Villa writes that "contemporary agonists remind us that the public sphere is as much a stage for conflict and expression as it is a set of procedures or institutions designed to preserve peace, promote fairness or achieve consensus."[1] Agonistic democrats thus share both a concern that contemporary liberalism has bureaucratized and domesticated politics and an interest in reenlivening politics with the spirit of the agon. Likewise, they tend to reject both communitarian and deliberative alternatives to liberalism as similarly taming the agonistic ethos that lies at the heart of democracy. Beyond these shared concerns, agonistic democrats have a wide variety of political and theoretical commitments.

The term *agonistic* or *agonal* democracy dates at least to William Connolly's use of it in *Identity/Difference*. "Robust" and "agonal" democracy, Connolly claims, "operates to disturb the naturalization of settled conventions," "exposes settled identities to some of the contingencies that constitute them," and "increases the likelihood that the affirmation of difference in identity will find expression in public life."[2] By contrast, Wolin—who as we have seen is often described as advocating an agonistic sort of democracy though he himself does not use such terminology—is wary of the politics of identity and difference.[3] For Wolin, politics "refers to the legitimized and public contestation, primarily by organized and unequal social powers, over access to the resources available to the public authorities of the collectivity."[4] Rather than the play of identity and difference, democracy for Wolin is a "rebellious" moment in which "the political potentialities of ordinary citizens" are actualized in the self-fashioning of a demos acting to end its oppression. Such important differences aside, what Wolin, Connolly, and other agonistic democrats share is a sense of politics as, in Wolin's words, "continuous, ceaseless, and endless" contestation—whether over identity/difference or "resources."[5]

My reading of *Acharnians* and *Knights* locates Aristophanes closer to Wolin than to Connolly. The most basic point I want to make, though, is a broader one: Aristophanes complements the turn toward agonism in democratic theory by providing us with portraits of ordinary Athenian citizens engaged in political struggle with the elites who dominated Athenian democratic politics. At the same time, he can help us to think not only about "the political potentialities of ordinary citizens" but also about the limitations of ordinary citizens and of agonistic democracy generally. Some of these limitations are in fact suggested by those sympathetic to agonism. Villa thus notes that agonistic democracy is subject to "compelling liberal objections," especially for its tendency to "exacerbate the divisions within society" rather than promoting compromise; he seeks a "morally serious and publicly oriented agonism" and finds it in Arendt.[6] For his part, Connolly recognizes the "permanent possibility" that the problematization of identity in agonal democracy may well yield a "reactive politics of dogmatic identity."[7] This will surely occur absent a "peculiar respect for difference" which Connolly admits not everyone would be able or willing to adopt.[8]

Running parallel to this concern that agonistic democracy might produce unsavory results on the collective level is the possibility that it may in fact rarely yield anything on the collective level. Thus Wolin's depiction of democracy as "fugitive" rests on his conclusion that, particularly given the scale and institutionalization of the late modern polity, the contests of politics will only rarely yield truly political "moments of commonality" when "collective power is used to promote the well-being of the collectivity."[9] The challenges facing an agonistic democratic politics thus concern both the political aptitude of the ordinary citizen and the collective consequences—whether chaotic or reactionary or ultimately negligible—of an agonal political ethos.

In keeping with the fluid and complex political vector of his comedy, Aristophanes, too, both celebrates what we might call the agonistic potential of ordinary citizens and simultaneously recognizes the limitations of agonism as a political mode, as a way of finding and acting upon moments of commonality. Put differently, Aristophanes suggests the need to balance democracy's agonistic rebelliousness with its impulse toward collective action. His plays, that is, point us again and again toward what I have described as the central challenge of democratic citizenship. In *Acharnians* and *Knights*, Aristophanes's engagement with these matters emerges from his own agon with Cleon, which I consider in the following section. I then turn to the plays, focusing especially on their exploration of the ordinary citizen's cleverness in battling elites. In closing, I consider Aristophanes's gesture toward a properly clever and agonistic citizenry that might yet provide a check on elite domination, whatever the limitations of the individual ordinary citizen.

Aristophanes and Cleon

Aristophanes's first two plays—*Banqueters*, produced in 427 BCE, and *Babylonians*, produced in 426 BCE—have been lost, and we know relatively little of either. We do know that *Babylonians* included open mockery of Cleon, who subsequently indicted the playwright in the Athenian law courts. The prosecution failed and Aristophanes soon resumed his critique of Cleon and his policies, with *Acharnians* in 425 BCE and *Knights* in 424 BCE. Beyond tangling with Cleon, both plays engage, too, with fundamental issues of war and peace familiar from the foregoing chapters.

Acharnians suggests a broad critique of the Peloponnesian War, of those leaders like Cleon who encouraged its energetic prosecution, and of the war's impact upon the lives of ordinary Athenians. In the play, an Athenian named Diceapolis, unable to secure peace in the elite-dominated assembly, arranges and defends a private treaty with Sparta. The attack on Cleon is much more direct in *Knights*, the plot of which unfolds as an allegory of late-fifth-century Athenian politics. A certain "Demos of Pnyx," obviously in some sense representing the Athenian people, stars as the head of a household and the master of several slaves who represent various Athenian politicians. The action revolves around the defeat of a Paphlagonian slave, who represents Cleon, by a sausage-seller who manages to win the favor of Demos by means of the very tactics of demagoguery which had served Paphlagon/Cleon in his rise to power.

That part of Aristophanes's conflict with Cleon that survives for us, then, is situated in the playwright's consideration of democratic politics as the interaction of elites and common citizens. As a backdrop for what *Acharnians* and *Knights* suggest about this interaction, we can turn to what Thucydides has Cleon say about democratic politics in the famous Mytilene Debate, which Thucydides records as occurring in 427 BCE. This is admittedly a risky move. We cannot, of course, simply take the Cleon of the *History* as identical to the Cleon whom Aristophanes battled in real life or the Cleon he caricatures in *Knights*. At most we might take what Thucydides's Cleon has to say about democracy as suggestive of a view in the air in Athens around the time Aristophanes wrote *Acharnians* and *Knights*. At the very least, Thucydides's Cleon offers a vision of democratic politics that sharply and usefully contrasts with what we see in those plays.

Along with his arguments that justice demands harsh punishment for the rebellious Mytilenians, Cleon's demagogic, self-contradicting attack on the role of speech and speakers in democracy has drawn much attention.[10] I want to focus, though, on his broader assertion that "ordinary people [*phauloteroi tôn anthrôpôn*] run their cities far better than intelligent ones [*xynetôterous*]" (3.37). Cleon here uses the same Greek to describe ordinary people that Aristotle uses in the *Poetics* to describe the characters of comedy. He uses the term just this once, and his comments on democracy remain more polemics than careful analysis. Cleon does, though, offer a series of sharp contrasts between the Athenians' bad political habits and the ways in which proper citizens might act. Just before he presents the ordinary-intelligent dichotomy, he thus makes the more specific claim that the Athenians fail to recognize "that ignorance [*amathia*] combined with self-restraint [*sôphrosynes*] is more serviceable than cleverness [*dexiotes*] combined with recklessness [*akolasias*]" (3.37). We can, then, explore how ordinary citizens are, for Cleon, ignorant and moderate, and how the intelligent are clever and reckless.

In disparaging the cleverness of the intelligent citizen, Cleon would seem most obviously to be thinking of the clever speaker who (like his opponent Diodotus) is too "confident in his rhetorical power" (3.38). *Dexiotes* suggests the English dexterity and, particularly in the context of sophistic teaching, we might think of cleverness as a special dexterity with words. Indeed, in praising ordinary citizens, Cleon says that they "are less able to dissect arguments than those who speak well" (3.37). Yet Cleon's point is not simply that we should trust the ignorant listening citizen over the clever sophistic speaker. For clever citizens lurk in the audience as well, exercising a more active brand of listening than suits Cleon: "what each of you wants most of all is to be able to give speeches himself. If you can't do that, though, you get the idea of a clever phrase and applaud it in advance" (3.38). The ignorance which Cleon admires in the ordinary citizen, then, at least in part concerns rhetorical sophistication. We need not worry about ordinary citizens stringing together nifty but deceptive arguments themselves, nor recognizing and approving (but somehow being fooled) when others craft such arguments.[11]

The second contrast that Cleon draws—between the moderation of ordinary citizens and the recklessness of the intelligent—appears frequently in one form or another in Greek discussions of ethics. In the *Gorgias*, for example, Socrates argues that the orator must consider "how temperance [*sôphrosyne*] may be bred in [the souls of listeners] and licentiousness [*akolasia*] cut off and how virtue as a whole may be produced and vice expelled."[12] Though he uses the same terms, Cleon no doubt cares little for improving his listeners. In decrying the recklessness of the intelligent, he mainly has in mind the way they act toward existing laws, decisions, and ways of acting. The intelligent speaker, "wanting to appear wiser than the laws," argues against them in the Assembly. Intelligent listeners are "slaves to the improbable and flouters of the customary," addicted to "new turns of phrase." Ordinary citizens, on the other hand, "regard themselves as less learned than the laws." Intelligent citizens will not pay attention to "what's tried and true," but, with the inherent conservatism that Cleon counts as moderation, ordinary citizens will (3.38).

Cleon's speech suggests a further contrast between good, ordinary citizens and dangerous, intelligent ones. The two in general approach political deliberations with a different spirit. Once more, the category of the intelligent includes both speakers and listeners. Intelligent speakers, proud of their cleverness, "aim to outdo whatever nonsense is spoken in public assemblies." As a result, they become "excited by eloquence and combat of wits [*deinoteti kai xyneseôs agôni*]" and are likely "to give wrong-headed advice to the majority" (3.37). Such speakers find plenty of intelligent listeners among those who like to "watch [*theatai*] debates and hear about actions" (3.38). They take important matters—like the punishment of the Mytilenians—and "make a game" of them (3.38). Ordinary citizens, by contrast, are not "competitors [*agônistai*]" but "judges who are equal to each other" (3.37). Summarizing the attitudes of the two sorts of citizens, Cleon returns to the language of the theater, wishing for people who will act "like citizens deliberating about politics [*poleôs bouleuomenois*]" rather than "men who sit as spectators [*theatais*] at exhibitions of sophists" (3.38).

The contrast Cleon draws between the ignorant, moderate, and altogether ordinary person who alone can properly be called a citizen and the clever, reckless, and intelligent contestant or spectator points toward a choice between two very different kinds of democratic politics. We can have a politics that amounts to an agon of rhetorical skills where change and upheaval and rebellion are the rule. Or we can have a politics of firmness and stability, marked by the calm prudence of ordinary people who for the most part stick with what works. The differences between such imagined possibilities in ancient Athens and the realities of modern politics are, of course, vast. Still, there is a basic resemblance between the politics of firmness and stability that Cleon favors and the "politics of domestication, containment and boundary drawing" that agonistic democrats see in the liberal state and beyond which they seek to move.[13] Likewise, there is a basic resemblance between Cleon's critique of the clever and the contemporary concern that, if spurred to agonistic action, "the democratic demos may be unjust, racist, fickle, and capricious."[14] Cleon professes to worry in particular about the fickleness of clever, agonistic citizens, which in the case of Mytilene threatens an unjust leniency toward the captives. His response is to call on properly domesticated, ordinary citizens who will respect the boundaries of their own knowledge and so resist the impulse to rebel. In the end, such citizens will, Cleon hopes, follow the advice of elites like Cleon himself. Aristophanes, on the other hand, explores the possibilities of the agonistic alternative to this view of democratic politics—through a rethinking of the potentialities and the limitations of ordinary citizens.

Acharnians

In the parabasis of *Acharnians*, the chorus leader declares that Aristophanes has "never yet . . . come forward to tell the audience that he is intelligent [*dexios*]," thus using the same Greek that Thucydides's Cleon employs in deriding cleverness. Aristophanes does not go on to call himself intelligent here. Rather, he defends himself against his critics and brashly claims that for his work he "deserves rich rewards." He has, he says, saved the Athenians from being "*chaunopolitas*" (628–35). This term appears in no other surviving Greek text. Aristophanes has created it by joining the common Greek word for citizen, *polites*, with a form of *chaunos*, which takes the literal meaning of porous or spongy, and, figuratively, means empty or frivolous. Hence Aristophanes claims that he has prevented the Athenians from being "citizens vacant and vain" or "citizens of Simpletonia."[15] Later in the parabasis, Aristophanes also makes clear his disdain for Cleon, saying that he will never "be caught behaving toward the city as [Cleon] does, a coward and a punk-arse" (659–65). This critique aside, some of the basic complaints about the Athenians that Aristophanes includes in this parabasis sound like the criticisms of clever citizens offered by Thucydides's Cleon. Aristophanes thus suggests that the Athenians have in fact been *chaunopolitas* at times, falling victim to the fine words and flattery of speakers, especially those from allied states (635–45). And he allows the chorus—cast as elderly Acharnians—to forward a "complaint against the city." They find themselves being made "the sport of stripling speechmakers [*neaniskôn . . . rhetorôn*]" who drag them into court, taking advantage of their lack of rhetorical skill (675). In short, though he does not derisively label them intelligent or clever, Aristophanes is also concerned with speakers and listeners who are caught up in the joys of rhetorical jousting to the detriment of the city.

Furthermore, Aristophanes of course turns, as Cleon does in the Mytilene Debate, to the ordinary citizen as hero of the tale. *Acharnians* opens with Diceapolis sitting on a bench in the Athenian assembly, impatiently waiting for the proceedings to begin. Part of the charm of Diceapolis, part of what at once engages our sympathy and makes us laugh, flows from how very ordinary he is.[16] We see in him the epitome of the cantankerous old man who cannot help but draw a smile from a passerby, though perhaps a roll of the eyes or a shaking of the head as well. Diceapolis's first words are words of complaint: "How often I've been bitten to my very heart! My delights? Scant, quite scant—just four! My pains? Heaps by the umpteen million loads!" (1–3). After reciting a few of his complaints, he tells us how he spends his time as he waits for the Assembly to convene: "I sigh, I yawn, I stretch myself, I fart, I fiddle, I scribble, pluck my beard, do sums" (30–31). He gazes longingly into the countryside, he says, thinking of his home there, away from the bustle of the city. There is thus nothing particularly sophisticated about Diceapolis, no signs of thoughtfulness or great skill. Particularly given his age, attitude, and rural address, he might well be Cleon's model ordinary citizen, one whom we can expect to resist change instinctively.

Except that Diceapolis has come to the Assembly precisely to foment change. He wants peace and an end to the suffering brought by the Peloponnesian War.[17] More to the point here, he offers a critique of politics in wartime Athens. Of the "umpteen million loads" of pains he has, the greatest, Diceapolis says, comes from the Athenians' failure to put their political power to use to end the war: "they don't care at all about making peace" (25–26). Most of his fellow citizens can in fact be found not in the

Assembly but "gossiping in the market." As for the Prytanes, the officials responsible for conducting Assembly meetings, they never even arrive at Assembly meetings on time (20–24). Neither the mass of Athenians nor their leaders can be expected to act responsibly enough to bring the costly war to an end any time soon. Ordinary though he may be, Diceapolis will not simply go along with this complacency. At its most basic, the opening of *Acharnians* thus suggests that Cleon's generalizations about ordinary citizens are wrong: some in fact would seek change. The war and the suffering it brings drag on because the peace-seeking citizen faces seemingly insurmountable obstacles in the form of elites and the *chaunopolitas* whom they dominate in the Assembly.

Acharnians soon adds an element of fantasy to this critique of Athenian politics and policy. Diceapolis has come to the Assembly this day with a plan to reclaim some of his political power. "So now I'm here," he says, "all set to shout, interrupt, revile the speakers, if anyone speaks of anything except peace" (38–39). Many of those in the theater audience will have recognized Diceapolis's frustration and liked the idea of upsetting the normal order of things by quieting those who dominate the Assembly. We can imagine them cheering as Diceapolis tries valiantly to make good on his plan. As the Assembly gets underway, he tangles with the Prytanes. Immediately upon the opening of the Assembly, one Amphitheus enters, claiming immortality and a charge from the gods to conclude peace between Athens and Sparta. As the authorities drag Amphitheus away, Diceapolis shouts out that they "wrong the Assembly" (56–58). Now enter in envoys sent by Athens to the king of Persia. Diceapolis disrupts their report, calling them "peacocks" for their preening manner and gorgeous dress and trying mightily to expose them for the frauds and cheats they are (62). He does much the same to Theorus, who has just returned from a mission to Thrace. Diceapolis dismisses him as a "phony" who has only tarried so long on his mission because of the salary he has drawn (135).

Ultimately, Diceapolis's noisemaking in the Assembly comes to little; the Athenians still will not speak of peace. Thoroughly rebuffed, he declares in a spur of the moment ruse that he has felt a raindrop and thus causes the Assembly to adjourn. And then he does something truly extraordinary. Having sent Amphitheus to the Spartans to sue for a private peace, Diceapolis now accepts a thirty-year treaty with the enemy and promptly removes to his home in the countryside. Having tried, in the face of elite domination and mass quiescence, to confront the Athenians with their blindness to peace, he attempts to leave Athenian politics altogether. This declaration of a private peace moves the fantasy of *Acharnians* to a new level, again inviting those watching to put themselves in Diceapolis's place by imagining the joy of leaving behind the deprivations of war and the machinations of democratic politics.

In fact, though, Diceapolis's escape from Athenian politics is not yet complete. As he celebrates his victory and the joys of peace by holding, with his wife and daughter, a family-sized rural Dionysia, he is accosted by the play's chorus of Acharnians, who want revenge against Sparta, not peace. Thrown back into conflict with fellow citizens, Diceapolis seeks a return to the central mode of Athenian politics, asking for the opportunity to speak in support of his own course of action. "But shouldn't you know my reasons for making peace," he cries, "please listen" (294). Rhetoric, then, will decide the main conflict of the play. To prevail, Diceapolis will need some of the rhetorical sophistication that Cleon derides. In fact, he already has at least a touch of such cleverness. Ordinary though he is, he knows his audience and, further, knows that an orator must tailor any appeal to the audience: "And yet I'm apprehensive: I know the way country people act, deeply delighted when some fraudulent personage eulogizes them and the city, whether truly or falsely; that's how they can be bought and sold all unawares. . . . So now, before I make my speech, please let me array myself in guise most piteous" (372–84). Anticipating that the Acharnians will hate the message, he tries to soften them by changing the messenger. He will appear as a beggar, like the title character in Euripides's *Telephus*. This requires an appeal to Euripides who, after much haggling, consents to loan Diceapolis Telephus's rags. Apparently this ruse succeeds, for after Diceapolis speaks, the chorus relents.

Has Diceapolis, this newly successful orator, thus become the clever citizen Cleon disdains? Yes and no. Certainly he displays considerable dexterity, both in the speech itself, which is a careful, if comic, account of the beginnings of the war, and in the machinations preceding it.[18] Yet he does not become foolishly enamored of this skill. He thus wears Telephus's rags only as a temporary disguise: "For the beggar must I seem to be today: to be who I am, yet not seem so. The audience [*theatas*] must know me for who I am, but the chorus must stand there like simpletons, so that with my pointed phrases I can give them the finger" (440–44). Like Telephus's rags, cunning words and schemes remain, for Diceapolis, something other than himself. He does not, at least in this part of the play, fully take on the identity of the orator.[19] He and the audience both know that this is still plain old Diceapolis. He will take up rhetoric and trickery and deception in order to defend his peace, for that is how one deals with Athenians, but they do not overwhelm his character.

As the plot of *Acharnians* reaches its dramatic climax, Diceapolis thus appears to upset Cleon's simplistic categories. He is indeed ordinary, but he wants change, seeing that both his own good and the good of the city may in fact require a periodic rethinking. He lacks the sophistication of those who play rhetorical games with important matters—he is neither a sophist nor a *chaunopolite*—but he sees that a little skill with words is necessary at times, and he can be persuasive when he has to. Funny but not himself ridiculous, Diceapolis at once embodies a satirical jab at Cleon's depiction of the ordinary Athenian and offers a model of the rebellious ordinary citizen who takes matters into his own hands. For contemporary democrats—and agonistic democrats in particular—he holds considerable appeal as well. Here is a non-elite citizen who follows the course of public affairs, takes a principled stand for peace, finds the skills he needs to challenge the powers-that-be, and, finally, brings about the results he seeks—all the while maintaining a good sense of humor. Diceapolis is, from this point of view, an embodiment of the possibility that ordinary citizens can become "political beings through the self discovery of common concerns and of modes of action for realizing them," with the first and foremost mode of action involving a rejection of existing elites.[20]

Of course, we may well harbor some doubts about Diceapolis's attachment to *common* concerns, since his course of action has already led him away from the collective politics of his city. We might, that is, worry that he is somewhat too responsive to democracy's rebellious impulse. Such doubts can only build in the second half of the play as Aristophanes fully develops what Dover calls a "fantasy of total selfishness," which the audience no doubt enjoyed.[21] We might say that this fantasy itself works to puncture any preceding fantasy of Diceapolis as an agent of democratic transformation. We now see Diceapolis enjoying the fruits of his victory. He reopens trade with the city of Megara, rebukes rascally Athenian informers, and ends up in the arms of beautiful young dancers. Once concerned with his fellow citizens favoring the market over the Assembly, Diceapolis himself now seems chiefly focused upon private matters. What is more, he seems increasingly on the verge of becoming what Cleon calls a "competitor," one who enjoys conflict for its own sake. Thus when Lamachus, an Athenian general with whom Diceapolis clashes throughout the play's second half, stumbles back on stage having been injured on a mission, Diceapolis mercilessly mocks his suffering (1190–91). He seems here to show the same kind of anger that animates Peisetaerus in the second half of *Birds*.

We should perhaps like to see these developments in Diceapolis as themselves skewering any fantasy of total selfishness. The message to the ordinary citizen will then be something like, "were you to indulge your wish to leave it all behind, look how selfish and uncivil you might become." Aristophanes, though, will not let us escape our discomfort so easily. The play ends not with disappointment, but with joy. Diceapolis exhorts the chorus to "Hail the Champion [*kallinikos*]," and they gleefully comply (1231–35). Everyone exits dancing. Diceapolis may well have become a self-interested competitor but he is a victorious competitor, and the play gives no indication that he is anything but happy with his victory. His name—which means something like "What is Just for the City"—might easily enough be taken by the audience to refer not to Athens but to the new city he has founded for himself and his family. Better to live in the country in seclusion and peace than to bear the burden of membership in political life in Athens.

It should come as no surprise that the work of Aristophanes should call forth complex responses, especially from an audience whose members brought and still bring to his plays a wide-ranging set of wishes and concerns. As we have seen, *Acharnians* sends a mixed message in particular for the contemporary proponent of a more active, agonistic democratic politics. At times ordinary citizens may be more than willing to rebel against the status quo, and they may indeed have, or be ready to gain and wield, the political skills necessary to make a difference. At the same time, the play reminds us of the limits, often recognized by agonistic democrats themselves, of relying upon heroic action by individual ordinary citizens. Such citizens, though they may despise elite domination, may well be most interested in the joys and comforts of private life, making moments of truly political action, to borrow again from Wolin, "episodic" and "rare."[22] Or they may be distracted from their nobler goals by the sheer pleasure of contestation, losing the "agonistic respect" which Connolly sees as necessary.[23] In the end, if we refuse simply to dance with the chorus in celebration of Diceapolis's victory, we will have to think about how we might draw citizens like Diceapolis back into the political life of the city, back into the demos as a collective agent seeking effective change. We can read *Knights* as offering Aristophanes's fuller exploration of this challenge.

Knights

Knights opens with two of Demos's slaves, usually identified as Nicias and Demosthenes, worrying over the rise of the newly purchased Paphlagonian slave who represents Cleon. After the two briefly consider fleeing their household to escape "this damn new-bought Paphlagonian" with "all his schemes" (1–3), Demosthenes, in a playful—and very Aristophanic—bit of direct exposition, reveals the basic comic situation, focusing on the skillful manipulation of the unwitting Demos by his newest slave. The Paphlagonian "sized up the old man's character . . . crouched before the master and started flattering and fawning and toadying and swindling him" (48–49). Such tactics work, and the other slaves suffer accordingly. This exposition complete, Demosthenes turns back to Nicias in search of a plan for ousting the new arrival. Soon they have determined to steal an oracle from the Paphlagonian's private supply. That oracle predicts the defeat of the Paphlagonian by the sausage-seller, who miraculously turns up at precisely the right moment.

Much as *Acharnians* offers up Diceapolis, *Knights* thus quickly sets up as its most obvious hero a very ordinary citizen. When the sausage-seller wonders how he could possibly be destined for great power, Demosthenes reassures him that he fits the prophecy of the oracles perfectly, for he is "loudmouthed, low class and down market" (180). The sausage-seller himself warns Nicias and Demosthenes, "I'm uneducated except for reading and writing, and I'm damn poor even at those" (189–90). The humor here draws in part on some familiar satirical elements. Both the dialogue and the basic allegory of the play—with politicians as whimpering or manipulative slaves—skewer the Athenian political elite. Demosthenes thus says that "political leadership's [*demagôgia*] no longer a job for a man of education and good character, but for the ignorant [*amathe*] and disgusting" (192–93).[24] If rogues like Cleon can have such power in Athens, then the ordinary citizen, however ignorant, might just as well rule; indeed, they would be better than the current crop of leaders.

To realize his potential, the sausage-seller will, much like Diceapolis in *Acharnians*, need the sorts of political skills necessary to defend oneself in Athens. He will, that is, need the sorts of skills with which Thucydides's Cleon credits the intelligent citizen and which *Knights* suggests the Paphlagonian used to gain power: the skills of the demagogue. Unconvinced by the prophecies of the oracles, the sausage-seller wonders how he will defeat the Paphlagonian and thinks it "an amazing idea, me being fit to supervise the people." Demosthenes reassures him, "Nothing's easier [*phaulotaton*]. Just keep doing what you're doing: make a hash of all their affairs and turn it into baloney, and always keep the people on your side by sweetening them with gourmet bons mots. You've got everything else a demagogue needs: a repulsive voice, low birth, marketplace morals—you've got all the ingredients for a political career" (213–19).

Again like Diceapolis, the sausage-seller begins with a certain modicum of the qualities needed for challenging the existing elite. And, just as Diceapolis's skills emerge more fully as *Acharnians* unfolds, we see the sausage-seller growing in cleverness and confidence as he defeats Cleon/Paphlagon in one rhetorical battle after another. The chorus serves as his chief ally and cheerleader. As he first tangles with the Paphlagonian, they exclaim "how well and adroitly [*poikilôs*] you've mounted your verbal attack" (459–60), and after hearing of the sausage-seller's second victory, before the council, the chorus proclaims that he excels the Paphlagonian "in greater rascality and intricate schemes [*poikilois*] and wheedling words" (685–87). The word used by the chorus here—*poikilos*—has deep roots in Greek literature, tracing back to the wily Odysseus.[25] Our ordinary citizen has come far from his initial hesitancy.

Diceapolis and the sausage-seller thus follow a familiar trajectory. From political obscurity, both emerge to challenge powerful elites by honing latent political skills—most notably cleverness and guile—and drawing upon a rebellious, agonistic spirit. Aristophanes thus makes the same point more explicitly in *Knights* that he makes less directly in *Acharnians*. Cleon cannot depend on ordinary citizens to acquiesce apathetically to his domination of Athenian politics. *Knights*, like *Acharnians*, also offers up the fantastical possibility of an ordinary citizen standing up to demagogues.[26] From this point of view, *Knights* differs from *Acharnians* chiefly in the site of the contest. Here the ordinary citizen's agon occurs within the bounds of Athenian politics. Insofar as he competes for the attentions of Demos, the sausage-seller cannot, as Diceapolis does, withdraw from the Assembly. He must fight there; he does, and he wins.

This seems like a great victory for the ordinary citizen over the elite. As with Diceapolis, though, some doubts linger about the sausage-seller as a model of ordinary democratic citizenship. Though Diceapolis eventually fled from the political arena and seemingly lost himself in private concerns, he at least began with the noble goal of peace for the city. By contrast, the sausage-seller's motives from the start are murky at best. He seems motivated chiefly by power or by sheer love of conflict or, simply, by the adventure promised by the dubious oracles which Nicias and Demosthenes present. And, of course, to defeat Cleon, he must in some sense become Cleon, must out-demagogue the demagogue—hardly what we might hope for a hero of democracy.

Knights does offer another possible hero. In the character of Demos, Aristophanes presents the body of Athenian citizens in the body of one very ordinary Athenian. Demosthenes's description of him might well be a description of Diceapolis: "we two have a master with a farmer's temperament, a bean chewer, prickly in the extreme, known as Mr. Demos of Pnyx Hill, a cranky, half-deaf little codger" (40–43). In a sense, of course, Demos, ordinary or not, begins not as powerless, but as all-powerful. He is, after all, the master of the house. His decisions (or his whims) determine the status of the various slaves/politicians. His appetites and quirks shape their actions. But *Knights* problematizes this power. The chorus confronts Demos on his susceptibility to manipulation, noting both his "tyrannical power" and the unfortunate fact that he enjoys "being flattered and thoroughly deceived" and that "every speechmaker has [him] gaping [*kechenas*]." The chorus concludes that, "You've a mind / But it's out to lunch" (1113–20). Demos, in turn, responds that he in fact skillfully manipulates orators for his own pleasure: "I pick one thieving / Political leader to fatten; / I raise him up, and when he's full, / I swat him down" (1121–30). By such means Demos, so he says, retains control of Athenian politics and satisfies his own gluttony.

Though they acknowledge that Demos possesses "very deep cunning [*pyknotes*]" if he schemes in this way, the chorus members are not entirely convinced, nor are we. Aristophanes himself suggests a more nuanced understanding of Demos's cunning. As he makes ready to witness the decisive agon, which will end with the victory of the sausage-seller, Demos insists that everyone "move forward to the Pnyx." This greatly discourages the sausage-seller: "Oh blast my luck, I'm finished! When he's at home the old fellow's the shrewdest [*dexiôtatos*] of men, but when he's sitting on that rock, he gapes [*kechenen*] like a chewer of dried figs!" (752–55). This passage strains the basic allegory of *Knights* to the breaking point.[27] Aristophanes presents Demos to us as the head of a household; presumably the play, then, deals with matters of the *oikos*. From this point of view, it makes little sense to refer to another setting in which Demos is "at home"; he is at home throughout the play. This passage only makes sense if we think of Demos "at home" as the Athenians when they are at their homes. Here they are not one Demos, but many Athenians. In this private plurality, they possess the requisite cleverness to resist elite manipulations.

We have seen in *Acharnians* precisely such cleverness on the part of an individual Athenian in his private life. Diceapolis shows us what the ordinary citizen can accomplish at home. He also, though, points out the chance that the clever ordinary citizen will choose to stay at home, leaving us with the question of how we might encourage an ordinary citizen like Diceapolis to bring his political skills back into politics. *Knights* points to a more complex question. How might we move from a plurality of citizens who, like Diceapolis, are clever enough in their private concerns, to a properly clever citizenry that might, rather than being a mass of *chaunopolites*, show more care in exercising its collective political power?

Knights offers its own solution, as the sausage-seller, in the final scene, works a magical transformation in Demos. Or, rather, he works this transformation offstage just before the final scene. Having given himself over to the care of the sausage-seller, the two exit while the chorus offers the second parabasis. The sausage-seller then returns to announce a miraculous change in Demos, who has been "transformed . . . from ugly to handsome" (1321). When the chorus asks for a fuller description, the sausage-seller replies that Demos now appears "as when his messmates were Aristides and Miltiades" (1325). Here is the demos of the glory days of the Battle of Marathon, when democracy was younger and less radical. Dover argues that the new Demos points toward "a sentimental unity of social classes against politicians like Cleon."[28] And indeed Demos now offers something for everyone: for the lower classes, prompt pay for rowers in the Athenian fleet; for the better-off hoplites, a fair policy on transfers.

Such civic unity and solidarity need not be incompatible with lively democracy; some would of course argue that they are necessary precursors for democracy.[29] At the same time, the transformation of Demos hardly reflects a moment of democratic renewal. It is, rather ironically, the work of a benevolent elite. Just before Demos and the sausage-seller, whose name we now know is Agoracritus, move offstage for the final transformation, we witness the following exchange:

> Demos: Then to Agoracritus' stewardship I commit myself, and to his custody I commit this Paphlagon here.
>
> Sausage Seller: And you can count on me, Demos, for fine service, so you'll agree you've never seen anyone better fit than me for the city of Suckerthenians [*Kechenaion*]. (1259–63)

We should particularly note the way the sausage-seller describes Demos. *Kechenaion* is another Aristophanic coinage, playing on the sound of *Athenaion*. Its root, *kechena*, means "yawn" or "gape"; as we have seen, the chorus and sausage-seller have previously used it to describe Demos. Having won his victory and thus having risen from the ranks of the ordinary, the sausage-seller sees his ward as the same gaping fool—we might well say the same *chaunopolite*—as ever. The transformation worked in Demos, then, will presumably be based on more elite manipulation—only here it happens, by chance, that the particular member of the elite involved has retained rather lofty motives. Nor should we forget that at the play's end Demos retreats to the countryside, presumably leaving political matters behind in the city to be tended by the sausage-seller. Again, *Knights* ends on a note of joyous celebration that masks a more nuanced perspective on democratic possibilities.[30]

A Clever Citizenry?

Aristophanes offers a more complex and more hopeful portrait of the ordinary citizen than does Thucydides's Cleon. We need not gloomily or cynically dismiss the ordinary citizen as opposed to change, as lacking basic political skills, or as too conflict averse to challenge the existing order of things. We can aim at something more than the drearily stable pseudo-politics of elite machinations before a complacent, demobilized mass of citizens. In Diceapolis and Agoracritus, we see ordinary citizens who are willing and able to rebel against the existing order by standing up for themselves and defeating elites in combats of cleverness, rhetorical wit, and political maneuvering. And yet, lest we lose ourselves completely in dreams of transformations worked by the ordinary individual citizen turned hero of agonistic democracy, Aristophanic irony brings us back to ground in a way that recalls the "sore feet" on which Trygaeus returns to earth in *Peace*. The ordinary citizen may, in the end, seek simply to disengage from public life. The ordinary hero who, like the sausage-seller, stays in the arena to battle elites may prove victorious, though the victory may in effect require becoming an elite; and should the victor remain public spirited, he may embrace his fellow citizens in an undemocratic paternalism. As I have suggested, in this insistence upon the potential of ordinary citizens combined with a sense of their limitations as heroes in the struggle against domination, Aristophanes stands in basic accord with recent proponents of agonistic democracy.

Aristophanes also points to the particular challenge of crafting an agonistic politics on the collective level. In the character of Demos, he suggests that the individual cleverness of Athenians tends to disappear in the Assembly. Here too there is a basic affinity with agonistic democrats, who struggle to imagine a vision of the political—understood broadly as "the mutual seeking of some commonality in the context of difference"[31]—that remains both properly agonistic and appropriately sensitive to the realities of contemporary politics. Thus Wolin, building on his recognition that moments of democracy are rare, concludes that democracy "cannot be a complete political system." Wolin sees some hope in local democratic moments organized around "common concerns of ordinary lives," and he gestures toward the possibility of "a broader political" with the Polish Solidarity movement as a model, but he is resigned to the fact that such "rebellious moments" cannot endure.[32] Likewise, Connolly cites the need for a "politics of forbearance, generosity and selective collaboration between interdependent constituencies," but, thinking again of the challenge of "agonistic respect," admits that the "ethical dimension of political life" that would allow such collaboration is "indispensable and fragile."[33] Aristophanes, I think, has similar concerns in mind—and expresses them with greater clarity and more force—when he portrays the demos (as Demos) as either losing its agonistic edge and becoming the easy prey of manipulative elites or reveling in its power to manipulate those elites for selfish ends. Then, too, there is the anger that *Wasps* and *Birds* suggest abides even when ordinary citizens appear to rule. This anger lurks in the background and emerges, for example, when the clever Diceapolis has carried the day.

Aristophanes does gesture toward a different possibility, another way in which ordinary citizens might come together not simply as individual, angry rebels but as a demos acting to effect change. His model, perhaps not surprisingly, is the theater audience. Just as the demos in the Assembly holds power over the careers of politicians, so the demos in the theatre holds power over the success or failure of the comic poet. And sometimes, much like Demos, the demos-as-audience manipulates and mistreats its poets. Such was the case, the chorus says in the first parabasis of *Knights*, with the great playwright Crates, who "used to send you home with a low-cost snack, baking up very witty ideas from his dainty palate" but who like all Athenian poets also endured "violent rebuffs" and "barely survived, sometimes losing, sometimes not" (535–43). Elsewhere in this first parabasis, the chorus says that the "tastes" of the demos-as-audience "change every year" (517–18). Aristophanes himself wisely remained anonymous for his first productions, fearing the whims of the Athenian audience, just as the politicians/slaves fear the whims of their master.

As a poet, then, Aristophanes has his concerns about the malleability of the Athenians. As in his portrayal of Demos, though, Aristophanes credits the Athenians-as-audience with a sort of cleverness. Just before the Paphlagonian makes his first appearance in *Knights*, slave/Demosthenes attempts to soothe the sausage-seller's fear of his opponent: "And never fear, he's not portrayed to the life: none of the mask makers had the guts to make a portrait mask. He'll be recognized all the same, because the audience [*theatron*] is smart [*dexion*]" (230–33). Aristophanes here uses the familiar *dexios* to describe a different kind of cleverness. The members of the audience, like those ordinary citizens who fill the assembly, do not, of course, speak. Their cleverness is not a matter of the rhetorical ability or verbal dexterity of Diceapolis or the sausage-seller. Rather, Aristophanes credits the audience with a sharpness of vision, a capacity for seeing things as they really are. Though they will not literally see his face or even a mask painted to resemble it, they will know Cleon when they see him. Though they may change their minds often and though they may manipulate and be manipulated in turn, they can be counted on to recognize Cleon's demagogic ways in the words and actions of the Paphlagonian. As we have seen, Diceapolis makes a similar claim in *Acharnians*. Cloaked in the rags of Telephus, he says the audience will nonetheless "know who I am" (442) seeing through his disguise.

We might see this faith in the cleverness of the audience—understood as a faculty for recognizing the truth beneath the masks of elite actors—as Aristophanes's bottom line response in these early plays to the sort of demagogic portrayal of the ordinary citizen offered by Thucydides's Cleon. Cleon, too, made reference to the Athenians as audience, suggesting that at their worst the Athenians in the Assembly acted not as citizens but as an audience for the exhibitions of sophists, as mere spectators, *theatais*. Perhaps as an occupational hazard, Aristophanes has more faith in spectators. He does not explicitly suggest transferring this faith to the political realm, but we might well see agonistic possibilities in a cleverness that allows ordinary citizens to act as more sophisticated observers of the spectacle of elite politics. Citizens with this brand of cleverness would lack the heroic potential of individuals like Diceapolis or the sausage-seller. In the absence of moments of fundamental democratic renewal or in the intervals between such moments, though, citizens as clever spectators might provide a stopgap check on the machinations of elites.

Aristophanes's faith in the potential (if not always the current state) of his audience fits well with what I in chapter 1 described as his invitation to his audience to embark on uncertain comic voyages in search of the place of the ordinary Athenian. In the context of Athenian democratic politics, this sort of voyage, we can now say, demands precisely the sort of cleverness that Demos—the Athenian demos—lacks. In the context of my reading of comic voyaging in chapter 1, we ought not to expect Aristophanes to present a pedagogy of cleverness; cleverness instead we might expect to come in and through the voyage itself. But, again, in the case of Diceapolis in particular, this cleverness may come not with agonistic respect but with a kind of anger and vengefulness familiar from the previous chapter's discussion of *Wasps* and *Birds*. These darker political emotions suggest the possibility that the agonistic mobilization of rebellious ordinary citizens may at times slide into a ranker sort of enraged populism. This suggests, I think, that the wry, ironic vision that cleverness yields—that ability to see through masks, to see elites for precisely what they are—is not by itself a sufficient response to the challenge of democratic citizenship. And so I turn in the next chapter to explore fantasy as a counterpoint to irony and what I will call *comic recognition* as a supplement to mere cleverness.

Chapter 5

FANTASY, IRONY, AND ECONOMIC JUSTICE

ASSEMBLYWOMEN AND *WEALTH*

The last chapter ended with the suggestion that cleverness, while central to the sort of ordinary citizenship that might resist elite domination, may coexist with the kind of anger considered in chapter 3. Chapter 3, for its part, ended with the idea of moving beyond the limitations of a reality in which the maddening contingency of *archē* inspires rage. This chapter returns to the possibility of new beginnings, offering a reading of Aristophanes's final two surviving comedies, *Assemblywomen* and *Wealth*. I find emerging from a juxtaposition of these two plays a kind of comic recognition that, I argue, works by holding fantasy and irony in perpetual and productive tension with one another.

The English term "fantasy" has etymological roots in the Greek *phantazomai*, to appear, and *phantasia*, imagination. Though Aristophanes uses neither term, I here draw from *Assemblywomen* and *Wealth* an understanding of fantasy as imagining possibilities that involve overcoming limits or boundaries imposed by everyday reality. In this sense, the fantasy of fundamental material redistribution stands as a central element of the comic appeal of both plays. In *Assemblywomen*, the intrepid Praxagora leads the women of Athens in a plot to seize control of the city from the men; once in power, they institute a scheme of communal property designed to ensure economic equality for all. The hero of *Wealth*, an ordinary citizen named Chremylus, discovers that the just souls among us are poor because the god Wealth is, literally, blind; after he manages to restore the god's sight, the just become wealthy and the unjust soon enough change their ways so that they too might regain their riches. Beyond their appeal as a particular mode of comedy, these fantasies of social justice can be seen in part as responses to the economic realities of early fourth-century-BCE Athens. Alan Sommerstein has gone so far as to see in *Assemblywomen* and *Wealth* a radical transformation in the politics of Aristophanes, away from the traditional aristocratic posture of his earlier work and toward a greater sympathy for the suffering of the ordinary Athenian citizen.

Sommerstein's insistence that the plots of *Assemblywomen* and *Wealth* reflect Aristophanes's sincere interest in economic reform stands against a more widespread reading of the plays as deeply ironic.[1] Here the plays point in one way or another toward the impossibility of fantasies of change ever becoming reality. Thus Douglas Olson, for example, writes that whatever is suggested by a cursory examination of its basic plot, *Wealth* is "an essentially conservative text, whose deeper ideological aims are not necessarily identical with its apparent surface concerns."[2] For those with a proper feel for the ironic, *Assemblywomen* and *Wealth* in fact continue to preach Aristophanes's aristocratic politics.

This latter reading no doubt has wide appeal for a variety of reasons. It promises admittance to the elite group of those "in the know," allowing us to participate in the sort of "presumed superiority" that often marks irony;[3] it perhaps resonates with what Rorty calls "our increasingly ironist culture";[4] and, more particularly for the political theorist, it falls in line with the long-standing philosophical interest in irony from Socrates to some postmodern thinkers.[5] Still, I find ironic readings of *Assemblywomen* and *Wealth* lacking, in part, because they typically rest on a narrow understanding of irony as denoting the presence of alternative meanings that are more or less the *opposite* of the plays' apparent meanings. In particular, such readings tend to see the plays as subtly reinforcing the real impermeability of the limits or boundaries that fantasy imagines overcoming. As I suggest later, a more serviceable definition of irony allows for a wider range of alternative meanings that need not simply oppose or supplant the apparent meaning. More broadly, merely choosing one way of reading the comedy and thus the political upshot of *Assemblywomen* and *Wealth* seems too simple to me. Instead, I will argue that we must with Sommerstein retain a sense of the power of fantasy while at the same time recognizing that the two plays do indeed offer material for the ironic puncturing of the fantasies they present.

To a certain extent, a sense of Aristophanes's interest in both fantastic possibilities and ironic reminders of limitations has been implicit throughout the previous chapters. Still, my argument, particularly in the last two chapters, has tended toward a certain emphasis on irony. The kind of cleverness chapter 4 located in *Acharnians* and *Knights* involved a seeing through masks that we might think of as connected to irony's penchant for recognizing multiple possibilities, for seeing something beyond or in addition to what lies on the surface. Similarly, chapter 3 argued that *Wasps* and *Birds* pointed toward the fact that the *logos* of *archē* may be something other—something less certain—than it appears. Alongside the clear centrality of irony, though, there remains always Aristophanes's fundamental fascination with extraordinary—fantastic—possibilities. Put differently, the comic disposition upon which Aristophanic comedy depends and which it seeks to instill in its audience is not simply about seeing beneath the surface to what is real, it is also about imagining different realities. It is not simply about diagnosing and rebelling against the existing conditions but about working together to create a different world.

In this chapter, again, I explore this juxtaposition of irony and fantasy in the context of *Assemblywomen*'s and *Wealth*'s engagement with issues of social and economic justice. As I have in previous chapters, I work here in conversation with contemporary concerns. I thus orient my argument about Aristophanic comic recognition in the context of the recent debate among social theorists regarding the relationship between economic redistribution and cultural politics in "postsocialist" political action.[6] Obviously, we must proceed with care in making comparisons across admittedly very different contexts. Still, a broad concern flows through both Aristophanes's final plays and the recognition-redistribution debate: how ought we to understand the possibility of economic change in and through democratic politics, particularly in the face of potentially competing political or cultural goals?

I turn in this chapter to *Assemblywomen* and *Wealth* with this broad concern in mind. I claim here that we can use social theorists' arguments about recognition and redistribution as an interpretive heuristic for understanding Aristophanes's engagement with issues of economic justice in *Assemblywomen* and *Wealth*. I also claim that the plays can, in turn, make a particular contribution to the recognition-redistribution debate. True to the complex character of Aristophanes's art as it has appeared in previous chapters, though, this theoretical contribution comes not through analytical argument but through a poet's reflection on the comic disposition appropriate to ordinary citizenship.

Class, Status, and Politics—Ancient and Contemporary

Aristophanes produced *Assemblywomen* in the late 390s BCE and *Wealth* in 388 BCE. We can identify both long-term and more immediate contexts that might account for his engagement in these plays with issues of material distribution. Josiah Ober emphasizes the clear and consistent distinction drawn in Greek texts of various periods between rich (*plousioi*) and poor (*penetēs*), suggesting at the least an ongoing acknowledgment of material inequality.[7] No doubt the issue of inequality—and more generally the basic matter of material suffering—took on particular significance for Aristophanes in the 390s BCE. Athens at the time still felt the more lasting effects of the Peloponnesian War, including the loss of its lucrative empire, the dislocation of its rural population, and the destruction wrought by the Spartan army during its annual invasions of the Attic countryside. Some scholars disagree over just how far Athens's fortunes fell and just when they began to rebound, and we cannot say with absolute certainty that inequality in fact grew worse during the period because the fortunes of wealthy Athenians will themselves have declined.[8] Clearly, though, Aristophanes

wrote his final plays with an eye toward the suffering of the ordinary Athenian in particular and, more generally, toward the issue of distribution.[9]
This suggests the basic potential relevance of *Assemblywomen* and *Wealth* to a
contemporary engagement with economic change.

That potential, though, will remain limited if Aristophanes's understanding of the economic and its relationship to the cultural and the political differs too drastically from our own. Following the pioneering work of
Karl Polanyi, the prevailing primitivist approach to the study of economic
activity in the ancient world raises precisely this possibility.[10] Polanyi argues
that in "primitive societies" like classical Greece "the elements of the economy [were] embedded in noneconomic institutions."[11] As a result, economic activities and attitudes were shaped by cultural practices and values.
The Greeks, for example, "took pains to describe the only activity that in
addition to war and politics they deemed worthy of a free man, that is,
the working of the land."[12] The resulting "hierarchy of occupations" consistently placed agriculture above the "banausic" activities of trade and
manufacturing, but this distinction was based more on cultural or moral
considerations than on purely economic calculations.[13] To this sort of
intermingling of the economic and the cultural, Polanyi contrasts the
vaunted independence of the "disembedded" capitalist economic sphere.
There market mechanisms supposedly shape production and consumption
without interference from "blood-tie, legal compulsion, religious obliga-
tion, fealty or magic."[14]

Although Polanyi rejects this latter way of thinking as an "obsolete market mentality," its continued prevalence lends credence to the idea that
the Greeks may have had a fundamentally different understanding of economic life. Classicists and historians, again, have taken this idea quite seriously. Both de Ste. Croix and Finley, though they react in widely divergent
ways to the insights of the primitivist approach, thus depict Aristophanes in
particular as focusing chiefly on extra-economic matters of status. Finley in
fact defends "status" as an appropriate concept for the study of embedded
ancient economic activity, calling it "an admirably vague word" that can
capture a person's place in a tangle of "criss-crossing categories," including citizenship and landownership.[15] In contrast, de Ste. Croix insists on
the relevance of a Marxist analysis of ancient class struggle, centering on
the exploitation of the working class (both free and slave), and freed from
the ideological misdirection that follows from paying too much attention
to matters of status, as our elite ancient sources do. He thus dismisses Aristophanes as an aristocratic "snob" who judged material life according to
precisely the sort of status markers Finley emphasizes, though one who
occasionally showed a patronizing sympathy for the poor.[16] From the perspective of either Finley or de Ste. Croix, Aristophanes's reflection of the
embeddedness of ancient economic life, or at least his participation in the

ideology of status that masked ancient economic realities, limits his contemporary relevance.

Other work, although adhering to the basic insights of the primitivist approach, opens more interpretive space. Ellen Meiksins Wood thus explores the potentially fruitful contrasts to be drawn between the interrelation of the economic, cultural, and political in the ancient world and the supposed independence of the economic in capitalism. Writing of democratic Athens, Wood concludes that "as in capitalism, the right to citizenship was not determined by socioeconomic status, but unlike capitalism, relations between classes were directly and profoundly affected by civic status."[17] As this formulation suggests, Wood, unlike Finley and de Ste. Croix, finds concepts of both status and class relevant to the ancient world. The status of citizen was, of course, particularly central in ancient Athens. The definition of the citizen, while it did not depend on class and so allowed for the empowerment of what Wood calls the "peasant citizen," did turn on other status markers including gender, free birth, and, after the imposition of Pericles's citizenship laws in 450/451 BCE, Athenian lineage.

As Ober makes clear, other status markers—noble birth, education, and the like—continued to matter in interactions among those defined as citizens.[18] Despite this centrality of status, though, the basic class division between rich and poor remained alive as a chief concern of the political activity of the polis. The Athenians through their democratic politics routinely redistributed wealth by requiring wealthy citizens to undertake liturgies, such as the trierarchy and the *choregia*, and by paying citizens for attending the assembly or serving on juries.[19] Then, too, Polanyi depicts the Athenian agora, or marketplace, not as an independent institution driven by the laws of supply and demand, but as an "an artificial construct" of the polis. The agora, Polanyi argues, had equalizing effects both of a directly material nature—by ensuring a steady supply of cheap food—and of a more indirect political or social sort—by creating within its bounds a certain "equality of status."[20] In this context, the question for those granted the status of citizen was not whether to redistribute but how and how much to redistribute. My suggestion will be that Aristophanes engages with the question of redistribution understood in this way and, more generally, with the intertwining of what we sometimes separate as the political, the cultural, and the economic.

This more complex approach to the place of economic matters in ancient Athenian life and so at least potentially in Aristophanes's plays also makes the ongoing debate among social theorists over the relative priority of recognition and redistribution a useful point of contemporary contact. I have in mind in particular the controversy spawned by the work of Nancy Fraser on the relationship of cultural recognition and economic redistribution.[21] In *Justice Interruptus*, Fraser identifies three aspects of the postsocialist condition: first, the "absence of any credible progressive vision" of comprehensive social justice; second, the renewed strength of economic liberalism; third, and most centrally for Fraser's work, a "shift in the grammar of political claims making" toward calls for "the recognition of group difference" which at times "eclipse" calls for redistribution.[22] Worried that this last development imposes a false choice between pushing for economic redistribution or seeking recognition for excluded groups, Fraser argues for a comprehensive understanding of social justice that encompasses both goals, while properly holding them as analytically distinct. In developing this argument about the distinctiveness of redistribution and recognition, Fraser acknowledges the influence of Weber's discussion of class, status, and party.[23] Issues of redistribution, then, focus on class, whereas issues of recognition properly focus on status. Fraser also imagines a third dimension of social (in)justice concerned with specifically political exclusion and corresponding to Weber's idea of party, though to date this third dimension remains underdeveloped.[24]

Fraser insists that the distinctions she wants to draw work only at the analytical level. In political practice, recognition and redistribution are inevitably intertwined in the pursuit of "participatory parity" for all members of society, which Fraser calls the "normative core" of her conception of justice.[25] Although her argument has met serious criticism from a variety of directions,[26] I here want briefly to highlight the critique offered by Axel Honneth, who argues that the analytical distinctions Fraser draws are artificial and thus untenable. Honneth contends that attempts to bring about redistribution can in fact be understood as struggles within the three "spheres of recognition"—love, law, and achievement—that together constitute the "capitalist recognition order."[27] In particular, redistribution struggles aim at "mobilizing social rights" by appeal to the law or are "definitional conflicts over . . . the current application of the achievement principle."[28] In either case, they fundamentally aim at recognition—of the equal legal status of the oppressed or at their achievement of the status of productive citizens—with redistribution following as rights are recognized or principles redefined.

Broadly speaking, the redistribution-recognition debate hinges on an issue familiar from the contemporary study of the ancient economy: the relationship between economic life and matters that fall under the broad rubrics of culture, status, or identity. That is, in thinking about our own time no less than in thinking about the ancient world, we must at the very least call into question the notion of a separate and distinct economic sphere of human activity. The debate among Fraser, Honneth, and others suggests that in considering the possibility of redistribution, we must consider whether such fundamental economic change is in fact separable, analytically or otherwise, from changes in the cultural sphere—in matters of status and identity. I mean to suggest that Aristophanes did something akin to this in *Assemblywomen* and *Wealth*, responding both to changed economic circumstances and to the intertwining of class, status, and politics as described in particular by Wood. Borrowing contemporary language, we might say that in these late plays, Aristophanes explored the possibility of radical economic redistribution and its intertwining with issues of recognition in and through democratic politics. Of course, such a claim risks serious anachronism unless, in addition to the broad similarities I have been emphasizing, we take stock of some important differences between Aristophanes's time and our own. Before turning to the plays, I want to give proper play to those differences.

Redistribution and Recognition

That we can usefully relate Aristophanes's plays to our contemporary concerns makes them relevant; that the conceptual fit will always prove imperfect makes such a move interesting rather than simply pedantic. Two concepts, redistribution and recognition, are particularly crucial to my reading of *Assemblywomen* and *Wealth*. Of the two, redistribution poses relatively few difficulties, though some important differences between Aristophanes's time and our own emerge that are worth noting. In discussing redistribution, Fraser distinguishes between "transformative strategies," which aim to "change the division of labor, the forms of ownership and other deep structures of the economic system" and "affirmative strategies," which seek "to redress maldistribution through income transfers" and thereby "to increase the consumption of the disadvantaged."[29] Drawing on his argument that class in a Marxist sense had little or no meaning in the ancient world and referring in particular to Aristophanes, Finley argues that "ancient Utopian schemes . . . concentrated on consumption" rather than on changing the relations of production.[30] Again, the reminder that there can be little point in attempting to make a Marxist of Aristophanes is important. He indeed emphasizes the potential pleasures of redistributing food, drink, and other consumer goods, and especially in *Assemblywomen* the changes he imagines assume the continued existence of slavery. And yet Finley perhaps overstates the case. In both *Assemblywomen* and *Wealth*, Aristophanes imagines a redistribution of land, surely a fundamental factor of production in the Greek world. In this and other details, he seems to envision, to borrow Fraser's term, transformative changes in the life of the ordinary citizen.

Differences in contemporary and Greek ideas of recognition are more central to my argument that Aristophanes, by exploring a sort of comic recognition, might usefully complicate the terms of contemporary

debates about social justice. Two contemporary understandings of recognition are relevant here. The first might be called *identity-based recognition*. Articulated most influentially in Charles Taylor's "The Politics of
Recognition," it draws ultimately on Hegel and focuses upon individuals'
mutual recognition of one another based on a "presumption of equal
worth" of their cultural identities. Such proper recognition of one's identity works as a salve for the "real damage, real distortion" imposed by
"non-recognition or misrecognition" by others, which "can inflict harm,
can be a form of oppression, imprisoning someone in a false, distorted,
and reduced mode of being."[31] Now, comedies frequently enough rely on
the plot device of mistaken identity followed by recognition, and Aristophanes is no exception. Both *Assemblywomen* and *Wealth* include moments
of misrecognized individual identity. Aristophanes, though, shows little
interest in the psychic consequences of mistaken identity, and so the type
of recognition that appears in the plays will be of little comfort to those
contemporary theorists who do have such concerns.

A second recent understanding of recognition, which I will refer to
here as *status-based recognition*, emerges from Fraser's critique of the politics of recognition as depicted by Taylor and others. As I have already suggested, Fraser thinks of recognition as "a question of social status," thus
rejecting what she calls the "identity model of recognition," which she sees
as tending to reify group identity in dangerous ways.[32] The relevant harm
done by misrecognition or nonrecognition for Fraser consists not in some
sort of psychic distortion or injury but in preventing those denied proper
recognition from "participating as a peer in social life."[33] Recognition in
turn aims "not at valorizing group identity but at overcoming subordination."[34] Along with an element of basic mistaken identity, I will suggest that
Assemblywomen envisions something like Fraser's status-centered and parity-
focused recognition occurring for the women of Athens.

In turning to *Wealth*, though, we will need a more particularly Greek
notion of recognition. Markell's recent work on *tragic recognition*, or tragic
acknowledgment, serves as something of a model for me on this score. By
considering the centrality of recognition to Sophoclean tragedy, Markell
means to challenge the contemporary idea of recognition as an exercise
of sovereign agency over one's identity, reflected in particular in the work
of Taylor. Against this, he considers Aristotle's analysis of *anagnôrisis* in the
Poetics and the action of Sophocles's *Antigone*. He finds there an understanding that gaining recognition of one's identity, including and especially self-
recognition, is both "impossible and dangerous."[35] Tragedy thus depends
on the prevalence, even inevitability, of misrecognition and, paradoxically,
on the dramatic power of moments of recognition—though the paradox
fades somewhat when recognition is conceived not only as coming to know
oneself (as commanded by the Oracle at Delphi) but also as a dawning

awareness of every human's powerlessness over matters of action and identity. Alongside this fundamental impossibility of achieving true recognition of one's identity, tragedy for Markell ultimately points to the possibility that some assertions of identity and their accompanying demands for recognition—including Creon's "tyrannical" insistence on his inviolable role as ruler—in fact serve to support "social relations of subordination."[36]

What we might call a kind of comic recognition emerges in Aristophanes's late plays and especially in *Wealth*. Like Greek tragic recognition, it directs our attention to moments in which particular individuals struggle to assert their agency and in the process gain insight into their own being and their place in the cosmos. These moments reveal the fragility of particular humans, and they raise questions about the power or powerlessness of humanity. As Markell suggests of tragic recognition, a consideration of Aristophanic comic recognition can ultimately help to complicate the contemporary debates I have been considering. More precisely, the sort of recognition that occurs in *Wealth*, appearing most clearly as the hero of the play argues with the goddess Poverty, deals not with status or identity among humans but with the relationship between humans and forces beyond their control. This recognition draws on a different understanding of the cultural and thus a possible intertwining of the cultural and the economic for which contemporary discussions of recognition and redistribution cannot easily account. True to the complexity of Aristophanes's artistic spirit, this comic recognition allows for a measure of fantasy and thus holds out somewhat more hope than tragic recognition—though not foolish hope, for Aristophanes always juxtaposes fantasy with irony.

Again, the latter two types of recognition—status-based recognition and comic recognition—figure prominently in my readings of *Assemblywomen* and *Wealth* and particularly in my understanding of three interrelated movements from the former to the latter. Given the complexity of those movements, let me present them schematically here using the language of recognition and redistribution. First, Aristophanes moves from a presentation of redistribution and recognition as distinct dramatic and political moments in *Assemblywomen* to a presentation of redistribution subsumed in a moment of recognition in *Wealth*. The vision of social and economic change in *Assemblywomen* is thus broadly analogous to that offered by Fraser, with a change in the status of women followed by a redistribution that erases the class distinction between rich and poor. *Wealth*, though, does not somehow return to the position defended by Fraser's critics, for it, much more than *Assemblywomen*, relies on the sort of comic recognition just sketched. That is to say that the second movement I find from *Assemblywomen* to *Wealth* takes us toward an understanding of recognition that reflects some of the deepest questions of Greek culture. Finally, Aristophanes's portrayal of comic recognition in *Wealth* reflects a different deployment of fantasy and irony. In *Assemblywomen,* fantasy and irony stand juxtaposed as different perspectives on the possibility of radical change; in *Wealth,* they stand in tension with one another as elements of comic recognition and of the sort of sensibility Aristophanes seems to have hoped for in his fellow Athenians.

Assemblywomen

Ironically enough, the action of *Assemblywomen* [*Ecclēsiazousai*], despite the play's name, never takes us to the Athenian assembly (or *ecclesia*). The play's plot hinges on a decision made in a particular meeting of that assembly to give all political power to the women of the city. But rather than show that meeting, Aristophanes has the character Chremes offer an after-the-fact account of the proceedings. Chremes describes the subject of that day's assembly as "the salvation [*sōtērias*] of the city" (396). In practicing the speech she intends to give at the assembly, Praxagora—the leader of the women—similarly promises her imagined audience, "trust my counsels and you may be saved [*sōthēsesth'*]" (210).[37] Whatever elements of irony or satire we find in the play, and there are many, *Assemblywomen* thus most basically presents a fantasy. Aristophanes asks the theater audience to imagine and to enjoy the wondrous results of two fantastic transformations in the collective life of the city: the granting of political power to women and the use of that power to enact a scheme of communal property. Drawing on contemporary terms, we might say that the fantasy of *Assemblywomen* thus depends on a moment of status-based recognition, followed by a moment of redistribution. Each of these moments admits of an ironic as well as a fantastic reading. Taken together, the interplay of fantasy and irony in the play's presentation of recognition and redistribution serves to thematize the limits or boundaries of democratic politics understood as persuasion among fellow citizens about the city's well-being.

The opening lines of *Assemblywomen* make clear the centrality of recognition of some sort to the play's comic situation. Praxagora walks on stage, speaking to the lamp she carries through the dark night. She both demands that the lamp "broadcast now the fiery signal" summoning her coconspirators and praises the lamp's discretion: "You alone we make privy to our plot, and rightly, for also in our bedrooms you stand close by as we essay Aphrodite's maneuvers; and when our bodies are flexed, no one banishes from the room your supervisory eye . . . and you stand by us when stealthily we open pantries stocked with bread and the liquor of Bacchus; and you're an accomplice that never blabs to the neighbors" (5–15). The lamp, as "supervisory eye," sees or sheds light on that which is usually hidden—here sex and theft—but also, as an "accomplice" whose light spreads only so far, allows for the keeping of secrets. Here the lamp serves as a means by which the women of Athens might recognize one another as they emerge from the private space of their homes to embark on a most public scheme, but, Praxagora insists, the lamp alone can be trusted to witness the enactment of that scheme. Praxagora's address to the lamp points toward the complex strategy that she has urged upon the women of Athens.[38] She has told them to get "false beards" and to "swipe their husbands' clothes," for they are to appear in the Athenian assembly as men and, thus disguised, to carry their proposal that power be given over to women. As the women gather round Praxagora and her lamp, there ensues a rehearsal scene that demonstrates both the comic potential and the practical difficulties of such a scheme.[39] The women find it relatively easy to take on the physical appearance of men: "I threw my razor out of the house right away, so that I'd get hairy all over and not look female at all," one exclaims (65–66). But it proves rather more difficult for them to mimic male mannerisms and ways of speaking. As they practice speaking before the Assembly, one woman mistakenly swears "by the Two Goddesses" (155), another, "by Aphrodite" (189), as no man would. Another to Praxagora's dismay greets the "assembled ladies" (165–66). Frustrated, Praxagora insists that everything be "exactly right" before they proceed (163).[40]

In offering up the idea that women somehow gaining political power in Athens might be key to the city's salvation, Aristophanes introduces one of the key elements of the play's fantasy.[41] But these opening scenes also suggest much about the reality of citizenship in Athens. The playwright clearly points toward the fact that full participation in the affairs of the polis requires recognition as a citizen and toward the additional fact that gaining the status of citizen requires appearing to one's fellow citizens as a man. Without recognition as a man-citizen, one may not enter the Assembly, where speeches are made and heard and decisions are taken. This poses a seemingly paradoxical necessity to Praxagora and the other women: they must first make sure to be misrecognized if they are to achieve proper recognition as citizens. In contemporary terms, we might say that to achieve recognition as political equals (or, as it turns out, rulers), the women must forfeit recognition of their identities as women. From such a contemporary perspective, we might see *Assemblywomen* as suggesting a basic tension between status-based recognition and identity-based recognition. But, again, Aristophanes shows little concern with the consequences of mistaken identity for the women as individuals. Instead, he uses the strategy of mistaken identity as a comic point of entry for exploring status-based recognition as a boundary on democratic politics.

Precisely what Aristophanes means to say about this boundary remains unclear. On one hand, we might see these opening scenes as revealing how ridiculous the Athenian exclusion of women *qua* women is. After all, the differences between men and women appear remarkably superficial, turning out to be a matter of physical attributes that can be artificially recreated and ways of speaking and bearing oneself that can be learned or at least imitated tolerably well. On this level, the play invites the audience to imagine the fantastic possibility of getting beyond these differences and thinking solely about what is best for the city. On the other hand, we might read these scenes as enacting standard stereotypes of women as fundamentally scheming, deceptive beings who also, somewhat incongruously, struggle to find a proper political pitch as they try to implement their plans. In any event, a more ironic reading would emphasize that Praxagora and her followers have to become men in order to gain power for women. In a sense, the apparently fantastic overcoming of boundaries they achieve in fact reinforces the presence of those boundaries in the real world.[42]

Whether we lean more toward fantasy or irony in understanding the recognition of the women of Athens as citizens will ultimately depend in part on what we make of the scheme of communal property that Praxagora enacts.[43] Put simply, the success of that scheme would lend credence to the idea that Aristophanes means us to see the empowerment of women as a good thing, to view it through the lens of a joyous fantasy rather than with a knowingly ironic, even cynical eye. The meaning of status-based recognition and redistribution are in this sense inextricably linked in *Assemblywomen*.[44]

And yet Aristophanes seems to go out of his way to establish the two as dramatically distinct moments. Despite the frustrations she endures during the women's rehearsal, Praxagora's strategy of mistaken identity works amazingly well, and she will soon move to implement her plan for radical redistribution in Athens. As noted previously, though, Aristophanes does not have us witness the actual assembly meeting in which the women present and carry their proposal. He instead has a neighbor named Chremes relate the remarkable outcome of the meeting to Praxagora's husband, Blepyrus. Chremes tells of how a "pale, good-looking young man"—in fact, the disguised Praxagora—"made a case for handing the city over to women" (427–30) and, in the end, carried the day. Hearing this, Blepyrus soon turns to give to Praxagora, who has shed her beard and man's cloak and who feigns surprise, the news of her own success. One effect of this bit of indirection is to reinforce the complexity of the issue of recognition or, for the contemporary reader, to point again toward the tension between identity-based and status-based recognition. Even as they gain political status, we who know the true identity of the conspirators as women are not to see them acting politically.

A more immediate effect is to distance the strategy of mistaken identity from the scheme of redistribution, at least dramatically. Though she still does not take credit for bringing women to political power, Praxagora soon introduces her central reform: "I propose that everyone should own everything in common [*koinōnein*], and draw an equal living. No more rich man [*ploutein*] here, poor man [*athlion*] there, or a man with a big farm and a man without land enough for his own grave, or a man with many slaves and a man without even an attendant. No, I will establish one and the same standard of life for everyone" (588–92). The following scenes by and large bear out Finley's conclusion that ancient Utopian schemes focused essentially on consumption. Blepyrus does, it is true, briefly raise the issue of production, asking "who will there be to farm the land" once it is held in common. Praxagora responds simply "the slaves," thus affirming that, however much the life of the free farmer or peasant may change under her scheme, the basic mode of production will remain the same. If, with de Ste. Croix, we see the ancient world as a site of class-based exploitation—drawing, again, on a Marxist notion of class as defined by relation to the means of production—then Praxagora's scheme, and Aristophanes's outlook, is hardly revolutionary. On the other hand, her aim in equalizing distribution is nothing less than a fantastic alteration in the motivations of human action. Her central claim is that "No one will be doing *anything* as a result of poverty [*penia*] because everyone will have all the necessities" (605–6) and so there will be "no more mugging, no more envying the next guy, no more wearing rags, no more poor people, no more wrangling, no more dunning and repossessing" (565–67). She thus, for example, meets Blepyrus's concern about whether those who lose lawsuits will be able to pay the judgments imposed by noting that there will be nothing left to sue over (335).

Praxagora wins over Blepyrus with her fantasy of a work- and conflict-free existence, but Aristophanes soon introduces a more abiding challenge to the redistributive scheme. As the two make their way off to the agora so that Praxagora can collect everyone's private property, there ensues a conversation between their neighbor and a "Dissident" who doubts the very basis of Praxagora's plan.[45] The neighbor will eventually cry out against the "total skepticism [*apistōn*] of this man." In part, the Dissident's skepticism follows from a claim about what drives human beings in general and Athenians in particular: it is "not in our national character," he says, "to give up private goods" (777–78). This skepticism about the possibility of removing the desire for gain (or, in Praxagora's formulation, the goad of poverty) merges with a skepticism about the worth of grand claims like Praxagora's. The Dissident thus concludes that "on the strength of mere words I'm hardly about to throw away the fruits of my sweat and thrift in this sort of mindless way" (750) and declares, "I intend to be cautious, until I see what most people do" (770). At the core of the Dissident's concerns, then, are doubts about the power of "mere words" to change "what most people do." Chremes, Blepyrus, and most of their fellow citizens hurry off to the agora to turn in their private property, but the Dissident remains recalcitrant.

He, for one, thinks it absurd to imagine the citizens of Athens willingly parting with their goods.

Much depends on what importance we attach to the presence of the Dissident in *Assemblywomen*. Perhaps Aristophanes means his skepticism as a convenient foil soon overtaken by the power of Praxagora's fantastic vision. Or perhaps the Dissident reflects the ironic undercurrent of the play, pointing toward the ultimate unfeasibility of any radical redistribution of wealth in the face of both basic human greed and the somewhat more palatable human attachment to treasured goods. If we resist simply choosing between these two possible readings, we can see their juxtaposition as both locating and problematizing redistribution as the outer limit of democratic politics.[46] Praxagora sees the fantasy of a redistribution that fundamentally alters the basis of human action as possible through persuasion. The Dissident, and readers more attuned to irony, will see the material motivations of humans as marking the bounds of persuasion's power.[47] The dramatic separation of recognition and redistribution in *Assemblywomen* thus coexists with a thematic link. The two appear as boundaries at opposite ends of democratic politics. The dynamics of status-based recognition determine the constitution of the body of citizens (and bodies of citizens) that will be party to the process of persuasion. Ideas of redistribution, in turn, test just how far such persuasion can go.

Read in this way, *Assemblywomen* suggests a view of Athenian democracy that accords with Wood's arguments, discussed earlier, about the place of status and class in ancient politics—matters of status determining who has a political voice, issues of class providing much of the fodder for political debate and action. We can also see a resemblance to Fraser's argument that in contemporary politics recognition and redistribution are analytically distinct though often pragmatically related in progressive political action. Iris Marion Young emphasizes this pragmatic relationship in concluding that "what Fraser calls 'recognition' is a means to the economic and social equality and freedom that she brings under the category of 'redistribution.'"[48] Similarly, *Assemblywomen*'s fantasy of social change involves a movement for redistribution that follows on a movement to recognize the equality of a group previously relegated to lower cultural, social, and civic status. Still, the dramatic distance between recognition and redistribution in the play suggests that the link between the two remains, as in Fraser's analysis, pragmatic and contingent rather than inherent or necessary.

In his recent reading of *Assemblywomen*, Ober has explored a similar set of themes in the play and arrived at an interpretive conclusion similar in some ways to my own. Ober argues that the critical force of the play comes from Aristophanes's "comic exaggeration" of political principles that most Athenians accepted without much thought. The play thus takes the basic Athenian commitment to equality to two logical conclusions: equal (or more) political power for women and the equal distribution of property and wealth. As the Dissident's doubts suggest, Praxagora's scheme also takes to the extreme the Athenian idea that the social order and even nature itself can be reorganized through politics as persuasion. For Ober, these comic exaggerations serve to invite "members of the audience to confront their contradictory norms and values."[49] Again, I have something similar in mind: by enabling both fantastic and ironic readings of the central moments of recognition and redistribution in *Assemblywomen*, Aristophanes renders the boundaries of democratic politics problematic. In effect, he encourages the audience to consider how firm those boundaries are and whether they can or ought to be overcome.

But Ober's emphasis on the revelation to the audience of *contradictions* in their ways of thinking poses a potential problem—which is to say it raises an interesting question. On Ober's reading, *Assemblywomen* ultimately suggests to the Athenians that they are not as committed to equality as they think, for they are also, for example, committed to private wealth. Their holding equality dear thus means something other—something less— than they think it does. If irony involves the recognition of an alternative meaning beyond the apparent meaning, then we might say that *Assemblywomen* for Ober ultimately aims to make the Athenians see the irony in their political thinking. In the end, that is, Ober's reading seems to emphasize *Assemblywomen*'s ironic impact or the way in which the play can be seen to highlight the hidden contradictions, and thus the limits more than the possibilities, of democratic politics in Athens or elsewhere.[50] Perhaps that is inevitable—perhaps once a spectator or reader sees ironic limits, the possibilities of fantasy fade. If so, then my reading of *Assemblywomen*, in emphasizing the juxtaposition of irony and fantasy rather than choosing one or the other, stops one step too soon. To think further about whether one can in fact simultaneously hold on to both fantasy and irony—particularly in thinking about issues of recognition and redistribution—we need to turn to *Wealth*.

Wealth

As with *Assemblywomen*, the opening scene of *Wealth* revolves around vision and light, secrecy and revelation. The play begins with the complaints of Cario, slave to the hero of the play, an Athenian named Chremylus. Cario points to his master, who enters behind an old man as all three make their way home from a visit to the Oracle at Delphi. Chremylus is, Cario tells us, "following a blind person, exactly the opposite of what he should be doing: we who can see should lead the blind" (12–15).[51] What is more, Cario complains, Chremylus refuses to reveal his true motives. Faced with

Cario's demands, Chremylus finally agrees to tell all, saying "I won't keep you in the dark." Chremylus says that he had gone to Delphi out of concern for the future of his only son. Though he considers himself "a just and god-fearing man," he nonetheless has "always been poor and unsuccessful" (26–28). His question to the Oracle was whether his son should follow his just ways or "become a criminal, unjust, completely unwholesome, considering that's the way to get ahead in life" (37–38). The god's answer was, of course, a riddle: "the first person I encountered on leaving the shrine I was told to stick to and persuade to come home with me," Chremylus explains. That first person was none other than the blind old man he follows, whose identity remains unknown until with some not-so-gentle prodding by Chremylus and Cario he reveals himself to be the god Wealth.

This revelation of the identity of Wealth marks the general thematization of what we might, again, consider broadly as matters of recognition. Beyond the struggle to resolve Wealth's originally mistaken identity, Aristophanes casts the blindness of Wealth as a problem of recognition. He has the god explain to Chremylus and Cario: "Zeus did this to me because he resents mankind. You see, when I was a boy I vowed that I'd only visit the houses of just, wise and decent people, so Zeus made me blind, to keep me from recognizing [*diagignôskoimi*] any of them. That's how much he resents good [*chrēstoisi*] people" (87–92).[52] Two things are worth noting here. First, from the outset, *Wealth* presents issues of recognition and (re)distribution not as dramatically distinct though thematically connected— as in *Assemblywomen*—but as inherently intertwined. Second, recognition and redistribution are in turn bound up in *Wealth* with issues of justice and goodness. As things stand, there cannot be a just or good distribution of wealth because Wealth cannot recognize whom he should and should not "visit."[53] In *Assemblywomen*, recognition centered on determining who qualified as a citizen; redistribution, a separate and distinct issue, might (or might not) result from the deliberations of those recognized as citizens. In both cases, the overriding goal was not justice per se, but rather the salvation of the city. By contrast, the setup of *Wealth* holds out the possibility of a single dramatic moment in which a just redistribution of wealth is bound up with a restored capacity for the recognition of the goodness of particular human beings. Seeing the meaning of the riddling message of the oracle, the obvious solution occurs to Chremylus. He tells Wealth, "I think, yes I think, and I hope to god [*theō*] it's true, that I can cure this sickness and restore your sight" (115).

The hope lurking at the center of Chremylus's plan reflects, broadly speaking, the fantasy of economic change that *Wealth* shares with *Assemblywomen*; it also points to another key difference between the two plays. It remains unclear precisely to which god Chremylus appeals, but the play obviously revolves not around the affairs of the polis, as *Assemblywomen* does, but rather around the interaction of humans and gods. This reinforces the sense that a different notion of recognition is at work here. The action of *Wealth* does not hinge on the sort of recognition that occurs in *Assemblywomen*, which involves the granting of properly equal status to previously marginalized groups. Nor, however, does it turn, as many contemporary accounts of recognition do, on human beings acknowledging the equal worth of one another's authentic identities. Rather, the fantasy of *Wealth* sees just redistribution as requiring the mutual recognition of gods and humans. That is, Wealth must come to recognize good human beings like Chremylus, and Chremylus must recognize Wealth and the power that he, along with Zeus, exerts over human life. The restoring of Wealth's sight provides the impetus for the play's plot; but the deeper interest of *Wealth* lies in Chremylus's complex—and, I will suggest, comic—recognition of human beings' relationship with the gods, or, more generally, with forces beyond their control.

Chremylus's hope marks him as a basically pious man. So, too, do his initial decision to seek guidance from Apollo and his frequent invocations of various gods by name (364, 359, 396). Often enough, Aristophanes uses these invocations to draw a laugh, as he does in the following exchange between Chremylus and his friend Blepsidemus, who questions Chremylus's claim to have found Wealth:

> Blepsidemus: You swear by Hestia?
> Chremylus: By Poseidon, yes.
> Blepsidemus: The sea god, right?
> Chremylus: If there's another Poseidon, I swear by him, too. (393–96)

Chremylus's willingness to swear by Poseidon—by *any* Poseidon, even if he hasn't previously heard of him—suggests the potential absurdity of extreme piety. But the plot and action of *Wealth* call for its audience to have some respect and sympathy for the desperation felt by Chremylus and those he describes as allies: "righteous people [*dikaiois*] who've gone without their daily bread" (219).

Given his suffering and his desperation, Chremylus's piety has its limits. Certainly it does not prevent him from entering into quarrels with and among the gods. He thus does not hesitate to take up the cause of restoring the vision of Wealth even though it will pit him against Zeus.[54] It is Wealth himself who hesitates, saying that Zeus "scares the pants off me" (122). Chremylus, though, sees Wealth as "the most puissant [*krastiste*] of all divinities [*daimonōn*]," for he has power over both men and gods. In Chremylus's view of the world, everything humans do derives from their desire for wealth. "All crafts and skills known to mankind were invented for your sake," he says in trying to persuade Wealth of his own power (160–1). Later he concludes that "it's you and you alone who motivate everything, the good and the bad alike; you can be sure of that" (180–1). In the course of the play, this will mean that Wealth, his sight restored, not only rewards the just, but in doing so also motivates the unjust to change their ways.[55] Because his power extends beyond humans to the gods, the effects of this transformation are far reaching. Wealth motivates Zeus himself in two ways. First, Zeus's rule over the gods, Chremylus claims, rests on his riches, because "he's got the most" (130). Second, the steady flow of sacrifices offered to Zeus from humans depends upon their having sufficient wealth to make sacrifices and on their continued need to ask Zeus to bless them with wealth, which is always "their very first prayer" (133). If Wealth regains his sight and eventually visits all humans as they become just, Chremylus argues, there will be no prayers or sacrifices to Zeus and the power of Zeus's own wealth will diminish.

Beyond the economic redistribution it promises, Chremylus's scheme for restoring Wealth's ability to recognize goodness and justice thus portends a radical, fantastic reworking of relationships among the gods and between gods and humans. With off-stage help from Asclepius, the god of healing, this is precisely what happens. The slave Cario reports the story of the healing in the temple of Asclepius to Chremylus's wife, Chremylus himself having slept through it. The tale is a mixture of lowbrow humor mingled with comedy's respect for magical transformations:[56] "Panacea wrapped [Wealth's] head and whole face in crimson cloth. Then the god whistled, and two serpents darted from the temple, extraordinarily large ones. . . . They slipped quietly beneath the crimson cloth and started licking his eyelids, I suppose. And sooner than you could drink five pints of wine, mistress, our Wealth stood up and could see" (730–38).

Wealth's sight restored, the expected effects on both humans and gods follow forthwith. In typical Aristophanic fashion, the second half of the play encompasses several short scenes reflecting the results of the resolution of the plot's main conflict. First there enters a character known simply as Just Man, "once ruined, but now fortunate" (825), who brings his tattered old cloak to dedicate to Wealth (840). Next comes an Informer, whose scurrilous activities in Athens had brought him riches but will no more. Not all the consequences are so straightforwardly salutary. An Old Woman who, with her riches had attracted the attention of a Young Man, now finds herself scorned by him. Though it is difficult to join in the joy and laughter of the Young Man, Aristophanes seems to have expected his audience to do precisely that. But, finally, there comes the god Hermes, who reports that Zeus is indeed furious, for the newly wealthy humans have stopped making sacrifices: "no incense, no bay, no barley cake, no victim, not a single thing" (1115–16). The play ends with Zeus and the Olympian gods powerless and with a singing, dancing procession following the newly ascendant Wealth to the treasury of Athena on the Acropolis, where he will be installed as guardian and attended accordingly.

This joyous ending suggests that Chremylus has found a way to overcome the limits of human action in the face of the divine, reinforcing the sense of fantasy and possibility that undergirds much of the play's action. Having recognized the source of his suffering in the quarrels of the gods, our hero has on his own initiative reversed Zeus's blinding of Wealth and thereby brought about a reordering not just of economic reality among humans but of the power structure among the gods as well. As with *Assemblywomen*, though, *Wealth* admits of a reading that sees Chremylus's triumph as absurd and thus Aristophanes's intent in the play as ironic. The ironic reading finds its strongest support in an earlier scene involving an exchange between Chremylus and his friend Blepsidemus, on the one hand, and, on the other, the god Poverty. Rather than simply undermining the play's fantasy, though, that exchange reveals the true complexity of Chremylus's understanding of the relationship of gods and humans, pointing toward the comic nature of the recognition Chremylus achieves. That comic recognition, I will argue, sees both the power of the gods and the real promise of human action from a perspective that holds fantasy and irony in productive tension with each other.

Poverty, appearing as an old woman with a "crazed and tragic look" (423),[57] in effect offers an alternative to Chremylus's worldview, arguing that humans are driven not by the allure of wealth but by the goad of poverty. Aghast at Chremylus's scheme to restore Wealth's sight and banish her from Greece, Poverty claims to be "the sole source of all your blessings" (470–1). In this view of things, Poverty "sits by the artisan like a taskmaster, compelling him . . . to seek his livelihood" (533–34). Although with Wealth "you'll find men with gout, potbellies, bloated legs and disgustingly fat, . . . with [Poverty] they're lean, wasp-waisted and hard on the enemy" (557–59). Poverty brings "good behavior," whereas Wealth breeds "arrogance," as witnessed in politicians, who when poor "do right by the people" but "when they get rich on public funds immediately become wrongdoers, plotting against the masses and warring against the people" (565–70). In place of Chremylus's vision of a world where wealth rewards justice, Poverty depicts a world where hunger, need, and the fear of deprivation not only motivate the productive behavior necessary for human life but also ensure some semblance of personal and civic virtue.

To the arguments of Poverty, Chremylus and Blepsidemus offer responses that are alternatively halfhearted and bombastic. The broad consensus among scholars is that Poverty wins this rhetorical agon; it is a short interpretive step from this reading to the conclusion that Aristophanes means by Poverty's victory to point to the hollow absurdity of Chremylus's later success.[58] Whatever dreams men like Chremylus may have of transcending this world with the unjust suffering it imposes on the good and the material rewards it heaps on the bad, his exchange with Poverty, on this reading, pulls us back to reality. Here wealth and corruption go hand in hand, and only the threat of poverty motivates humans to act productively. Nothing humans do can, or from Poverty's point of view should, change this. This is in a way a return to, or perhaps a development of, the perspective of the Dissident in *Assemblywomen*. The Dissident had thought it unlikely that his fellow citizens would give up the security of their private property in favor of the possible common good of shared wealth. Poverty offers what amounts to a theory of human motives to buttress this concern. What the Dissident only senses is precisely what Poverty clearly identifies as the universal human desire to avoid being poor. Better to rely on the power of this desire than to hope for some miraculous future in which all humans become just and, when recognized by the gods as just, come to enjoy universal and equal wealth. Better to remain in *this* world, dealing with one another through reasonable, rational persuasion bounded by a respect for limits imposed by the realities of human nature.

Once again, the lure of the ironic reading is powerful. If we see the relative effectiveness of Poverty's arguments, then the temptation is to think we have seen through Chremylus's fantasy—and thus to dismiss that fantasy as mere entertainment for the more simpleminded spectator. At first glance, Chremylus's final response to Poverty and the worldview she presents provides little reason to think otherwise, for it borders on the nonsensical: "now get lost and stop your grumbling," he shouts, "not another word! You won't persuade [*peiseis*] me even if you convince [*peisēs*] me" (599–600). Henderson's translation of the last sentence tends to downplay the paradoxical nature of the claim Chremylus makes. The double appearance of forms of *peitho* suggests that we read the line more literally as "you won't persuade me even if you persuade me." The line no doubt drew a laugh in performance. And we might well read it, in accord with the common interpretation of the *agon* in general, as reflecting the weakness of Chremylus's reasoning skills in the face of Poverty's more realistic arguments. But, before leaving *Wealth*, I want to try to take Chremylus's claim more seriously.

At the beginning of the *Republic*, Socrates responds to the group that seeks to detain him for a conversation by suggesting the possibility that he try to persuade them to let him go. The young Glaucon retorts, "but could you persuade us, if we won't listen?"[59] In this context, the implication is that the group so firmly intends to detain Socrates that they would resort to force rather than risk even listening to his quite probably persuasive arguments. By the time Chremylus makes his paradoxical claim, he has, in fact, already heard Poverty's arguments; he cannot simply mean that he will refuse to listen. One possibility is that Chremylus, having listened, simply thinks himself able to stop the process of persuasion before it really comes to fruition. That is, he can somehow sense that he is about to be persuaded and yet refuse to allow it—hence his demand that Poverty stop speaking. If this is what happens, it would in itself be a remarkable feat involving some capacity on Chremylus's part for seeing and standing apart from himself as a target of rhetorical ploys. But Chremylus in fact makes a stronger claim: he suggests that even if the process of persuasion has achieved its end, he will still not be persuaded. That is, he can at the same time *both* be persuaded *and* not be persuaded. In the specific context of the play, this means that he can both return to the world of normal politics, recognizing the power of arguments that, like those of Poverty, remain within the limited field of vision that demarcates that world and—while doing this—still transcend that world by recognizing possibilities that go beyond the limits it tries to impose. In other words, we can see Chremylus as claiming that he somehow combines faithfulness to his fantastic redistributive schemes with an ironic sense that they are indeed fantasies.

We might dismiss this possibility of holding fantasy and irony together as itself a fantasy: insofar as irony reveals fantasy as an absurd ignoring of limits, no one can do what Chremylus claims. And this is true in a literal sense: if we believe the arguments of Poverty, then we cannot also believe in the possibility of Chremylus's fantasy becoming a reality. Aristophanes is not so foolish as to suggest anything of this sort. Rather, as I have suggested throughout this book, I think he means to point toward the possibility of somehow holding fantasy and irony together as a particular sensibility, an attitude toward the world and toward change that might allow an ordinary citizen like Chremylus to recognize both the possibilities and the limits of human action.

From this perspective, *Wealth* offers at least two more concrete clues as to the sensibility Chremylus brings to matters of economic justice. First, both Chremylus's sense of the world Poverty depicts and his hope for better things to come are connected to his recognition of the mundane realities of human suffering, which goes beyond the mechanistic motivational world view of poverty. To Poverty's claim that she motivates humans to produce all that they need and want, Chremylus replies:

What benefits can *you* provide, except blisters in the bathhouse and masses of hungry children and old ladies? Not to mention the lice, gnats, and fleas, too numerous to enumerate, that annoy us by buzzing around our heads and waking us up with the warning, "get up or you'll go hungry!" And on top of that, you have us wearing rags, not coats, and sleeping not on a bed but a bug-infested twine mat that doesn't let you get any sleep, under threadbare burlap instead of a blanket, with our heads not on a pillow but a hefty stone. And to eat, not bread but mallow shoots, not cake but withered radish leaves. We sit not on chairs but on broken crocks, and instead of a kneading trough we get one side of a barrel, and that's broken too. Now haven't I revealed the many blessings you bring to all humanity? (535–47)

Second, Chremylus' reaction to this sense of suffering is guided by his on-again, off-again piety. As we have seen, he reveres the gods and their power in human life, but he does not hesitate to become involved in their quarrels in order to bring about change. Chremylus's understanding of the material life of humans, then, is deeply intertwined with his understanding of and relationship to the gods. His experience of the economic is indeed deeply embedded in his cultural reality. He sees the material life of human beings as shaped not only by the cruel tyranny of Zeus but also, at least potentially, by the quasi-Promethean sympathy for humankind shown by Wealth.

More generally, we might say that Chremylus arrives at a complex under-standing of the limits of human action that merges cultural and economic considerations. He acknowledges that we are ruled by forces that seem in the course of everyday life to elude us, whether they appear as gods or as supposed dictates of (human) nature. Chremylus, though, rejects the idea that these forces are purely and simply beyond our control. His apprecia-tion of both the possibility and the challenge of alleviating human suffering through redistribution thus simultaneously depends on and reflects a deep recognition of the human condition. We might, again, call that recognition comic insofar as it requires a sensibility that allows for fantastical possibilities without simply becoming absurd. Brought to the rhetorical agon, this comic recognition allows the ordinary citizen like Chremylus to resist the sort of arguments made by Poverty, arguments to this day marshaled by those who would persuade us of the impossibility of fundamental change.

Comic Recognition

Earlier, I suggested a basic parallel between the complex relationship of the economic to the cultural in the ancient world and the contemporary controversy over the relationship between recognition and redistribution. Important though it is to remain wary of reading the present into the past, that parallel proves useful in working through the complex issues that emerge from *Assemblywomen* and *Wealth.* In contemporary terms, we can see Aristophanes moving from a treatment of recognition and redistribu-tion as distinct dramatic and political moments in *Assemblywomen* toward a vision of economic justice in *Wealth* that sees redistribution and recogni-tion as indissolubly linked. With this movement comes the emergence in *Wealth* of what I have here termed comic recognition.

That comic recognition, not surprisingly, differs significantly from the sort of recognition that figures in contemporary struggles for social justice. Recognition today (whether identity based or status based) tends to focus on the shared identities of particular groups—gender, ethnicity, sexual orientation. Although *Assemblywomen* considers the struggle of Athenian women to overcome their exclusion from Athenian politics (and the ironies implicit in their strategy of deliberate mistaken identity), the sort of recognition we find in *Wealth* tends, if anything, to elide differences among identity-based groups.[60] In particular, the latter play does not address the status of women as the former does. This is not to say that *Wealth* somehow moves toward the sort of abstract liberal individualism rejected by advocates of the politics of recognition. The action of *Wealth* hinges upon the recognition—by gods and humans alike—of the status of the ordinary human being who suffers unjust deprivation and yet dreams of justice. As the central role of Chremylus's slave Cario suggests, other markers of social status matter less in *Wealth* than the shared fact of suffering under the misrule of Zeus.[61] The great fantasy of *Wealth* is that ordinary human beings might join together to achieve recognition of their shared status—and thus, through the consequent redistribution, to ameliorate their suffering.

As we have seen, it would be wrong to say that Aristophanes offers the fantasy of *Wealth* as a realistic solution to the predicament of ordinary citizens in his day. Fantasy, as I have used the term in this book, imagines an escape from the limits of everyday reality. Those aspects of both *Assemblywomen* and *Wealth* that support ironic readings of the plays serve to remind us of this basic fact, tend to bring us back to earth. As I have tried to insist on here, though, it would be equally wrong to conclude that the irony embedded in the plays marks their fantasies as meaningless—as so much entertainment for the weaker wits in the audience who lack the ability to see the playwright's true, more cynical message. Such a conclusion rests on an understanding of irony in which the apparent meaning of an utterance or text or action is in fact the *opposite* of its intended meaning. But that, again, seems an overly restricted way of reading irony in general and Aristophanic irony in particular. Irony, as I said earlier, can also point more vaguely to a meaning that is simply *different* from the apparent meaning.[62] And so in the case of *Assemblywomen* and *Wealth*, we can reject the idea that Aristophanes sees sudden, radical redistribution as a realistic possibility without drawing the opposite conclusion that he must support the maintenance of the unequal, unjust status quo. Instead, the plays suggest a different possibility of some sort.

Assemblywomen's simultaneous enabling of both ironic responses and the sincere celebration of fantasy points toward that different possibility. It finds fuller expression in the comic recognition that emerges in *Wealth* and the attendant sensibility displayed by Chremylus. That sensibility takes the hope that fantasy promises and the appreciation of the limits of reality that irony demands and brings them together, holding them in an ongoing imaginative tension with one another.[63] Rather than falsely promising easy answers or, on the other hand, suggesting the ultimate inevitability of the status quo, Aristophanes offers Chremylus's sensibility as a sort of model. In our "postsocialist condition" with its "exhaustion of utopian energies,"[64] we might draw on that model as inspiration for a kind of theory that imagines seemingly fantastic possibilities without falling back into the sort of metanarratives that our age, with its penchant for irony, has come to mistrust. Ultimately, though, Aristophanes suggests that the best possibility for progressive change can be found in the underlying good sense of ordinary citizens sensitive to the realities of economic injustice, on guard against rhetoric that suggests the impossibility of reform, and alive with the hope for a better future. I turn in the conclusion to think about how this comic recognition, and the broader comic disposition of which it is a manifestation, can help us to reorient our thinking about the challenge of democratic citizenship.

CONCLUSION

DEMOCRATIC POSSIBILITIES

Ultimately, this book seeks to advance three related claims. First, I mean to encourage a rethinking of democratic citizenship. Democracy, as I argued in the introduction, presents citizens with two fundamental demands that exist in tension with one another. In the context of contemporary debates between agonal and liberal or deliberative understandings of democracy, I have referred to these competing demands as democracy's rebellious impulse and democracy's impulse toward responsible and effective collective action. On one hand, democracy calls citizens to resist the institutionalization of rule. On the other hand, democracy calls citizens to participate in collective democratic action, which, if it is to be both effective and responsible, may well demand institutions. The tension between democracy's impulses or demands thus shapes the basic challenge of democratic citizenship.

Second, I argue that Aristophanic comedy suggests the need for a particular comic disposition among ordinary citizens if they are to meet the challenge of democratic citizenship. In Aristophanes's Athens, that challenge revolved around the interaction of a handful of elites with the mass of ordinary citizens. It was heightened by the suffering brought by the Peloponnesian War and its aftermath. In this context, Aristophanic comedy developed, deployed, and looked to instill in its audience a comic disposition manifested in comic voyaging, cleverness, and comic recognition. These three manifestations of the Aristophanic comic disposition are, at a conceptual level, complementary. All three point to a willingness to embrace and an ability to navigate the multiple meanings, the contingency, and the tension that mark the challenge of democratic citizenship. Together, they suggest what is required of ordinary citizens who must respond to democracy's competing demands.

Third, I mean to claim that Aristophanes's surviving plays can speak to the possibilities of democracy, not only in Aristophanes's day, but also in our own time. Even given the important differences between democracy in Athens and democracy today, the basic contours of the challenge of democratic citizenship remain the same. Today, as in Aristophanes's

Athens, what passes for democratic politics often consists of the interaction of vocal elites with the mass of ordinary citizens who listen and from time to time exercise political power. In this context, today's ordinary citizens are called by democracy both to participate in collective action—channeled, controlled, and hedged as it often is by institutional forms and their potential capture by elites—and, at the same time, to resist being ruled as the antithesis of democracy. At the most basic level, my argument is that, given the ongoing realities of the challenge of democratic citizenship, ordinary citizens in contemporary times need the kind of comic disposition that we find in Aristophanes's surviving plays.

All this is, of course, to put the basic claims of this book in their simplest, most abstract form. Drawing on the arguments of the last five chapters, I aim in this conclusion to explore and develop these claims. I begin by considering more carefully the relationship between comic voyaging, cleverness, and comic recognition as manifestations of an Aristophanic comic disposition. This leads to an engagement with the relationship between Aristophanes and his comic heroes and heroines. I then turn to the link between Aristophanes's comic heroes and his audience as a way to think again about how Aristophanic comedy works as political thought. I next consider what my reading of Aristophanes suggests about the relationship of spectators and citizens, something which bears directly upon how Aristophanic comedy might be a response to the challenge of democratic citizenship. Finally, I close by thinking about the contemporary usefulness of turning to an Aristophanic comic disposition, in part, by considering the relationship between democracy in Athens and democracy today.

The Poet and His Characters

In the *Ethics*, Aristotle defines virtue as a state or disposition or *hexis*: "Virtue then is a settled disposition [*hexis*] of the mind determining the choice of actions and emotions, consisting essentially in the observance of the mean relative to us, this being determined by principle, that is, as the prudent man would determine it."[1] In broad terms, I have been using the language of disposition in a similar way. Aristophanic comedy on my reading draws upon and aims to instill in its audience a settled comic disposition that is manifested in comic voyaging, cleverness, and comic recognition. That comic disposition locates the citizen in, or enables the citizen to occupy, the tension-filled space between democracy's rebellious and institutionalizing impulses.

Aristotle's claim that the mean is "relative to us" suggests that in the pursuit of virtue each individual will struggle to avoid his or her own extremes.

The *Ethics* thus counsels us to "examine what we ourselves drift into easily" and then "drag ourselves off into the contrary direction."[2] This dragging of ourselves is part of what Aristotle has in mind when he concludes that it is "hard work to be excellent."[3] The hard work also follows from the complex contexts in which we pursue virtue; thus, acting virtuously "to the right person, in the right time, for the right end, and in the right way" is not "easy."[4] My reading of Aristophanes similarly suggests that is it difficult to be a good democratic citizen. Democracy makes complex, dynamic, and sometimes contradictory demands of citizens. Though Aristophanic comedy suggests that a particular disposition can meet those demands, it also makes clear that achieving that disposition is no easy thing.

Part of the difficulty of being "excellent," Aristotle suggests, lies in the fact that virtue is pursued by particular individuals in particular contexts. The same virtue will look different for different individuals, and for the same individual at different moments.[5] This means that "the right way" of being angry, for example, will vary. I have something analogous in mind in thinking about the relationship of an Aristophanic comic disposition to its particular manifestations. If, as I suggested in the previous section, comic voyaging, cleverness, and comic recognition appear complementary on the conceptual level, they remain in practice distinct manifestations of an Aristophanic comic disposition. Along these lines, each seems to be particularly central to Aristophanes in different contexts and at particular moments in Athenian history.

Consider, for example, cleverness as an ability to see through masks or disguises to what lies beneath them. Cleverness as I have here understood it bears upon a specific, central aspect of Athenian democratic politics: the rhetorical interaction of elite speakers and the mass of ordinary citizens. It emerges most clearly in Aristophanes's earliest surviving plays, which of course were written as part of Aristophanes's battle with Cleon. As we have seen, *Acharnians* and *Knights* are to a considerable extent concerned with the possibility of cleverness as a potential antidote to the power of the demagogue. Neither play can be read as praising ordinary Athenians for their cleverness; indeed, both might be read as suggesting the absence of that quality in the Athenian demos. Nor do these early plays depict cleverness as unproblematic. Both, in fact, point toward the clever ordinary citizen as potentially angry and manipulative. Put differently, both *Acharnians* and *Knights* point to the need for something more than pure cleverness. Still, it makes sense that during these early years of both Aristophanes's career and the Peloponnesian War, cleverness emerges as the central manifestation of his comic disposition.

We can say something similar about comic voyaging. In chapter 1, I drew on *Peace* and *Lysistrata* to describe comic voyaging as a willingness to abide the presence of multiple possibilities, multiple meanings, even multiple senses of one's fundamental identity. Again here, we can hardly read Aristophanes as suggesting in these plays that ordinary Athenians regularly display this willingness. We might think of Trygaeus as coming through his own fantastic travels to something like an openness to comic voyaging. But comic voyaging in *Lysistrata* emerges more from the juxtaposition of the men's and women's semichoruses and from the unfolding of the play's plot than through any one character. Aristophanes, again, does not so much praise any particular Athenian or the Athenian demos for taking joy in comic voyaging as he suggests the desperate need for such voyaging. And we might well think that this makes sense given the production dates of *Peace* and *Lysistrata*, both written as the war dragged on, frustrating expectations, confounding any simple explanation, complicating and confusing any simple understanding of the world.

Finally, comic recognition seems particularly suited to the context in which Aristophanes wrote *Assemblywomen* and *Wealth*. Holding in tension fantasy and irony, comic recognition respects both the realities of this world and dreams of a better world. So understood, comic recognition makes good sense as a response to the plight of the ordinary Athenian in the years following the Peloponnesian War. No longer confronted by the sharp crisis of a war brought about by manipulative elites and lingering beyond anyone's worst fears, Athens faced challenges less dramatic but more enduring: the struggle for basic material well-being and the question of whether democratic politics might be fit for that struggle. If these challenges were in a sense more mundane, we might think that they for Aristophanes highlighted the need for a more profound if still fundamentally comic response. And so we find him in *Assemblywomen* and *Wealth* imagining the possibility of such a response in the form of a complex sort of recognition that is neither naïve nor cynical.

Contextualizing Aristophanes's portrayal of cleverness, comic voyaging, and comic recognition in this manner suggests the complexity and fluidity of the comic disposition that flows through his work. In this manner, the comic disposition I have in mind reflects the challenge of democratic citizenship, which is itself not static, but dynamic. The ordinary citizen is pulled in different ways at different moments. When demagogues seem to dominate, the pull of democratic citizenship is toward resistance and rebellion. Cleverness is particularly appropriate to this context. When the question becomes whether democratic politics can respond to shared suffering, ordinary citizens especially need comic recognition's ability to balance resistance to the way things are with the idea that common action is both possible and necessary. In short, in response to the changing challenges and possibilities of democratic politics, a properly comic disposition will manifest itself in different ways at different moments.

This is not to say that at any one moment citizens need only one particular manifestation of the comic disposition. Though cleverness, comic voyaging, and comic recognition seem particularly central to Aristophanes at particular moments, each of the three appears throughout his surviving plays. I have drawn the idea of cleverness from a close reading of *Acharnians* and *Knights*, but the theme of seeing through masks or disguises of course appears in later plays, too. Praxagora's plan in *Assemblywomen* to have the women of Athens dress as men surely plays on the ability or inability of the ordinary Athenian citizen to see beyond appearances (either to see the women of the play as women or to see the politically excluded women of Athens as, in fact, more than capable of full citizenship). We could say something similar of the kinsman's appearance as a woman in *Women at the Thesmophoria* or the appearance of the goddess Poverty in *Wealth*.

The same holds for the other manifestations of the comic disposition of ordinary citizenship. *Birds* surely asks after the possibility of comic voyaging—or perhaps the inability of Athenians to embark on such voyaging. And we have seen that *Knights* remains open to rather diametrically opposed readings that demand of the spectator the ability to abide multiple possible meanings: is the rejuvenation of Demos a victory for democracy or a reestablishing of elite domination? As for comic recognition, nearly all of Aristophanes's plays work with the tension between fantasy and irony. In *Acharnians*, Diceapolis fantastically escapes from the city but finds that the reality of rhetorical contests follows him. And *Peace* clearly makes thematic the juxtaposition between transcending the boundaries of normal political life and being brought soundly back to earth by the limits of reality.

Democratic citizenship at different moments thus requires different configurations and combinations of cleverness, comic voyaging, and comic recognition. All this suggests, again, that we ought to think of the comic disposition of ordinary citizenship as complex and dynamic. It is manifested in distinct but complimentary ways, pointing to different democratic possibilities at different moments. Any particular aspect of the comic disposition may be marked as much by its absence in a particular play as by its presence—think here of the anger that emerges in *Acharnians*, *Wasps*, and *Clouds*, indicating perhaps the absence of that balancing of fantasies of change and acceptance of reality that marks comic recognition. Finally, it is worth emphasizing that none of Aristophanes's heroes and heroines in some sense perfectly manifest the comic disposition. None of them show the challenge of democratic citizenship resolved, though their portrayal can help spectators to grasp elements of comic disposition needed to meet that challenge. The full democratic possibilities of Aristophanic comedy, then, will be found not in an individual character or a particular play but, in large part, in the relationship between poet, characters, and spectators.

Characters and Spectators

If, as I have just suggested, no one of Aristophanes's characters fully and unproblematically embodies the comic disposition I have drawn from his plays, then what becomes of the idea that ordinary citizens as spectators of Aristophanic comedy might be expected in some way to identify with the ordinary people who are his heroes and heroines? I suggested this sort of identification in the introduction, drawing on Henderson:

> But there, onstage, is a rather likeable person. Not an actual person, and in fact not the sort of person who would be prominent at all: a farmer, a seller from the markets, the debt-ridden victim of a socialite wife and a social-climbing son, a juror, the target of too many lawsuits who has decided to try his luck elsewhere, a housewife. This person is in the same fix as most of us and it is pleasant to see someone like that in the spotlight for once.[6]

I argued in a preliminary way in the introduction that Aristophanes means spectators both to identify with and stand at a distance from the heroes and heroines of his comedies. I said this in the context of longstanding interpretive debates over Aristophanes's own politics. Was he a conservative warning Athenians about the dangerous excesses of radical democracy? Or was he in fact more open to the schemes of his protagonists and so to more fundamental democratic reforms? Does he, then, hold Diceapolis, Praxagora, Trygaeus, and all the rest up to mockery, as a way to warn the Athenians of their own potential for foolishness? Or does he mean for ordinary citizens to take some share of inspiration from their schemes?

All the arguments of preceding chapters suggest that these are the wrong questions to ask about the relationship between Aristophanes, his characters, and his audience. Ultimately, such questions pose false choices that the plays consistently disrupt and move beyond. Aristophanes's heroes and heroines are both compelling and flawed protagonists. While each of them contributes something to our understanding of the comic disposition of ordinary citizenship, none of them are simply models for us to emulate. Likewise, while their schemes hold a certain appeal, the plays consistently introduce complications by raising questions about whether those schemes will work and, if so, whether we will like the consequences that follow. These sorts of complications should by now be familiar. Demos is clever enough to see the Paphlagonian for what he is but readily enough plays along with the game of mutual manipulation. Strepsiades rightfully enough worries over the place of pompous, self-proclaimed elites in the democratic city but veers toward a dangerously angry cultural populism. Praxagora boldly pursues what we might recognize as justice, but we end with serious doubts about whether her reforms can succeed. All this, as always, suggests that we ought not to turn to any one of Aristophanes's characters as a model of democratic citizenship.

We will be better served by focusing on the particular way Henderson expresses the idea that spectators might identify with Aristophanes's characters. Those characters are, Henderson writes, in the "same fix as most of us." The particular fixes in which Aristophanes's protagonists find themselves—facing manipulative demagogues, struggling through an interminable war, facing economic suffering and political inequality—are all depressingly familiar. On the reading I have offered, the fixes in which ordinary citizens find themselves on and off stage point toward the underlying and shared challenge of ordinary citizenship in democracy. How can an ordinary citizen balance a wariness of claims about leadership with the quite real possibility that elite advice may be helpful in exercising the collective capacity of the demos? When faced with wrongheaded or simply wrong democratic decisions, how can the ordinary citizen resist without simply withdrawing? Ought the ordinary citizen to work within the seemingly fixed parameters of political reality or to try to fashion a new reality? Can one do both at the same time?

These, I think, are the sorts of questions Aristophanic comedy raises. In doing so it reflects the "fix" or the challenge facing the ordinary citizen of democratic Athens. This, in turn, helps to clarify what might be gained by the sort of identification Aristophanic comedy encourages between its characters and its spectators. Aristophanes offers no answer to the particular political problems his plays address or to the broader challenge of democratic citizenship they reflect. Rather, by putting on stage characters for spectators to identify with and to laugh both with and at, Aristophanic comedy calls his audience to appreciate the challenge or fix in which ordinary citizens find themselves and to recognize that that challenge or fix is widely shared. The plays invite reflection upon their heroes' and heroines' attempts to meet the challenges they face and on their successes and failures. And, ultimately, the plays call upon and seek to call forth the complex and dynamic comic disposition I have aimed to describe.

In chapter 1, I drew on Rancière's account of the emancipatory potential of art, which he thinks lies in the preservation of the distances between artist, art work, and spectator. Rancière links this idea of emancipatory art with his earlier work on emancipatory pedagogy. He sees in both an antidote to the traditional, stultifying tendency of educators, artists, and especially philosophers to craft images of students, spectators, and ordinary people that generally work to keep everyone in their proper place. My claim in chapter 1 was that Aristophanic comedy avoids such stultification. On one level, what I have been saying here is consistent with that. The comic disposition of Aristophanic comedy works to disrupt any simple identification of the spectator with any one of Aristophanes's characters. Aristophanes, that is, does not create on stage model ordinary citizens. Nor does he do the opposite, creating antiheroes that, in their flaws and limitations, reveal what "good" citizens should be.

Instead he gives us complex protagonists facing or revealing the challenge that democracy poses to its citizens, and he points toward the kind of disposition with which they might respond to that challenge. Rancière might, of course, counsel us to be wary of the potentially "stultifying" effects of a poet seeking to instill a disposition among spectators. But part of the genius of Aristophanic comedy is that it consistently turns its comic disposition upon itself. As we saw in chapter 1, the complex play of distances in the surviving comedies works to disrupt any supposed relationship between poet, characters, and spectators. Ultimately, too, the comic disposition of ordinary citizenship calls into question the very idea of the ordinary itself. Far from celebrating some reified vision of the ordinary citizen, Aristophanic comedy prompts reflection upon deep questions of identity, of what it means to be man, woman, Athenian, Greek, human.

This openness of Aristophanic comedy and the comic disposition it reflects and nurtures does not suggest the absence of some core commitments. Far from tolerating anything and everything from ordinary people, the vision of ordinary citizenship I have described here is quite demanding. It asks that ordinary citizens tolerate and even embrace contingency, uncertainty, imperfection, and delay. It calls upon them to eschew simple answers and either-or choices. It welcomes tension and requires a tacking back and forth between possibilities (and impossibilities). It suggests the necessity of trying and failing and trying again. And it flows from and asks for an attentiveness to one's own suffering and to that of others without giving up joy or hope or humor.

None of this is easy, and Aristophanes clearly thinks that his fellow Athenians often failed to be good citizens of democracy. At the same time, his surviving plays reflect a deep faith in spectators and, more generally, in the potential of ordinary human beings. One aspect of this faith is that the comic disposition that emerges from his plays will resonate with them. There is here, of course, the faith of the would-be civic teacher, and Aristophanes frequently enough claims that role. He does so, though, not in the manner of Rancière's pedantic Old Master, but with the kind of playfulness that he seems to have found in his fellow Athenians as they came to the theater.

Spectator and Citizen

Aristophanes's plays ultimately rely upon and themselves seek to call forth a particular sort of spectator. The spectator who seeks either mere laughs or straightforward instruction will be disappointed; one who approaches the comedies with the right kind of comic disposition or develops such a disposition in watching them will be both entertained and challenged. To the extent that the experience and practice of being a spectator is closely related to the experience and practice of democratic citizenship, that disposition, in the end, may resonate not only in the theater but also in political life more broadly. In other words, beyond questions about the relationship of Aristophanes to his characters and the relationship of his characters to spectators, the political import of Aristophanic comedy on my reading in no small part depends upon the relationship between spectators and citizens.

That link no doubt seemed natural enough in ancient Athens. The theater was, after all, deeply intertwined with the politics of the city. We should recall here of course that Aristophanes's plays, like those of all other comic as well as tragic poets, were produced at the expense of the city. As we saw in the introduction, this need not mean that poets were thereby bound to adhere to common opinion or parrot conventional wisdom. It does seem, though, to have contributed to Aristophanes's sense that he might be a civic educator of sorts. Beyond this place of politics in the theater, we can easily enough see elements of the theater in politics. The workings of the Athenian assembly and the lawcourts involved a few political actors appearing before citizens who watched and from time to time decided. In short, the line between citizen and spectator was blurred in Athenian political practice.[7]

This intertwining of the roles of spectator and citizen was seen as problematic by a range of observers. In the *Republic*, Plato of course worries over the potential effects of dramatic poetry on the souls of citizens. Though more sanguine on the matter, a similar concern in part motivates Aristotle's *Poetics*. In chapter 4, I drew on the critique of citizens-as-spectators offered by Thucydides's Cleon. Though I there found Aristophanes to be much more hopeful about the potential of ordinary citizens, he has his own concerns about the tendency of Athenians to lose themselves in spectacle. This is most obvious in *Knights* with its questions about Demos as spectator encouraging the most outrageous of elite rhetorical displays.

Then, too, there is Diceapolis, who becomes a spectator in a different way by withdrawing into his own political space, to gaze from afar with distrust and disgust on the spectacle of Athenian democracy. Here we might recall the description Walter Lippmann offers—and which I quoted in the introduction—of the plight of the citizen in modern mass democracy:

> The private citizen today has come to feel rather like a deaf spectator in the back row, who ought to keep his mind on the mystery off there, but cannot quite manage to keep awake. He knows he is somehow affected by what is going on. Rules and regulations continually, taxes annually

and wars occasionally remind him that he is being swept along by great drifts of circumstance. Yet these public affairs are in no convincing way his affairs.[8]

The kind of sleepy apathy that worries Lippmann appears as less of a concern in Aristophanic comedy. Still, Diceapolis seems beset by a similar sense that being a spectator means feeling the effects of political decisions without having real, meaningful input.

We have, then, twin concerns about the spectator-citizen as, on the one hand, actively contributing to the reduction of political life to rhetorical spectacle and as, on the other hand, passively experiencing politics and its effects. These concerns are surely as serious in our day as they were in Aristophanes's or in Lippmann's. But the presence of these twin—and potentially rival—concerns also points toward how the comic disposition of ordinary citizenship might be suited particularly well to a kind of citizenship practiced in large part as spectating.

Concerns about the citizen-spectator as both actively encouraging political spectacle and as passively observing it reflect the fact that the role of the spectator is in fact simultaneously passive and active. Put differently, to be a spectator—whether in the theater or in nominally democratic political life—is at once to undergo an experience and to engage in a practice. We might think of a disposition as that which brings experience and practice together. In Aristotelian terms a disposition or hexis marks a habitual way of moving from perception to wish to decision to action. I have used the idea of a disposition in a broadly similar way here; now we might say that a disposition links a settled way of experiencing the world with a settled way of acting in the world. Thinking in this way about a disposition of citizenship can thus help us to make sense of the fact that spectator-citizens are simultaneously passive and active, that they simultaneously experience and practice democratic politics. Thinking in particular of a comic disposition needed by the ordinary citizen as spectator means thinking, paradoxically enough, of a settled way of experience and practice that itself constantly works to unsettle one's experience and alter one's practice.

This idea of a comic disposition of the spectator-citizen that can respond to the tension-filled demands of democracy differs from common conceptions of citizenship. Following Richard Bellamy,[9] we can broadly think of arguments about citizenship as unfolding along three lines. Citizenship in some accounts appears as active participation. In other accounts, it is a matter of belonging to a political whole; we might say it is the experience of membership. Finally, particularly in the liberal tradition, citizenship involves the possession of rights, something we might think of either as the (potentially active) deployment of protections against oppression or, alternatively, as the experience of a particular status of political equality. Thinking of a comic disposition of the citizen-as-spectator does not expressly conflict with these ideas. In its appreciation of democracy's impulse toward collective action, the comic disposition connects with the idea of membership, of belonging to something (the demos) beyond oneself. Its appreciation of democracy's impulse toward rebellion, in contrast, partakes of the idea of active participation and surely resonates with the idea of defending one's rights. The comic disposition of ordinary citizenship, though, moves beyond these (to my mind partial) definitions and thinks about democratic citizenship as simultaneously an experience and a practice and as simultaneously contributing to collective action and rebelling against domination.

Aristophanes and Democratic Citizenship Today

As I noted at the outset, in drawing a vision of ordinary citizenship from Aristophanes's surviving comedies, I mean to contribute to contemporary debates in democratic theory. More specifically, my arguments aim to move beyond the choice sometimes posed by contemporary theorists between democracy as rebellious disruption and democracy as ordered and responsible collective action. I have argued that rather than considering rebellion and collective action as alternative definitions of democracy, we might best think of them as competing democratic impulses. In the context of this understanding of democratic citizenship as a tension-filled practice and experience, Aristophanes points us toward a comic disposition attuned to the tensions, contingencies, and uncertainties of democratic political life. His comedies also consistently remind us that it is no easy thing to face the challenge of democratic citizenship and develop and deploy the complex and fluid disposition necessary to meet that challenge.

The effort of democratic citizenship will be worthwhile if it leads to a reinvigoration of democratic politics. Can a disposition—a particular way of experiencing and responding to the world—really do this? Here we might usefully return to the broadly similar argument offered by Steven White, upon which I briefly touched in the introduction. White, as we saw there, explores the possibility of an ethos appropriate to what he calls late modern citizenship. White roots this ethos in his notion of "weak ontology," in which we hold to particular understandings of the world and our place in it, while knowing that we cannot be absolutely certain. In this context, White's late modern ethos manifests itself both in a moral attentiveness to others who are in a similar fix and in a related self-restraint. This ethos, White claims, can help orient citizens toward the conditions of late modernity, including deep questions about the self and subjectivity, the challenge to the nation-state as the chief source of political identity and action, and what White calls "democracy's predicament." That predicament he describes in terms of the growth of economic inequality, the blurring of class as a basis for democratic mobilization, and the related loss of the ideal of the demos as "a collective macrosubject of democracy."[10]

In the context of this predicament, White suggests that the turn to an ethos is more promising than traditional hopes for energizing the demos as a collective actor. Those traditional hopes for White seem increasingly unrealistic insofar as it is harder to "craft commonality" in contemporary societies. This greater difficulty is in part due to the greater recognition of pluralism. To the extent that we recognize difference, commonality may be harder to find. The difficulty also follows, White argues, from changes in socioeconomic distributions. Traditional ideas of democratic mobilization, dating back to Aristotle's observation that the poor are many while the wealthy are few, presume a pyramid-shaped distribution.[11] By contrast, today's relatively affluent Western societies are, as White puts it, "diamond shaped," with a large, relatively comfortable middle class. Where democrats might once have sought to unite the poor against the wealthy, today they must seek different sources of collective action. As White puts it, "democratic political ties are harder to weave together and maintain than, for example, when a fifth-century Athenian politician was trying to draw the demos together."[12]

White's "late modern ethos," with its emphasis on contingency and generosity, bears some similarity to the comic disposition I find in Aristophanes and perhaps in particular to comic recognition. His account of the irrelevance of the Greek experience to democracy's contemporary predicament, though, raises the question of whether an Aristophanic understanding of democratic citizenship can ultimately speak to today's politics. On my reading, Aristophanes depicts democratic politics as the struggle between ordinary citizens and elite political actors or, put differently, as a matter of ordinary citizens trying to navigate a nominally democratic politics in which a small group of active and vocal "leaders" play a central and often troubling role. How well can an Aristophanic comic disposition meet the demands of contemporary democracies in which the struggle between the wealthy few and the many who are poor has been replaced by the politics of pluralism?

The answer in part hinges on the extent to which White misreads the meaning of democracy in Athens. He accords too much weight, I think, to the equation of the demos with the poor and so perhaps to a reading of a particular—though particularly insightful—passage in Aristotle. As my arguments in this book suggest, I find in Aristophanes an appreciation for the multiple possible meanings of democracy. Those multiple possible meanings are captured in the term *demos* itself, which can mean the entire people, the poor, or the common or ordinary citizens. I have here, of course, emphasized the idea of democracy as the power of ordinary people. But I also find in Aristophanes an insistence on the fluidity of the ordinary. His plays call on spectators to consider just who is ordinary. Those without great political power? Men and women? Just Athenians or Spartans, too? Or perhaps all Greeks or even all humans? Maybe even the gods? In prompting these questions about who counts as ordinary, Aristophanic comedy points not toward a fixed struggle of the poor against the rich, but instead toward the fluidity of democracy and the changeable (if not always changing) meaning of the demos as a collection of ordinary people and as a collective actor.

In grappling with these issues of democratic plurality and democratic commonality, it may be significant that, where White uses the term *ethos*, I favor *disposition*. In White's usage, an ethos is something widely shared, a source itself of the kind of commonality that might make democratic action possible in contemporary conditions of plurality. By contrast, the idea of a disposition works on the level of the individual ordinary citizen. I of course do not have in mind here the rational, self-interested, negotiating individual of classical liberalism. An Aristophanic comic disposition, instead, characterizes the democratic individual. That individual is called to a rebellious defense of democratic freedom but also called to be one of many ordinary citizens who come together to act, sometimes against elites, sometimes uneasily led by elites. Part of the power of Aristophanes's engagement with democratic citizenship on my reading lies precisely in its focus on the challenge the individual democratic citizen thus faces.

Aristophanes, though, is equally alive to democracy's impulse for the citizen to be one of many, to share in the sufferings and joys of fellow citizens, to work together to address common concerns. This impulse connects most strongly with comic recognition and its shared sense of humanity. From this point of view, the comic recognition I have described might seem to risk a kind of plurality-denying humanism that risks obliterating (or simply remaining oblivious to) difference by treating everyone as ordinary. But here comic voyaging and cleverness return and, with them, the balanced and productive tension that marks Aristophanic comedy. If the comic disposition of ordinary citizenship I have here described might well welcome democratic action as a rallying of each of us as ordinary, it also maintains a wariness of any and all such rallying cries issued in the name of democracy. Thinking through and sorting out claims about what we share and how we differ, about who counts as ordinary and who is elite, about what the demos is and is not—all of this is the stuff of democratic politics for Aristophanes. His comedies do not offer us answers, but they suggest the disposition with which we should approach the questions. And they constantly remind us that democratic citizenship is hard work.

NOTES

Introduction

1. See, for example, the work of Connolly, *Identity/Difference*, 192–93; Connolly, "Critique of Pure Politics"; Honig, *Political Theory*; Laclau, *On Populist Reason*; Mouffe, *On the Political*; and Rancière, *Disagreement*. For overviews of the debate surrounding agonal democracy, see Markell, "Rule of the People"; and Olson, "Friends and Enemies."

2. For liberalism here, I have in mind of course the work of John Rawls, among many others. For deliberative democracy, I have in mind, among many others, the work of Jurgen Habermas, Amy Guttmann, Dennis Thompson, and Seyla Benhabib.

3. See, for example, de Ste. Croix, *Origins of the Peloponnesian War*, 357–59; Dover, *Aristophanic Comedy*, 33–34; and Cartledge, *Theatre of the Absurd*, chap. 5. See also Handley, "Generation Gap." I discuss this reading of Aristophanes as an Athenian conservative in more detail in section 3 of this introduction.

4. Gutmann and Thompson, *Why Deliberative Democracy?*, 6.

5. Mouffe, *On the Political*, 32.

6. Two collections of essays have played a particularly important role in encouraging this sort of work: Euben, Wallach, and Ober, *Athenian Political Thought*; and Ober and Hedrick, *DĒMOKRATIA*. Others examples include Euben, *The Tragedy of Political Theory*; Euben, *Corrupting Youth*; Euben, *Platonic Noise*; Saxonhouse, *Athenian Democracy*; Monoson, *Plato's Democratic Entanglements*; Frank, *Democracy of Distinction*; Zumbrunnen, *Silence and Democracy*; and Salkever, *Ancient Greek Political Thought*.

7. For an overview of what we currently know about Athenian democracy, see Rhodes, *Athenian Democracy*.

8. See, for example, the essays by Xenos, Kateb, Dallymyer, Taylor, and White in Botwinick and Connolly, *Democracy and Vision*.

9. Wolin, "Fugitive Democracy," 31.

10. Wolin, "Norm and Form," 43.

11. Ober, *Democracy and Knowledge*, 12.

12. Herodotus, *Histories*, 5.69. Compare here Herodotus's description of the Athenians' response to Isagoras and Kleomenes seizing the Acropolis: "The rest of the Athenians united in their resolve and besieged them for two days" (5.72).

13. Ober, *Athenian Revolution*.

14. Wolin, "Norm and Form," 41.

15. Wolin, "Fugitive Democracy," 31.

16. Ober, *Athenian Revolution*, 20.

17. Ibid., 19.

18. Lippman, *Phantom Public*, 3.

19. Ober, *Mass and Elite.*

20. Finley, *Politics in the Ancient World,* 27.

21. Lippmann introduces the idea of "the manufacture of consent" in *Phantom Public.* Noam Chomsky (among others) picks up and criticizes this formulation in Herman and Chomsky, *Manufacturing Consent.*

22. Here see Finley's discussion in *Democracy Ancient and Modern* of the constant "tension" that "characterized the condition of being a political leader in Athens" and his comparison of that condition to the analogous position of political elites in contemporary representative democracy (60).

23. Pericles's first speech appears in book 1, chapters 140–44 of Thucydides, *The Peloponnesian War;* Pericles last speech appears in book 2, chapters 60–64. I have offered my own reading of these speeches and of the interaction of elite speakers and the Athenian demos in Thucydides in Zumbrunnen, *Silence and Democracy.*

24. Aristotle, *Nicomachean Ethics,* 1105b25.

25. White, *Ethos,* 4.

26. Ibid., 6, 77.

27. For good introductions to the context of Aristophanic comedy, see Dover, *Aristophanic Comedy;* and MacDowell, *Aristophanes and Athens.*

28. See especially Strauss, *Socrates and Aristophanes;* Saxonhouse, *Fear of Diversity;* Euben, *Corrupting Youth.* Strauss's work is, to my knowledge, the last book by a political theorist or philosopher to offer readings of all of Aristophanes's extant comedies. Though his concerns—which involve reading the other ten plays as a backdrop for understanding the portrait of Socrates in *Clouds*—differ significantly from my concerns (which are closer to those of Euben and Saxonhouse), I have nonetheless found Strauss's close readings of the plays most useful.

29. I borrow the language of domestication of Euben, *Corrupting Youth,* 114, who describes and rejects it as an adequate rendering of Aristophanes's relationship to Athens.

30. Heath, *Political Comedy in Aristophanes,* 40–41. See also Gomme, "Aristophanes and Politics"; Halliwell, "Aristophanic Satire"; Konstan, *Greek Comedy and Ideology;* and Edwards, "Aristophanes' Comic Poetics."

31. Aristophanes, *Clouds, Wasps, Peace.* Throughout this book, I cite Aristophanes's plays by line number. I have relied upon the Greek text and, unless otherwise noted, the English translations found in the Loeb Classical Library editions, edited and translated by Jeffrey Henderson.

32. See the works cited in note 3 above.

33. Konstan, *Greek Comedy and Ideology,* 27.

34. Along similar lines, see Olson's argument in "Economics and Ideology" that whatever is suggested by a cursory examination of its basic plot, *Wealth* is "an essentially conservative text, whose deeper ideological aims are not necessarily identical with its apparent surface concerns" (225).

35. Goldhill, "Great Dionysia"; Goldhill, *Poet's Voice;* Halliwell, "Freedom of Speech"; Longo, "Theater of the Polis"; and Reckford, *Old and New Comedy.*

36. Sommerstein, "Demon Poverty."

37. Ober, *Political Dissent.*

38. Henderson, "Comic Competition," 309. See also Henderson, "Comic Hero versus Political Elite"; McGlew, *Citizens on Stage;* and Ehrenberg, *People of Aristophanes.*

Chapter 1

1. Blume, *Lysistrata Project.*
2. Kotzamani, "Artist Citizens," 108.
3. Kotzamani, "Artist Citizens," 104.
4. See Kotzamani, "Artist Citizens," 104; and Donegan, "Remediating Dionysos."
5. Saxonhouse, *Fear of Diversity,* for example, reads Aristophanes as lamenting the essentially private nature of Lysistrata's path to peace. Though she finds Aristophanes tracing the manner in which war turns the city "on its head," Stroup, in "Designing Women," nonetheless sees the play as ending with "a state of marital normalcy returned to the polis" (39). Konstan similarly notes in *Greek Comedy and Ideology* that the play's end finds "the women comfortably dispersed under the authority of the household" and so undermines the "utopian ideal of social integration" (60). See also Foley, "The 'Female Intruder' Reconsidered." None of these readings denies that *Lysistrata* opposes war, but both raise questions about the idea that Aristophanes presents an achievable or desirable alternative to war. It is worth keeping in mind, too, the argument that Aristophanic comedy is not designed to forward serious proposals for ensuring peace: here see MacDowell who asserts in *Aristophanes and Athens* that "there can be no doubt that [Aristophanes] wishes that the hostilities would come to an end, but he has no practical suggestion for bringing that about" (246).
6. Stein, comparing the *Lysistrata Project* to a performance of the play by the Greek National Theater in "Review: The *Lysistrata* Experience," suggests that the latter showed a much greater degree of trust in Aristophanes's art than did the former: "Unlike the spirit of *The Lysistrata Project,* the production by the National Theater of Greece made no attempt to help the play project its relevancy or immediacy. The organizers of the event trusted Aristophanes to make those connections without any additional cues" (136).
7. MacDowell, *Aristophanes and Athens,* 181–82.
8. Nussbaum, "The Comic Soul," 176.
9. See MacDowell, *Aristophanes and Athens,* 180.
10. Here compare Thucydides's glowing evaluation in *The Peloponnesian War* (2.65) of Pericles as one who could stand up to the demos, raising spirits when times were harsh and bringing the people to heel when they grew overconfident. Where Thucydides suggests that Pericles could control the demos that then overwhelmed his successors, Aristophanes points to the opposite conclusion: that Pericles was controlled by the demos, which then accepted whatever the flattering orators who followed had to say. See also, of course, Plato's critique of Pericles in the *Gorgias.*
11. Rancière, *Politics of Aesthetics,* 12.
12. Rancière, *On the Shores of Politics.*
13. Rancière's work thus fits with other work that rejects the notion of democracy as a type or rule or political order or regime, including, for example, Wolin's idea of "fugitive democracy" as developed in "Norm and Form," and "Fugitive Democracy." I take up this theme more directly in chapter 3.
14. Rancière's reading thus stands opposed to recent work that finds democratic possibilities or resources in Plato or at least means to dislodge the idea that Plato is

simply an antidemocrat. One among many examples is Monoson, *Plato's Democratic Entanglements*. Though I find Rancière a useful theoretical resource for thinking through Aristophanes, my use of his work does not imply my acceptance of his at times highly schematic reading of the Greek philosophers. On Rancière's (mis) reading of Plato, see Tarnopolsky, "Plato's Politics."

15. Rancière, *Disagreement*; Rancière, *On the Shores of Politics*.

16. Roughly speaking, in *Disagreement*, Rancière deploys the terms *archipolitics* and *parapolitics* for these strategies (with Marx marking the emergence of *metapolitics*).

17. Rancière, *The Philosopher and His Poor*.

18. Nussbaum, in "The Comic Soul," following Segal, suggests that "comedy reinforces certain traditional values having to do with family, bodily need, and communal solidarity." But this sort of reinforcement involves not simply an affirmation of the status quo, but the offering of "a brief pause in the flow of events," during which "different possibilities are at least contemplated" (176). Part of what marks this level of general reflection, then, is precisely its refusal to offer specific advice or certain solutions; hence my claim that Aristophanes explores challenges to the existing order, as opposed to any more clear-cut claim that he endorses—rejects—those challenges.

19. Stroup, in "Designing Women," casts Lysistrata's plan as enabled by the way that war itself makes "a protracted assault" on the city and its "normative ideological boundaries—the means by which conceptual and structural distinctions are made between 'interior' and 'exterior,' 'Athenian' and 'foreigner,' 'private' and 'public,' and . . . 'wife' and 'non-wife'" (39). For Stroup, that is, Aristophanes understands war as dissolving the distribution of the sensible and opening a space of empowerment for the excluded women of Athens. I here place more emphasis on Lysistrata's agency, an emphasis I see as in keeping with Aristophanic comedy's focus on the (fantastical) heroism of its protagonists. See also Foley, "The 'Female Intruder,'" 5. To these readings which focus on how *Lysistrata* plays with gender relations in Athens, compare Strauss who suggests in *Socrates and Aristophanes* the possibility that Lysistrata and her coconspirators "stand for the men favoring peace," so that the play points toward the fact that "the only possible way to obtain peace in the circumstances is by a change of regime in Athens" (212).

20. Dover, *Aristophanic Comedy*, 137; see also MacDowell, *Aristophanes and Athens*, 198; and Reckford, *Aristophanes' Old and New Comedy*, 4.

21. Thucydides, *History of the Peloponnesian War*, 8.73.

22. Rancière, *The Emancipated Spectator*, 14.

23. Rancière, *The Ignorant Schoolmaster*, 21.

24. Ibid., 32.

25. Rancière, *The Emancipated Spectator*, 17.

26. Rancière, *On the Shores of Politics*, 1. Then, too, there is *Short Voyages*, where Rancière explores the unsettling effects for poets and philosophers and activists of their attempts to navigate the distance between themselves and the people. Here "associating and disassociating" occurs between "reality" and "utopia."

27. See note 14 above.

28. See Hubbard, *Mask of Comedy*. Most of Aristophanes's surviving plays include a parabasis, a moment in which the chorus abandons all pretense of dramatic

illusion and turns to speak directly to the audience, most often claiming to speak directly for the poet.

29. On this note, see the Funeral Oration of Pericles in Thucydides's *The Peloponnesian War*. Pericles famously declares that the Athenians "regard the man who takes no part in public affairs [*pragmata*] not as one who minds his own business, but as good for nothing" (3.40.2).

30. Along similar lines, Reckford, in *Aristophanes' Old and New Comedy*, describes Trygaeus's voyage with its "Olympian view" as enabling a certain "renewal of perspective" that allows for the "recognition" of Peace (11). I myself turn to the language of recognition in chapter 5.

31. See MacDowell, *Aristophanes and Athens*, for a more detailed reading of Hermes's explanation of the war's causes. MacDowell emphasizes not the different explanations of the war in *Peace*, but the differences between the explanations offered here by Hermes and in *Acharnians* by Diceapolis (186–92).

32. Here compare Strauss's comment in *Socrates and Aristophanes* on Trygaeus's return to earth: "from on high the human beings looked smaller and less evil than they do when viewed from the earth. The gods have less reason, one is tempted to infer, for being indignant and punitive than men" (153). Strauss reads *Peace* as reproducing "the connection between the highest and the lowest and thus [fulfilling] its duty to what is between" (158). I should want to say that *Peace* works to hold high, low, and in-between in tension with one another, without being bound firmly to any of the three.

33. MacDowell, in *Aristophanes and Athens*, presents the identity of the chorus as remaining unclear and so as a "problem" (185). See also Dover, who concludes in *Aristophanic Comedy* that "the chorus itself is half regarded as Greek, half as Athenian, then as (unspecified) farmers, and finally as Athenian farmers" (139).

34. Here compare Saxonhouse's argument in "Men, Women, War and Politics" that "the pan-Hellenism of Aristophanes' women is due precisely to their attention to what is private; it is not an expansion of the concept of what is public" (72). See also Konstan's conclusion in *Greek Comedy and Ideology* that, because they focus solely on ending the war with Sparta, "the women do not effectively challenge the division of Greece into separate political entities" (60). By contrast, see Reckford's depiction in *Aristophanes' Old and New Comedy* of Aristophanes as forwarding in *Lysistrata* a vision of *communitas* in which "a general rejuvenation" works to restore and mutually reinforce both Athenian unity and panhellenism (308).

35. Thucydides, *Peloponnesian War*, 1.70.

Chapter 2

1. I have relied on the translation in Aristotle, *Aristotle: The Poetics*, 1449a.

2. Aristotle, *Poetics*, 1449a.

3. McGuigan, *Cultural Populism*, 4. A concern with the cultural experience of ordinary people has, in fact, animated cultural studies since its inception, and the issue of cultural populism remains central to the field today. McGuigan goes on to cite Raymond Williams's "resonant phrase, 'culture is ordinary'" (21). This

fundamental focus on the ordinary seeks to undermine the distinction between elite and popular culture and to direct our attention toward the latter as an object of study. See Storey's account in *Inventing Popular Culture* of the development of the idea of popular culture, which he refers to as "concept produced by mainly middle-class intellectuals" (121n1).

4. Along similar lines, in his polemic *One Market under God* Frank links the cultural populism he, too, finds in cultural studies to the "market populism" of contemporary American conservatism. Both, Frank argues, find democracy—understood as the exercise of choice by ordinary people—in the marketplace, including the cultural marketplace.

5. I consider this connection in more detail in the conclusion of this chapter and again in chapter 3.

6. Plato, "Apology," 18D, in *The Last Days of Socrates*, 41.

7. See Strauss, *Socrates and Aristophanes*, and compare Euben's discussion of *Clouds* in chapter 5 of *Corrupting Youth*. The approach to *Clouds* that I take here owes much to Euben's reading.

8. Zuckert, "Rationalism and Political Responsibility," 278.

9. On this passage see Bowie, *Aristophanes*, 103; and Euben, *Corrupting Youth*, 119.

10. Dover, *Aristophanic Comedy*, 112.

11. Dover, *Aristophanic Comedy*, 172. See also MacDowell, *Aristophanes and Athens*, pp. 261–62. On the Thesmophoria festival more generally, see the discussion in Tzanetou, "Something to do with Demeter."

12. See, though, Strauss's argument in *Socrates and Aristophanes* that "the *Thesmophoriasuzai* presents Euripides' success: the concession he makes to the women fades into insignificance if seen in the light of his escaping capital punishment" (235).

13. Dover, *Aristophanic Comedy*, explores the complex relationship of the women's assembly to the Assembly of Athens, pointing in addition to the final choral ode of *Women at the Thesmophoria* (at 1143–47). In that ode, Dover writes, "for a moment it sounds as if the chorus is discarding its role and speaking for the Athenian people; then [the phrase] 'of the women' pulls them back into their role as women; yet their return to this role is by no means smooth" (171). On the complex role(s) Euripides plays in this comedy, see Zeitlin, "Travesties of Gender and Genre," 304.

14. Henderson, "Introductory Note," 449. MacDowell, *Aristophanes and Athens*, 270, is less certain that Aristophanes means in this scene to show comedy as straightforwardly superior to tragedy, as is Zeitlin, "Travesties of Gender and Genre," 317–18. See also Strauss's broader claim in *Socrates and Aristophanes* that *Women at the Thesmophoria* "shows the superiority of the poet, at least of the dramatic poet, who is able to appear in various disguises, to the philosopher" (235).

15. See Nietzsche, "The Birth of Tragedy," in *Basic Writings of Nietzsche*.

16. Here see Reckford, *Aristophanes' Old and New Comedy*, 427–28.

17. In his introduction to the Loeb edition of *Frogs*, Henderson notes that the "anti-heroic and burlesque portrayal" of Dionysus was "long familiar in comedy and satyr drama" (4). See also Segal, "Character and Cults of Dionysus," 209–10.

18. Along these lines, see Habash, "Dionysus' Roles in Aristophanes' *Frogs*."

19. Here compare the sausage-seller in *Knights*, who confesses that the prospect of doing battle with the Paphlagonian slave who represents Cleon scares him to death. See my discussion of *Knights* in chapter 3.

20. Reckford, *Aristophanes' Old and New Comedy*, 407, describes Aristophanes's Dionysus as "fat, lazy and very cowardly."

21. McGlew, *Citizens on Stage*, makes a similar point and discusses this passage in more detail.

22. See Edmonds, *Myths of the Underworld Journey*.

23. Here see, again, Henderson's claim about the appeal of Aristophanic heroes to the Athenian audience, quoted above in the introduction to this book.

24. Bowie, *Aristophanes*, 243. See also Strauss, *Socrates and Aristophanes*, 243–44.

25. On the "problem" of the unity of *Frogs* and the transformation of Dionysus, see Whitman, *Aristophanes and the Comic Hero*, 230–31; Segal, "Character and Cults of Dionysus," 215; Reckford, *Aristophanes' Old and New Comedy*, 408; and Lada-Richards, *Initiating Dionysus*. On the connection between Dionysus's transformation, the Eleusinian Mysteries, and the unity of *Frogs*, see Bowie, *Aristophanes*, 238–39 and 244–45.

26. Here compare Strauss, who concludes in *Socrates and Aristophanes* more straightforwardly that "*Frogs* presents the education of Aristophanes' educator from an unqualified admiration for Euripides to a preference for Aeschylus" and that, as Aeschylus and Dionysus depart Hades for Athens, the play "intimates its hope for peace" (262).

Chapter 3

1. Rich, "Slumdogs Unite," WK10. See also Brinkley, "Railing against the Rich," W1.

2. Rich, "Slumdogs Unite!"

3. Hofstadter, *Age of Reform*, 82.

4. Ibid., 5.

5. National People's Party, "The Omaha Platform."

6. National People's Party, "Platform of 1896.

7. By comparison, William Jennings Bryan's famous "Cross of Gold" speech, given at the 1896 Democratic National Convention might be read as struggling mightily to contain its negative emotional undercurrent. While in the contest waged so far "the warmest ties of love and acquaintance and association have been disregarded," Bryan, speaking after a prominent Massachusetts Democrat, assures his audience that "not one person in all this convention entertains the least hostility to the people of the state of Massachusetts" and, more generally, that "we say not one word against those who live on the Atlantic coast." Still, as he builds toward his climactic declaration that "you shall not crucify mankind on a cross of gold," Bryan cannot help but declare the defiance of his followers, who will "beg no longer," "entreat no more." Ready to "fight to the uppermost," Bryan warns that those who would impose the gold standard face "the avenging wrath of an indignant people." Like the Party Platforms, the "Cross of Gold" speech is widely available online and

in print. The following site includes the text of the speech along with an audio recording of Bryan giving an encore performance of the speech in the early 1900s, something he apparently did with some regularity. Bryan, "Cross of Gold."

8. Aristotle, *Nicomachean Ethics*, 1126a.

9. He is, one of his slaves says, "*phileliastēs*," a term which Henderson translates as "addicted to jury service" (88).

10. Konstan, *Greek Comedy and Ideology*, 22, 172n19.

11. Allen, *World of Prometheus*, 133.

12. I again emphasize that my turn to Rancière here does not imply my acceptance of his readings of Plato and Aristotle. See note 14 in chapter 1.

13. Rancière, *Disagreement*, 22. Compare Wolin's arguments about the constitutionalization of democracy in "Norm and Form."

14. Rancière, *On the Shores of Politics*, 95.

15. Rancière, "Ten Theses on Politics."

16. Rancière, *Disagreement*, 39.

17. Rancière, "Ten Theses on Politics."

18. See along similar lines Olson, who argues in "Politics and Poetry" that Philocleon experiences jury duty "as a means to an extraordinary, almost unrivalled degree of power and pleasure" (133). Olson here contrasts his view with that of Konstan, "Politics of Aristophanes *Wasps*."

19. Here compare Reckford's argument in *Aristophanes' Old and New Comedy* that the anger of the jurors is the same anger with which they once, as soldiers fighting for Athens, "pursued invaders," and so jury duty is for them "surrogate warfare" (237–38).

20. The trial of dog parodies the real-life legal conflict between Cleon and the Athenian general Laches. See the discussions in Reckford, *Aristophanes' Old and New Comedy*, 251–63; Olson, "Politics and Poetry," 131–32; and Konstan, *Greek Comedy and Ideology*, 25.

21. With these scenes in mind, Strauss, in *Socrates and Aristophanes*, concludes that Philocleon "retains to the end his natural inclination to malice and mischief, his natural nastiness or bitterness" (134). Though it is hard to quibble with that description, my reading would question whether it is nastiness and bitterness or, rather, the search for certain *archē* that is natural to Philocleon.

22. Olson, in "Politics and Poetry," describes Philocleon in these final scenes as "completely out of control" or "uncontrollable" (144). My reading here is that his behavior, which might well be described as out of control, follows from his sense that he himself is not in control, that he has lost that *archē* that he enjoyed (or at least experienced himself as enjoying) when sitting in the lawcourts.

23. On this cosmogony, see MacDowell, *Aristophanes and Athens*, 207–8.

24. Arrowsmith, in "Aristophanes' *Birds*," argues that *Birds* makes thematic both fantasies of eros and "the hard, stubborn reality of terrestrial human nature and imperfection" and so points to "the aching gap between confident aspiration of mind and man's implacable feet of clay" (148).

25. Arrowsmith thus argues in "Aristophanes' *Birds*" that the two heroes of *Birds*, though they leave Athens, take with them "the corrosive, ineradicable strain of a national—and for Aristophanes, I believe, a generically human—character" (126). See also MacDowell, *Aristophanes and Athens*, who rejects readings that have

Aristophanes critiquing Athens or particular Athenians or, by contrast, celebrating Cloudcuckooland as utopian; he concludes instead that the play "shows this ordinary Athenian doing what the ordinary Athenians in the audience can only dream of doing: getting control over everyone else, and using it for his own personal pleasure" (228). Similarly, see Reckford, *Aristophanes Old and New Comedy*, 332. In a different vein, though, see Vicker's revival of the argument that *Birds* presents an allegory of Athenian (and Spartan) politics, with Peisetaerus representing Alcibiades in "Alcibiades at Sparta" (339–54) and *Pericles on Stage* (chap. 9).

26. Along similar lines, Pozzi, in "Pastoral Ideal," describes Peisetaerus's "scheme of power" as "a contrivance . . . that belongs to the domain of *logos* and can be made to succeed by *peithō*, the exercise of *logos*" (126). See also Arrowsmith, "Aristophanes' *Birds*," 144–46.

27. Pozzi, in "Pastoral Ideal," finds in the ending of *Birds* a resolution of the "ambiguity" between the fantasy (or "pastoral ideal") of a *topos apragmon* and the lure of *archē* (128). As I do throughout this book, I read *Birds* as preserving this ambiguity or, as I prefer, the productive tension between fantasy and irony.

28. Panizza, "Introduction: Populism and the Mirror of Democracy," 30. See also Canovan's discussion in "Trust the People!" of the "inescapable tension" between the "pragmatic" and "redemptive" faces of democracy, a tension that "makes populism a perennial possibility" (2). Ernesto Laclau, *Politics and Ideology*, insists that the mobilization of the people—though it may serve demagogic or even despotic ends—is also necessary to progressive or democratic collective action. Along similar lines, Rancière, in *On the Shores of Politics*, emphasizes the dual role of the *demos*, which possesses the power of "the two" and "the one." The power of "the people," that is, may lead to the sort of division that challenges domination or to the kind of dangerous unity that marks some forms of populist mobilization (32).

29. Markell, "Rule of the People," 12.

30. Along these lines, Arrowsmith argues in "Aristophanes *Birds*" that *Birds* "is designed to cope with Athenian hybris by self-recognition in the audience" (155). Part of what must be recognized is "the metaphysical physis of the human animal— the animal who wants to be god" (154). In chapter 5, I argue for my own version of the sort of deep Aristophanic comic recognition of the human condition. Compare here Strauss, who argues in *Socrates and Aristophanes* that, while *Birds* (and Aristophanic comedy more generally) "holds a mirror to the Athenian vices, it is as such a praise of Athens because it shows what wonderful things might be done by Athenians, even to the gods, as distinguished from what the gods have in fact done for Athens" (191).

Chapter 4

1. Villa, *Politics, Philosophy, Terror*, 108.

2. Connolly, *Identity/Difference*, 192–93. See also Connolly, "Critique of Pure Politics."

3. Villa, *Politics, Philosophy, Terror*, 107–8, thus includes Wolin and Connolly, along with Mouffe and Bonnie Honig, as agonistic democrats. See Mouffe, "Democracy,

Power and the Political"; and Honig, *Political Theory and the Displacement of Politics*. See also Benhabib's introduction to *Democracy and Difference*. On the politics of difference see Wolin, "Democracy, Difference, and Re-Cognition," 480; and Connolly's response in "Politics and Vision."

4. Wolin, "Fugitive Democracy," 31. See also Wolin, "Liberal/Democratic Divide."

5. Wolin, "Fugitive Democracy," 31.

6. Villa, *Politics, Philosophy, Terror*, 109. Though Villa criticizes Connolly and Wolin (and others) for failing fully to account for such objections, both show an awareness of the limits of agonism in democracy. See also Honig's discussion of the possibility of overcoming the *virtu*-virtue dichotomy she establishes in *Political Theory and the Displacement of Politics* (200–201).

7. Connolly, *Identity/Difference*, 193.

8. Ibid., 167.

9. Wolin, "Fugitive Democracy," 31.

10. For contrasting views on Cleon and Diodotus, see Saxonhouse, *Athenian Democracy*, 75; and Orwin, *Humanity of Thucydides*, 159–60. I have discussed the Mitylene Debate and its place in Thucydides's *History* in my *Silence and Democracy*. Hesk, *Deception and Democracy*, 248–58, adopts an approach broadly similar to mine in this chapter, using the Mitylene Debate as the backdrop to a reading of *Knights*, but his focus is upon the sincerity of speakers, whereas mine is on ordinary citizens.

11. On the contradiction inherent in Cleon's clever attack on clever speakers, see Ober, *Political Dissent*, 98.

12. Plato, *Gorgias*, 504e. The translation here is from Plato, *Plato: Lysis, Symposium, Gorgias*.

13. Benhabib, *Democracy and Difference*, 7.

14. Ibid., 8.

15. Rogers's translation of Aristophanes, *The Acharnians, the Knights, the Clouds, the Wasps*, offers "citizens vacant and vain." Henderson's translation of Aristophanes, *Acharnians, Knights*, has "citizens of Simpletonia."

16. Given the arguments of chapters 1 and 2, it may seem problematic to use the language of "ordinary" in this way, as if it had a stable and substantive meaning. Again, I return to the complicated question of what is ordinary and what is not in chapter 5. Here I work from the assumption that Diceapolis differs from elite Athenian political actors in a way that makes it possible to call him ordinary without, again, assuming some essence of the ordinary. He is ordinary, again, because of his relative status in Athens; Aristophanes's description of him is, I think, meant to suggest that status to us, without suggesting that all ordinary Athenians are just like Diceapolis.

17. On *Acharnians* as a "plea for peace," see Cartledge, *Theatre of the Absurd*, 55–58.

18. Heath, *Political Comedy ina Aristophanes*, 16–18, argues against taking the speech seriously.

19. On the role of disguise in *Acharnians*, see Hesk, *Democracy and Deception*, 264–67; Slater, "Space, Character and απαπη'"; and Hubbard, *The Mask of Comedy*, chap. 2.

20. Wolin, "Fugitive Democracy," 30.

21. Dover, *Aristophanic Comedy*, 88.

22. Wolin, "Fugitive Democracy," 42, attributes the rarity of the political to the modern centrality of the state. The end of *Acharnians* suggests a perhaps more basic challenge to the political: the real appeals of the nonpolitical life. Along these lines, White, in "Three Conceptions of the Political," though sympathetic to the critiques of liberalism offered by Wolin and others, reminds us that life in liberal polities is "not bad, either economically or politically" (173).

23. Connolly, *Identity/Difference*, 166–67, and "Critique of Pure Politics," 21.

24. As Henderson, "Comic Hero versus Political Elite," 309, notes, the sausage-seller does stand out among Aristophanes's heroes, for he is less "respectable," if just as ordinary, as Diceapolis.

25. Detienne and Vernant, *Cunning Intelligence*, 8–23.

26. Reckford notes in *Aristophanes' Old and New Comedy* that scholars "fail to appreciate, and to identify with the sausage-seller"—as the ordinary citizens in Aristophanes's audience would have (114).

27. For a similar point, see Dover, *Aristophanic Comedy*, 99.

28. Dover, *Aristophanic Comedy*, 99. See also Henderson, "Comic Hero versus Political Elite," 313.

29. As Wolin, "Fugitive Democracy," 44, notes, solidarity need not mean "dreary uniformity."

30. Hesk, *Deception and Democracy*, similarly notes the ambiguous status of the sausage-seller, suggesting that the play's ending leaves open the possibility that "Agoracritus has simply enacted a new strategy of manipulating the demos" (257). See also Bowie, *Aristophanes: Myth, Ritual and Comedy*, 74–77, on the sausage-seller's "villainy." For different views on the sausage-seller, see Strauss, *Socrates and Aristophanes*, 107; and Reckford, *Aristophanes' Old and New Comedy*, 105–20.

31. I borrow this language from White, "Three Conceptions of the Political," 175.

32. White, in "Three Conceptions of the Political," sees Wolin's political as "extraordinary in ways that render it too remote from the ongoing expression of democratic energies" (177).

33. Connolly, "Critique of Pure Politics," 21–22. White, in "Three Conceptions of the Political," on the other hand, worries that Connolly's idea of generosity is too "indiscriminate" (183).

Chapter 5

1. McGlew, "After Irony"; Rothwell, *Politics and Persuasion*; Sommerstein, "Aristophanes and the Demon Poverty."

2. Olson, "Economics and Ideology," 225.

3. Nehamas, *Art of Living*, 51.

4. Rorty, *Contingency, Irony, and Solidarity*, 94.

5. Nehamas, *Art of Living*; Vlastos, *Socrates: Ironist and Moral Philosopher*; Colebrook, *Irony in the Work of Philosophy*; and Colebrook, *Irony*.

6. Feldman, "Redistribution, Recognition and the State"; Fraser and Honneth, *Redistribution or Recognition?*

7. Ober, *Mass and Elite*, 17–19, 194–96.

8. Bowie, *Aristophanes: Myth, Ritual, Comedy*; and Strauss, *Athens after the Peloponnesian War.*

9. French, "Economic Conditions in Fourth-Century Athens"; Mossé, "Economist"; Sommerstein, "Aristophanes and the Demon Poverty."

10. Austin and Vidal-Naquet, *Economic and Social History*; Burke, "Economy of Athens"; Mossé, "Economist."

11. Polanyi, *Primitive, Archaic and Modern Economies*, 84; see also Polanyi, *Livelihood of Man*, 51–52.

12. Mossé, "The Economist," 24.

13. Austin and Vidal-Naquet, *Economic and Social History*, 11–12; see also Burke, "Economy of Athens"; Finley, *Ancient Economy*; and Ober, "Aristotle's Political Sociology."

14. Polanyi, *Primitive, Archaic and Modern Economies*, 81–2.

15. Finley, *Ancient Economy*, 51.

16. de Ste. Croix, *Origins of the Peloponnesian War*, 357; and de Ste. Croix, *Class Struggle in the Ancient Greek World*, 125.

17. Wood, *Democracy Against Capitalism*, 202.

18. Ober, *Mass and Elite*, 249–50.

19. Austin and Vidal-Naquet, *Economic and Social History*, 119–23; Finley, *Ancient Economy*, 36–37.

20. Polanyi, *Primitive, Archaic and Modern Economies*, 311–16.

21. Fraser, "From Redistribution to Recognition?"; Fraser, "Recognition or Redistribution?"; Fraser, *Justice Interruptus*; Fraser, "Rethinking Recognition"; Fraser, "Recognition Without Ethics?"; Fraser and Honneth, *Redistribution or Recognition*; and Fraser and Naples, "To Interpret the World."

22. Fraser, *Justice Interruptus*, 1–3.

23. Fraser, "Rethinking Recognition," 116; see Max Weber, "Class, Status, Party."

24. Feldman, "Redistribution, Recognition and the State"; Fraser and Naples, "To Interpret the World," 1116–17.

25. Fraser, "Recognition Without Ethics?" 29.

26. Butler, "Merely Cultural"; Phillips, "From Inequality to Difference"; and Young, "Unruly Categories."

27. Fraser and Honneth, *Redistribution or Recognition?*, 138–39.

28. Ibid., 154.

29. Ibid., 74.

30. Finley, *Ancient Economy*, 144.

31. Taylor, "Politics of Recognition."

32. Fraser, "Rethinking Recognition," 113.

33. Fraser, "Rethinking Recognition," 112–16; Fraser and Honneth, *Redistribution or Recognition?*, 26–27.

34. Fraser, "Rethinking Recognition," 114.

35. Markell, *Bound by Recognition*, 63. Markell's emphasis on the openness of identity and action fits well with the understanding of *archē* which he will later draw from Arendt and which I discussed at the end of chapter 4.

36. Markell, *Bound by Recognition*, 73, 89.

37. I here draw on the translation in Aristophanes, *The Complete Plays of Aristophanes.*

38. Bowie, *Aristophanes: Myth, Ritual, Comedy*, 255–57; Saxonhouse, *Fear of Diversity*, 4–7; Strauss, *Socrates and Aristophanes*, 263.

39. Ober, *Political Dissent*, 135–38; Saxonhouse, *Fear of Diversity*, 4–9.

40. In considering the efforts of Praxagora and the other women to take on the appearance and mannerisms of men, we should not overlook the fact that these "women" will themselves have been played by male actors on the Athenian stage. Thus Aristophanes manages to double the play on gender roles here, having men portray women portraying men. The playwright perhaps here also engages in the theatrical self-referentiality that marks old comedy in generally. See Dover, *Aristophanic Comedy*; Hubbard, *The Mask of Comedy*; and Segal, "Spectator and Listener."

41. That women gaining power in the city remained a fanciful idea in fourth-century-BCE Athens need not mean it was an unfamiliar one. Dover, in *Aristophanic Comedy* thus describes "the assumption of some degree of social and political initiative by women" as a "comic tradition" and reminds us that Aristophanes has already presented the possibility in *Lysistrata* and *Women at the Thesmophoria* (201). Then, too, the broad theme of women exceeding the limits imposed by their status in Greek society appears in tragedy as well, with Sophocles's *Antigone* as perhaps the most obvious example.

42. MacDowell, *Aristophanes and Athens*, 309; Rothwell, *Politics and Persuasion*, 82–92, 103.

43. Praxagora's scheme for communal property leads, too, to a communal scheme for sexual relations, though I focus my attention on the former sort of redistribution here. The latter scheme hinges on Praxagora's declaration that unattractive women and old men will have their choice of sexual mates first and thus will not lose out to the young and attractive (610–20); it ends with a weakening of family ties familiar from Plato's *Republic*. Scholars have long argued over the potential link between Plato's communal scheme and Praxagora's. A general consensus exists that while such ideas may have been in the air in Athens generally, Aristophanes is not parodying Plato's thinking in particular here, especially since he presented *Assemblywomen* some time before the *Republic* was written. See, for example, MacDowell, *Aristophanes and Athens*, 314; Ober, *Political Dissent*, 154–55; and Reckford, *Aristophanes' Old and New Comedy*, 348. On the significance of the dissolution of the boundaries between families in *Assemblywomen*, see especially Saxonhouse, *Fear of Diversity*, chap. 1.

44. Dover, in *Aristophanic Comedy*, explores the deeper links between the place of women and the nature of property in Greek society and thus the easy "confluence" of "two comic traditions" in *Assemblywomen* (200). MacDowell, in *Aristophanes and Athens*, in contrast, concludes that the "two main subjects" of the play—"women attending the Assembly to take control of the state, and the communistic organization of property and sex"—"have no necessary connection with one another" (320).

45. This character is in fact denoted simply as "man [*anēr*]." I follow Sommerstein, "Aristophanes and the Demon Poverty," 316; and Rothwell, *Politics and Persuasion*, 7, in using Dissident. Henderson's translation in Aristophanes, *Frogs, Assemblywomen, Wealth*, uses "selfish man."

46. See also Reckford, *Aristophanes' Old and New Comedy*, 353.

47. Although I focus on the doubts of the Dissident here, those who see an ironic undermining of *Assemblywomen*'s fantasy point to other aspects of the play as well. The scheme of sexual communism, for example, plays out in ways that suggest that its success may be threatened by the selfish desires of individuals. More generally, Saxonhouse, *Fear of Diversity*, argues that the implementation of that scheme reveals the consequences of attempting to abolish difference in favor of seamless unity in the city. On another note, despite the play's ending with the joyous announcement of a great communal feast, some focus on Blepyrus's apparent suggestion that everyone must "hurry home" if they are to enjoy that feast (1144–47) as evidence that the idea of providing for all from common stores is unrealistic. For discussion of the ironic reading of these scenes, see especially Sommerstein, "Aristophanes and the Demon Poverty"; and Rothwell *Politics and Persuasion*, 6–7.

48. Fraser, *Justice Interruptus*, 152.

49. Ober, *Political Dissent*, 154.

50. Ober, in *Political Dissent*, himself presents his reading as an alternative to seeing *Assemblywomen* as simply "an ironic or absurdist fantasy." My suggestion here is that his argument in fact implies a reading of the fantasy of *Assemblywomen* as inherently ironic. On irony as revealing the limits of any particular "vocabulary," see Rorty, *Contingency, Irony, and Solidarity*, chap. 4.

51. Especially given Aristophanes's frequent parodying of tragedy—most explicitly in *Frogs* but in fact throughout his comedies (Dover, *Aristophanic Comedy*, esp. 72–73; Segal, "Spectator and Listener")—*Wealth*'s condition suggests at least oblique reference to the centrality of blindness in Greek tragedy. The comparison with Sophocles's Oedipus is perhaps particularly telling on the different attitudes of tragedy and comedy. Where *Oedipus Rex* ends with Oedipus being led away, having blinded himself in the wake of realizing the horror of his deeds, *Wealth* begins with Wealth's blindness as posing the central dramatic conflict to be resolved.

52. Wealth, then, appears as something like a latter-day Prometheus, whom Zeus punished for giving to human beings the gifts of fire and technical skills. Although in Aeschylus's version Prometheus appears as a tragic hero, Heisod's version stresses his delivery of the drudgery of labor to humankind (Austin and Vidal-Naquet, *Economic and Social History*, 12; Wood, *Peasant-Citizen and Slave*, 140–1). Aristophanes's Wealth as humans' benefactor in a sense combines the best of both worlds (to considerable comic effect), benefiting humankind not by offering them the technical means to improve their lives but, rather, by directly alleviating their suffering simply by making them rich.

53. The Greek *diagignôskoimi*, translated as "recognize," carries connotations of diagnosing or, perhaps more to the point here, distinguishing between. Wealth's point is precisely that he is unable to see a central difference among humans: that some are good and some are not.

54. Bowie, *Aristophanes: Myth, Ritual, Comedy*, 278–84; Strauss, *Socrates and Aristophanes*, 285.

55. Some find in this movement from enriching those who have always been just to enriching everyone a significant inconsistency in the plot of *Wealth*. See, for example, Konstan and Dillon, "The Ideology of Aristophanes' *Wealth*," who take

this inconsistency as part of Aristophanes's subtle—and ultimately conservative—diffusion of tensions in Athenian ideology. Dover, *Aristophanic Comedy*, and Mac-Dowell *Aristophanes and Athens*, 345, note but remain relatively untroubled by the inconsistency here, which both see as common in Aristophanic comedy.

56. Reckford, *Aristophanes' Old and New Comedy*, chaps. 2–4.

57. McGlew, "After Irony"; and Sommerstein, "Aristophanes and the Demon Poverty." Both emphasize the frightful appearance of Poverty as designed in part to elicit the audience's sympathy with Chremylus and Blepsidemus. Aristophanes also plays here with gender stereotypes. Chremylus in admonishing Blepsidemus to stay for the agon with Poverty asks, "Do you want it said that two men fled in terror from one woman?" As in *Assemblywomen* and elsewhere, the joke can cut either way. On the one hand, it suggests a general sense of women as weaker than men, as nothing to be feared. On the other hand, it reminds the audience of the power of this particular goddess.

58. Bowie, *Aristophanes: Myth, Ritual, Comedy*, 290; Strauss, *Socrates and Aristophanes*, 295–96; MacDowell, *Aristophanes and Athens*, 334–35.

59. Plato, *Republic*, 327c.

60. Saxonhouse, *Fear of Diversity*.

61. Dover, *Aristophanic Comedy*, 204–8.

62. Colebrook, *Irony*, 27–8; Nehamas, *Art of Living*, 53–57.

63. As part of his exploration of "the principle of hope," Ernst Bloch, in *Principle of Hope*, describes "the utopian capacity" as "the point of contact between dreams and life, without which dreams only yield abstract utopia, life only triviality" (145–46). This, I think, suggests a similar sensibility to that Aristophanes creates in Chremylus. Bloch, though, sees Aristophanes as a "reactionary" who "created several of his best comedies at the expense of revolutionary hope," referring specifically to *Birds* and *Assemblywomen* (435–36).

64. Fraser, *Justice Interruptus*, 4.

Conclusion

1. Aristotle, *Nicomachean Ethics*, 1107a.

2. Ibid., 1109b.

3. Ibid., 1109a.

4. Ibid., 1109a.

5. This is not to deny the existence for Aristotle of an absolute mean or the possibility of the singularly good individual. It is merely to find in the *Ethics* a sense that the practical pursuit of virtue manifests itself in a variety of ways.

6. Henderson, "The Dēmos and the Comic Competition," 309.

7. On the centrality of the spectator to Athenian and Greek life, see Segal, "Spectator and Listener."

8. Lippman, *The Phantom Public*, 3.

9. Bellamy, *Citizenship*. See also Pocock, "The Ideal of Citizenship."

10. White, *Ethos*, 82. In defending this ethos, White considers the charge that it may be "eaten up by tentativeness and uncertainty" (p. 94) and so lead to political

passivity. His response, which bears some similarity to my arguments in the previous section, is that there is no necessary connection between an ethos that recognizes complexity, contingency, and uncertainty and political passivity.

11. In *Politics*, 3.8, Aristotle writes that "the real difference between democracy and oligarchy is poverty and wealth. Wherever men rule by reason of their wealth, whether they be few or many, that is an oligarchy, and where the poor rule, that is democracy. But in fact the rich are few and the poor are many" (1280a).

12. White, *Ethos*, 88–89.

BIBLIOGRAPHY

Allen, Danielle. *The World of Prometheus.* Princeton, NJ: Princeton University Press, 2000.

American Political Science Association Task Force. "APSA Task Force Report: American Democracy in an Age of Rising Inequality." *Perspectives on Politics* 2 (December 2004): 651–66.

Aristophanes. *Acharnians, Knights.* Edited and translated by Jeffrey Henderson. Loeb Classical Library 178. Cambridge, MA: Harvard University Press, 1998.

———. *The Acharnians, the Knights, the Clouds, the Wasps.* Translated by Benjamin B. Rogers. Cambridge, MA: Harvard University Press, 1924.

———. *Birds, Lysistrata, Women at the Thesmophoria.* Edited and translated by Jeffrey Henderson. Loeb Classical Library 179. Cambridge, MA: Harvard University Press, 2000.

———. *Clouds, Wasps, Peace.* Edited and translated by Jeffrey Henderson. Loeb Classical Library 488. Cambridge, MA: Harvard University Press, 1998.

———. *The Complete Plays of Aristophanes.* Edited and translated by Moses Hadas. New York: Bantam Books, 1962.

———. *Four Plays by Aristophanes: The Clouds, the Birds, Lysistrata, the Frogs.* Translated by William Arrowsmith, Richard Lattimore, and Douglass Parker. New York: Meridian, 1994.

———. *Frogs, Assemblywomen, Wealth.* Edited and translated by Jeffrey Henderson. Loeb Classical Library 180. Cambridge, MA: Harvard University Press, 2002.

Aristotle. *Aristotle: The Poetics; Longinus: On the Sublime; Demetrius: On Style.* Translated by Hamilton Frye and W. Rhys Roberts. Cambridge, MA: Harvard University Press, 1991.

———. *Nicomachean Ethics.* Translated by Terence Irwin. 2nd ed. Indianapolis, IN: Hackett, 2000.

———. *Politics.* Edited by Stephen Everson. Cambridge: Cambridge University Press, 1988.

Arrowsmith, William. "Aristophanes' *Birds*: The Fantasy Politics of Eros." *Arion* 1, no. 1 (Spring 1973): 119–76.

Austin, M. M., and P. Vidal-Naquet. *Economic and Social History of Ancient Greece: An Introduction.* Translated and revised by M. M. Austin. Berkeley: University of California Press, 1977.

Baumgartner, Jody, and Jonathan S. Morris. "The Daily Show Effect: Candidate Evaluation, Efficacy, and American Youth." *American Politics Research* 34, no. 3 (May 2006): 341–67.

Bellamy, Richard. *Citizenship: A Very Short Introduction.* Oxford: Oxford University Press, 2008.

Benhabib, Seyla, ed. *Democracy and Difference*. Princeton, NJ: Princeton University Press, 1996.

———. "Introduction." In Benhabib, *Democracy and Difference*, 3–18.

Bernadete, Seth. *Socrates' Second Sailing: On Plato's Republic*. Chicago: University of Chicago Press, 1992.

Bloch, Ernst. *The Principle of Hope*. Vol. 1. Translated by Neville Plaice, Stephen Plaice, and Paul Knight. Cambridge, MA: The MIT Press, 1995.

Blume, Kathryn, "Lysistrata Project." http://www.kathrynblume.com/LysProj.htm.

Botwinick, Arhey, and William E. Connolly, eds. *Democracy and Vision: Sheldon Wolin and the Vicissitudes of the Political*. Princeton, NJ: Princeton University Press, 2001.

Bowie, A. M. *Aristophanes: Myth, Ritual, Comedy*. Cambridge: Cambridge University Press, 1993.

Brinkley, Alan. "Railing against the Rich: A Great American Tradition." *Wall Street Journal*, February 8, 2009, W1.

Bryan, William Jennings. "Cross of Gold." Speech first delivered July 9, 1896. http://historymatters.gmu.edu/d/5354/.

Burke, Edmund M. "The Economy of Athens in the Classical Era: Some Adjustments to the Primitivist Model." *Transactions of the American Philological Association* 122 (1992): 199–226.

Butler, Judith. "Merely Cultural." *New Left Review* 227 (January–February 1998): 33–44.

Canovan, Margaret. "Trust the People! Populism and the Two Faces of Democracy." *Political Studies* 47 (March 1999): 2–16.

Cartledge, Paul. *Aristophanes and His Theatre of the Absurd*. London: Bristol Classical Press, 1990.

Colebrook, Claire. *Irony*. London: Routledge, 2004.

———. *Irony in the Work of Philosophy*. Lincoln: University of Nebraska Press, 2002.

Connolly, William. "A Critique of Pure Politics." *Philosophy and Social Criticism* 23, no. 5 (1997): 1–26.

———. *Identity/Difference: Democratic Negotiations of Political Paradox*. Ithaca, NY: Cornell University Press, 1991.

———. "Politics and Vision." In Botwinick and Connolly, *Democracy and Vision*, 3–24.

———. *The Origins of the Peloponnesian War*. Ithaca, NY: Cornell University Press, 1972.

Detienne, Marcel, and Jean-Pierre Vernant. *Cunning Intelligence in Greek Culture and Society*. Translated by Janet Lloyd. Sussex, UK: Harvester Press, 1978.

Dillon, Michael. "(De)void of Politics? A Response to Jacques Rancière's Ten Theses on Politics." *Theory and Event* 6, no. 4 (2003). doi:10.1353/tae.2003.0011.

Donegan, Tom. "Remediating Dionysos: The (Re)making Project and the Lysistrata Project." *Didaskalia* 6, no. 2 (Summer 2005). http://www.didaskalia.net/issues/vol6no2/donegan.htm.

Dougherty, Carol, and Leslie Kurke, eds. *The Cultures within Greek Culture: Contact, Conflict, Collaboration*. Cambridge: Cambridge University Press, 2003.

Dover, Kenneth J. *Aristophanic Comedy*. Berkeley: University of California Press, 1972.

Edmonds, Radcliffe G. *Myths of the Underworld Journey: Plato, Aristophanes, and the "Orphic" Gold Tablets*. Cambridge: Cambridge University Press, 2004.

Edwards, Anthony. "Aristophanes' Comic Poetics: TRUX, Scatology, SKO^ MMA." *Transactions of the American Philological Association* 121 (1991): 157–70.

Ehrenberg, Victor. *The People of Aristophanes.* Oxford: Blackwell, 1951.

Euben, J. Peter. *Corrupting Youth: Political Education, Democratic Culture, and Political Theory.* Princeton, NJ: Princeton University Press, 1997.

———. *Platonic Noise.* Princeton, NJ: Princeton University Press, 2003.

———. *The Tragedy of Political Theory.* Princeton, NJ: Princeton University Press, 1990.

Euben, J. Peter, John Wallach, and Josiah Ober, eds. *Athenian Political Thought and the Reconstruction of American Democracy.* Ithaca, NY: Cornell University Press, 1994.

Feldman, Leonard. "Redistribution, Recognition and the State: The Irreducibly Political Dimension of Injustice." *Political Theory* 30 (June 2002): 410–40.

Finley, M. I. *The Ancient Economy.* 2nd ed. Berkeley: University of California Press, 1985.

———. *Democracy Ancient and Modern.* Rev. ed. New Brunswick, NJ: Rutgers University Press, 1985.

———. *Politics in the Ancient World.* Cambridge: Cambridge University Press, 1983.

Foley, Helen. "The 'Female Intruder' Reconsidered: Women in Aristophanes' *Lysistrata* and *Ecclesiasuzae*." *Classical Philology* 77, no. 1 (January 1982): 1–21.

Frank, Jill. *A Democracy of Distinction.* Chicago: University of Chicago Press, 2005.

Frank, Thomas. *One Market under God: Extreme Capitalism, Market Populism, and the End of Economic Democracy.* New York: Doubleday Press, 2000.

———. *What's the Matter With Kansas? How Conservatives Won the Heart of America.* New York: Henry Holt, 2004.

Fraser, Nancy. "From Redistribution to Recognition? Dilemmas of Justice in a 'Postsocialist' Age." *New Left Review* 212 (July–August 1995): 68–93.

———. *Justice Interruptus: Critical Reflections on the "Postsocialist" Condition.* New York: Routledge, 1997.

———. "Recognition or Redistribution? A Critical Reading of Iris Young's *Justice and the Politics of Difference*." *Journal of Political Philosophy* 3, no. 2 (1995): 166–80.

———. "Recognition without Ethics?" *Theory, Culture & Society* 18, no. 2/3 (2001): 21–42.

———. "Rethinking Recognition." *New Left Review* 3 (May–June 2000): 107–20.

Fraser, Nancy, and Axel Honneth. *Redistribution or Recognition? A Political-Philosophical Exchange.* Translated by Joel Bold, James Ingram, and Christiane Wilke. London: Verso, 2003.

Fraser, Nancy, and Nancy A. Naples. "To Interpret the World and to Change It: An Interview with Nancy Fraser." *Signs: Journal of Women in Culture and Society* 29 (Summer 2004): 1103–24.

French, A. "Economic Conditions in Fourth-Century Athens." *Greece & Rome* 38 (April 1991): 24–40.

Goldhill, Simon. "The Great Dionysia and Civic Ideology." In *Nothing to Do with Dionysos? Athenian Drama in Its Social Context,* edited by John J. Winkler and Froma I. Zeitlin, 97–129. Princeton, NJ: Princeton University Press, 1990.

———. *The Poet's Voice: Essays on Poetics and Greek Literature.* Cambridge: Cambridge University Press, 1991.

Gomme, A. W. "Aristophanes and Politics." *Classical Review* 52 (July 1938): 97–109.

Green, Jeffrey Edward. *The Eyes of the People: Democracy in an Age of Spectatorship.* Oxford: Oxford University Press, 2009.

Gutmann, Amy, and Dennis Thompson. *Why Deliberative Democracy?* Princeton, NJ: Princeton University Press, 2004.

Habash, Martha. "Dionysus' Roles in Aristophanes' *Frogs.*" *Mnemosyne* 55 (January 2002): 1–17.

Halliwell, Stephen. "Aristophanic Satire." *The Yearbook of English Studies* 14 (1984): 6–21.

———. "Comic Satire and Freedom of Speech in Classical Athens," *Journal of Hellenic Studies* 111 (1991): 48–70.

Handley, E. W. "Aristophanes and the Generation Gap." In *Tragedy, Comedy and the Polis*, edited by Alan Sommerstein, 417–30. Bari, Italy: Levante Editori, 1993.

Heater, Derek. *What is Citizenship?* New York: Polity, 1999.

Heath, Malcolm. *Political Comedy in Aristophanes.* Göttingen, Germany: Vandenhoeck and Ruprecht, 1987.

Henderson, Jeffrey. "Comic Hero versus Political Elite." In *Tragedy, Comedy, and the Polis*, edited by Alan Sommerstein, 307–19. Bari, Italy: Levante Editori, 1993.

———. "The Dēmos and the Comic Competition." In *Nothing to Do with Dionysos? Athenian Drama in Its Social Context*, edited by John J. Winkler and Froma I. Zeitlin, 271–313. Princeton, NJ: Princeton University Press, 1990.

———. "*Frogs*: Introductory Note." In Aristophanes, *Frogs, Assemblywomen, Wealth*, 3–10.

———. "*Women at the Thesmophoria*: Introductory Note." In Aristophanes, *Birds, Lysistrata, Women at the Thesmophoria*, 444–45.

Herman, Edward S., and Noam Chomsky, *Manufacturing Consent: The Political Economy of the Mass Media.* New York: Pantheon, 2002.

Herodotus, *The Landmark Herodotus: The Histories.* Edited by Robert B. Strassler. Translated by Andrea L. Purvis. New York: Anchor Books, 2007.

Hesk, Jon. *Deception and Democracy in Classical Athens.* Cambridge: Cambridge University Press, 2000.

Hillygus, D. Sunshine, and Todd G. Shields. "Moral Issues and Voter Decision Making in the 2004 Presidential Election." *PS: Political Science and Politics* 38 (April 2005): 201–10.

Hofstadter, Richard. *The Age of Reform.* New York: Vintage, 1955.

Honig, Bonnie. *Political Theory and the Displacement of Politics.* Ithaca, NY: Cornell University Press, 1993.

Hubbard, Thomas. *The Mask of Comedy: Aristophanes and the Intertextual Parabasis.* Ithaca, NY: Cornell University Press, 1992.

Konstan, David. *Greek Comedy and Ideology.* New York: Oxford University Press, 1995.

———. "The Politics of Aristophanes' *Wasps*," *Transactions of the American Philological Association* 115 (1985): 27–46.

Konstan, David, and Matthew Dillon, "The Ideology of Aristophanes' *Wealth*." *The American Journal of Philology* 102 (Winter 1981): 371–94.

Kotzamani, Marina. "Artist Citizens in the Age of the Web." *Theater* 36, no. 2 (2006): 103–10.

Laclau, Ernesto. *On Populist Reason.* New York: Verso, 2005.

———. *Politics and Ideology in Marxist Theory: Capitalism, Populism and Fascism.* New York: Schocken Books, 1979.

Lada-Richards, I. *Initiating Dionysus: Ritual and Theatre in Aristophanes' Frogs.* Oxford: Clarendon Press, 1999.

Lippmann, Walter. *The Phantom Public.* New York: Transaction Publishers, 1993. First published 1927 by Macmillan.

———. *Public Opinion.* New York: New Vision Publications, 2007 First published 1922 by Macmillan.

Longo, Oddone. "The Theater of the Polis." In *Nothing to Do with Dionysos? Athenian Drama in Its Social Context,* edited by John J. Winkler and Froma I. Zeitlin, 12–19. Princeton, NJ: Princeton University Press, 1990.

MacDowell, Douglas. *Aristophanes and Athens: An Introduction to the Plays.* Oxford: Oxford University Press, 1995.

Markell, Patchen. *Bound by Recognition.* Princeton: Princeton University Press, 2003.

———. "The Rule of the People: Arendt, Archē, and Democracy." *American Political Science Review* 100, no. 1 (February 2006), 1–14.

Markovits, Elizabeth. *The Politics of Sincerity: Frank Speech and the Threat to Political Judgment.* University Park: Penn State University Press, 2009.

May, Todd. *The Political Thought of Jacques Rancière: Creating Equality.* University Park: Pennsylvania State University Press, 2008.

McClure, Kirstie M. "Disconnections, Connections and Questions: Reflections on Jacques Rancière's 'Ten Theses on Politics.'" *Theory and Event* 6, no. 4 (2003). doi:10.1353/tae.2003.0014.

McGlew, James. "After Irony: Aristophanes' *Wealth* and its Modern Interpreters." *American Journal of Philology* 118 (Spring 1997): 35–53.

———. *Citizens on Stage: Comedy and Political Culture in the Athenian Democracy.* Ann Arbor: University of Michigan Press, 2002.

McGuigan, Jim. *Cultural Populism.* New York: Routledge, 1992.

Meyer, Dick. "The Anatomy of a Myth: How Did One Exit Poll Answer Become the Story of How Bush Won? Good Question." *The Washington Post,* December 5, 2004, Sec. B, p. 1.

Monoson, S. Sara. *Plato's Democratic Entanglements.* Princeton, NJ: Princeton University Press, 2000.

Mossé, Claude. "The Economist." In *The Greeks,* edited by Jean-Pierre Vernant, translated by Charles Lambert and Teresa Lavendar Fagan, 23–52. Chicago: University of Chicago Press, 1995.

Mouffe, Chantal. "Democracy, Power and the Political." In Benhabib, *Democracy and Difference,* 245–56.

———. *On the Political.* New York: Routledge, 2005.

Mufti, Aamir R. "Reading Jacques Rancière's 'Ten Theses on Politics' after September 11th." *Theory and Event* 6, no. 4 (2003). doi:10.1353/tae.2003.0015.

Nagourney, Adam. "Democrats Entangled: So What Happened in That Election, Anyhow?" *New York Times,* January 2, 2005, Sec. 4, p. 3.

National People's Party. "The Omaha Platform of 1892." Adopted July 4, 1892. http://historymatters.gmu.edu/d/5361.

————. "People's Party Platform of 1896." Adopted July 24, 1896. http://projects. vassar.edu/1896/peoplesplatform.html.

Nehamas, Alexander. *The Art of Living: Socratic Reflections From Plato to Foucault.* Berkeley: University of California Press, 1998.

Nietzsche, Friedrich. *Basic Writings of Nietzsche.* Translated by Walter Kaufman and Peter Gay. New York: Penguin, 2000.

Nussbaum, Martha. "The Comic Soul: Or, This Phallus That Is Not One," in *The Soul of Tragedy: Essays on Athenian Drama,* edited by Victoria Pedrick and Steven M. Oberhelman, 155–80. Chicago: University of Chicago Press, 2005.

Ober, Josiah. "Aristotle's Political Sociology: Class, Status, and Order in the Politics." In *Essays on the Foundations of Aristotelian Political Science,* edited by Carnes Lord and David K. O'Connor, 112–35. Berkeley: University of California Press, 1991.

————. *The Athenian Revolution: Essays on Ancient Greek Democracy and Political Theory.* Princeton, NJ: Princeton University Press. 1966.

————. *Democracy and Knowledge: Innovation and Learning in Classical Athens.* Princeton, NJ: Princeton University Press, 2010.

————. *Mass and Elite in Democratic Athens: Rhetoric, Ideology and the Power of the People.* Princeton, NJ: Princeton University Press, 1989.

————. *Political Dissent in Democratic Athens: Intellectual Critics of Popular Rule.* Princeton, NJ: Princeton University Press, 2002.

————. "What the Ancient Greeks Can Tell Us About Democracy." *Annual Reviews in Political Science* 11 (2008): 67–91.

Ober, Josiah, and Charles Hedrick. *DĒMOKRATIA: A Conversation on Democracies, Ancient and Modern.* Princeton, NJ: Princeton University Press, 1996.

Olson, Joel. "Friends and Enemies, Slaves and Masters: Fanaticism, Wendell Phillips, and the Limits of Democratic Theory," *Journal of Politics* 71, no. 1 (2009): 82–95.

Olson, S. Douglas. "Economics and Ideology in Aristophanes' *Wealth.*" *Harvard Studies in Classical Philology* 93 (1990): 223–42.

————. "Politics and Poetry in Aristophanes' *Wasps.*" *Transactions of the American Philological Association* 126 (1996): 129–50.

Orwin, Clifford. *The Humanity of Thucydides.* Princeton, NJ: Princeton University Press, 1994.

Panagia, Davide. *The Poetics of Political Thinking.* Durham, NC: Duke University Press, 2006.

————. "Thinking with and against the 'Ten Theses.'" *Theory and Event* 6, no. 4 (2003). doi:10.1353/tae.2003.0016.

Panizza, Francisco. "Introduction: Populism and the Mirror of Democracy." In *Populism and the Mirror of Democracy,* edited by Francisco Panizza, 1–31. New York: Verso, 2005.

Phillips, Anne. "From Inequality to Difference: A Severe Case of Displacement?" *New Left Review* 224 (July–August 1997): 143–53.

Pizzigatti, Sam. *Greed and Good: Understanding and Overcoming the Inequality That Limits Our Lives.* New York: Apex Press, 2004.

Plato. *Plato: Lysis, Symposium, Gorgias.* Translated by W. R. M. Lamb. Cambridge: Harvard University Press, 1991. First published 1925 by Harvard University Press.

———. *Republic.* Translated by G. M. A. Grube. Revised by C. D. C. Reeve. Indianapolis: Hackett, 1992.

Pocock, J. G. A. "The Ideal of Citizenship since Ancient Times." In *The Citizenship Debates: A Reader,* edited by Gershon Shafir, 31–49. Minneapolis: University of Minnesota Press, 1998.

Polanyi, Karl. *The Livelihood of Man.* Edited by Harry W. Pearson. New York: Academic Press, 1977.

———. *Primitive, Archaic and Modern Economies: Essays of Karl Polanyi.* Edited by George Dalton. Garden City, NY: Anchor Books, 1968.

Pozzi, Dora C. "The Pastoral Ideal in 'The Birds' of Aristophanes," *The Classical Journal* 81, no. 2 (December 1985–January 1986): 119–29.

Rancière, Jacques. *Disagreement.* Translated by Julie Rose. Minneapolis: University of Minnesota Press, 1998.

———. *The Emancipated Spectator.* Translated by Gregory Elliott. London: Verso, 2009.

———. *The Ignorant Schoolmaster: Five Lessons in Intellectual Emancipation.* Palo Alto, CA: Stanford University Press, 1991.

———. *On the Shores of Politics.* Translated by Liz Heron. New York: Verso, 1995.

———. *The Philosopher and His Poor.* Translated by Andrew Parker, Corinne Oster, and John Drury. Durham, NC: Duke University Press, 2004.

———. *The Politics of Aesthetics.* Translated by Gabriel Rockhill, with an afterword by Slavoj Žižek. London: Continuum, 2004.

———. *Short Voyages to the Land of People.* Translated by James B. Swenson. Palo Alto, CA: Stanford University Press, 2003.

———. "Ten Theses on Politics." *Theory and Event* 5, no. 3 (2001). doi:10.1353/tae.2001.0028.

Rank, Mark Robert. *One Nation Underprivileged: Why American Poverty Affects Us All.* New York: Oxford University Press, 2004.

Reckford, Kenneth J. *Aristophanes' Old and New Comedy: Six Essays in Perspective.* Chapel Hill: University of North Carolina Press, 1987.

Rhodes, P. J., ed. *Athenian Democracy.* New York: Oxford University Press, 2004.

Rich, Frank. "Slumdogs Unite," *New York Times,* February 8, 2009, WK10.

Rorty, Richard. *Contingency, Irony, and Solidarity.* Cambridge: Cambridge University Press, 1989.

Rothwell, Kenneth S. *Politics and Persuasion in Aristophanes' Ecclesiasuzae.* Leiden, The Netherlands: E. J. Brill, 1990.

Salkever, Stephen, ed. *The Cambridge Companion to Ancient Greek Political Thought.* Cambridge: Cambridge University Press, 2009.

Saxonhouse, Arlene. *Athenian Democracy: Modern Mythmakers and Ancient Theorists.* Notre Dame, IN: University of Notre Dame Press, 1996.

———. *Fear of Diversity: The Birth of Political Science in Ancient Greek Thought.* Chicago: University of Chicago Press, 1992.

———. *Free Speech and Democracy in Ancient Athens.* Cambridge: Cambridge University Press, 2006.

————. "Men, Women, War and Politics: Family and Polis in Aristophanes and Euripides." *Political Theory* 8, no. 1 (February 1980): 65–81.

Scott, Janny. "Life at the Top in America Isn't Just Better, It's Longer." In *Class Matters*, with an introduction by Bill Keller, 27–50. New York: Times Books / Henry Holt, 2005.

Segal, Charles. "The Character and Cults of Dionysus and the Unity of the *Frogs*." *Harvard Studies in Classical Philology* 65 (1961): 206–42.

————. "Spectator and Listener." In *The Greeks*, edited by Jean-Pierre Vernant, translated by Charles Lambert and Teresa Lavendar Fagan, 184–215. Chicago: University of Chicago Press, 1995.

Sirota, David J. "The Democrats' DaVinci Code." *The American Prospect Online*, December 8, 2004. www.prospect.org/web/page.ww?section=root&name=View Print&articleID=8956.

Slater, Nial. "Space, Character and απапη': Transformation and Transvaluation in the Acharnians." In *Tragedy, Comedy, and the Polis*, edited by Alan Sommerstein, 397–415. Bari, Italy: Levante Editori, 1993.

Sommerstein, Alan. "Aristophanes and the Demon Poverty." *The Classical Quarterly*, New Series 34, no. 2 (1984): 314–33.

Ste. Croix, G. E. M. de. *The Class Struggle in the Ancient Greek World: From the Archaic Age to the Arab Conquests*. Ithaca, NY: Cornell University Press, 1981.

Stein, Howard. "Review: The Lysistrata Experience." *Arion*, 12, no. 3 (Winter 2005), 135–48.

Storey, John. *Inventing Popular Culture: From Folklore to Globalization*. New York: Blackwell, 2003.

Strauss, Barry S. *Athens after the Peloponnesian War: Class, Faction and Policy 403–386 B.C.* Ithaca, NY: Cornell University Press, 1986.

Strauss, Leo. *Socrates and Aristophanes*. Chicago: University of Chicago Press, 1996.

Stroup, Sarah Culpepper. "Designing Women: Aristophanes' Lysistrata and the 'Hetairization' of the Greek Wife," *Arethusa* 37, no. 1 (Winter 2004): 37–73.

Tarnopolsky, Christina. "Plato's Politics of Distributing and Disrupting the Sensible." *Theory and Event* 13, no. 4 (2010). doi:10.1353/tae.2010.0033.

Taylor, Charles. "The Politics of Recognition." In *Multiculturalism: Examining the Politics of Recognition*, edited by Amy Gutmann, 25–74. Princeton, NJ: Princeton University Press, 1994.

Thucydides. *History of the Peloponnesian War*. Translated by Charles Forster Smith. Cambridge: Harvard University Press, 1991.

————. *The Peloponnesian War*. Translated by Richard Crawley. Edited by T. E. Wick. New York: Modern College Library, 1982.

Tzanetou, Angeliki. "Something to do with Demeter: Ritual and Performance in Aristophanes' *Women at the Thesmophoria*." *American Journal of Philology* 123 (2002): 329–67.

Vickers, Michael. "Alcibiades at Sparta: Aristophanes' *Birds*." *The Classical Quarterly* 45, no. 2 (1995): 339–54.

————. *Pericles on Stage: Political Comedy in Aristophanes' Early Plays*. Austin: University of Texas Press, 1997.

Villa, Dana. *Politics, Philosophy, Terror: Essays on the Thought of Hannah Arendt*. Princeton, NJ: Princeton University Press, 1999.

Vlastos, Gregory. *Socrates: Ironist and Moral Philosopher.* Cambridge: Cambridge University Press, 1991.

Wallis, Jim. *God's Politics: Why the Right Gets It Wrong and the Left Doesn't Get It.* San Francisco: Harper Collins, 2005.

Weber, Max. "Class, Status, Party." In *From Max Weber: Essays in Sociology,* edited by Hans H. Gerth and C. Wright Mills, 180–95. Oxford: Oxford University Press, 1958.

Weir, Margaret. "Challenging Inequality." *Perspectives on Politics* 2 (December, 2004): 677–81.

White, Steven. *The Ethos of a Late Modern Citizen.* Cambridge, MA: Harvard University Press, 2009.

———. "Three Conceptions of the Political." In Botwinick and Connolly, *Democracy and Vision: Sheldon Wolin and the Vicissitudes of the Political,* 173–92.

Whitman, Cedric H. *Aristophanes and the Comic Hero.* Cambridge, MA: Harvard University Press, 1964.

Wilkinson, Richard G. *The Impact of Inequality: How to Make Sick Societies Healthier.* New York: New Press, 2005.

Wolin, Sheldon. "Democracy, Difference, and Re-Cognition," *Political Theory* 21 (1993): 480.

———. "Fugitive Democracy." In Benhabib, *Democracy and Difference,* 31–45.

———. "The Liberal/Democratic Divide: On Rawls's Political Liberalism," *Political Theory* 24 (1996): 97–119.

———. "Norm and Form: The Constitutionalizing of Democracy." In Euben, *Athenian Political Thought,* 29–58.

Wood, Ellen Meiksins. *Democracy Against Capitalism: Renewing Historical Materialism.* Cambridge: Cambridge University Press., 1995.

———. *Peasant-Citizen and Slave: The Foundations of Athenian Democracy.* London: Verso, 1988.

Wood, Ellen Meiksins, and Neal Wood. *Class Ideology and Ancient Political Theory: Socrates, Plato, and Aristotle in Social Context.* New York: Oxford University Press, 1978.

Young, Iris Marion. "Unruly Categories: A Critique of Nancy Fraser's Dual System Theory." *New Left Review* 223 (March–April 1997): 147–60.

Yunis, Harvey. *Taming Democracy: Models of Political Rhetoric in Ancient Athens.* Ithaca: Cornell University Press, 1996.

Zeitlin, Froma I. "Travesties of Gender and Genre in Aristophanes' *Thesmophoriasouzae.*" *Critical Inquiry* 8, no. 2 (Winter 1981): 301–27.

Zuckert, Michael. "Rationalism and Political Responsibility: Just Speech and Just Deed in the 'Clouds' of Aristophanes and the 'Apology' of Socrates. *Polity* 17 (1984): 271–97.

Zumbrunnen, John. "Elite Domination and the Ordinary Citizen: Aristophanes' *Acharnians* and *Knights.*" *Political Theory* 23, no. 5 (October 2004): 656–77.

———. "Fantasy, Irony, and Economic Justice in Aristophanes' *Assemblywomen* and *Wealth.*" *American Political Science Review* 100, no. 3 (August 2006): 319–33.

———. *Silence and Democracy: Athenian Politics in Thucydides' History.* University Park: Pennsylvania State University Press, 2008.

INDEX

Aeschylus, 52–57, 58
agon (as structural element of Aristophanes' comedies), 21, 26, 46, 55, 67–71, 94, 117–18
agonal democracy, 1, 2, 3, 8, 19, 81–83, 86, 90–91, 95–98, 123
Alcibiades, 56
Allen, Danielle, 64–67, 69
anger, 15, 52, 59, 90, 96, 98, 99, 125, 127; and *archē*, 77–80; in Aristotle, 11, 62; in *Birds*, 19, 71–77; and populism, 60–62, 81; in *Wasps*, 19, 62–71
archē, 19, 58, 99–100; as beginning, 78–80; in *Birds*, 71–77; in *Wasps*, 62–71
Arendt, Hannah, 79, 83
Aristophanes: *Acharnians*, 2, 12, 14, 19, 23, 28, 46, 48, 49, 84, 81–84, 86–94, 96–98, 100, 125, 127, 131; as apolitical, 13; *Assemblywomen*, 1–2, 13–14, 16, 20, 49, 99–102, 105–15, 118, 120–21, 126–27; *Birds*, 15, 19, 49, 71–80, 81, 90, 96, 98, 127; as civic educator, 14, 16, 38–40, 66, 98, 130–31; *Clouds*, 13, 19, 43–47, 52–53, 57, 127; as conservative, 2, 14–15, 17, 128; as domesticated, 13, 131; *Frogs*, 47, 52–57, 60, 81; *Knights*, 19, 49, 52, 74, 81–84, 91–98, 100, 125, 127, 131, 143n19; *Lysistrata*, 13, 18–19, 22–28, 29–30, 36–38, 38–40, 43, 45–46, 49, 125–26; *Peace*, 15, 18–19, 22–28, 28–38, 38–40, 43, 45, 49, 71–73, 125–127; as snob, 102; *Wasps*, 15, 19, 33, 52, 63–71, 72, 76–80, 81, 96, 98, 127; *Wealth*, 12, 20, 48, 69, 99–102, 105–08, 115–21, 126–27; *Women at the Thesmophoria*, 19, 47–52, 52–53, 57, 127

Aristotle, 4, 25–26, 65; *Ethics*, 11–12, 62–63, 124–25; *Poetics*, 41, 44, 84, 106, 131–32
audience. *See* spectators

Bloch, Ernst, 151n63
Bowie, A. M., 54–55, 142n9, 143n25, 147n30

chorus, 13, 14, 21–24, 28, 33–38, 46, 50, 52, 54, 56, 58, 63–64, 67, 70–71, 74–75, 86–87, 89–97, 126
citizenship, challenge of, 1–3, 5, 7, 10, 13, 17, 23, 39–40, 62–63, 71, 79–80, 81, 83, 98, 122–23, 127–30; common understandings of, 132–33. *See also* democracy
civic unity, 52–53, 58–59, 62, 94
Cleisthenic revolution, 6–7
Cleon, 23, 34, 46, 49, 97, 125; and *Acharnians*, 86–91; in *Knights*, 91–95; in Thucydides, 83–86, 131; in *Wasps*, 64, 68–71
cleverness, 18–19, 81–86, 95–98; in *Acharnians*, 86–91; and the comic disposition of ordinary citizenship, 123–27, 134–35; in *Knights*, 91–95
comic disposition of ordinary citizenship, 1–2, 7, 10, 11–12, 17, 20, 23, 39–40, 42–43, 58–59, 79–80, 82, 100–101, 122, 123–35. *See also* cleverness; comic recognition; comic voyaging
comic recognition, 12, 18, 20, 98, 115, 117; and the comic disposition of ordinary citizenship, 123–27, 134–35; and contemporary understandings of recognition, 105–8; in *Wealth*, 120–23. *See also* fantasy; irony

163

comic voyaging, 12, 18–19, 23, 25, 28, 43, 45–46, 51, 58–59, 78, 98, 123–27; and the comic disposition of democratic citizenship, 39–40, 134–35; in *Peace* and *Lysistrata*, 35–38
Connolly, William, 12, 82–3, 91, 96

deliberative democracy, 1, 3, 5, 8, 82, 123
democracy: and *archē* or rule, 64–71, 76–80, 96; and collective action, 1, 3, 5–7, 10, 11, 14, 40, 58, 63, 64–65, 71, 81, 83, 91, 96, 123–24, 126, 133–35; and institutions, 4–5, 10, 123–24; and rebellion or rebelliousness, 1, 3, 4–7, 10, 11, 14, 40, 42–43, 58, 62–63, 64–65, 71, 81–83, 86, 90–91, 96, 98, 123–24, 126, 133–35
demagogues/demagoguery, 2, 28–29, 34, 38, 52, 81, 92–93, 125–26, 129; Cleon as, 13, 23, 64, 68–69, 84, 97
dexios, 84–86, 94, 97
Diodotus, 85–86
Dionysus, 19, 52–57
Dover, Kenneth, 27, 45, 47, 90, 95, 137n3, 138n27, 141n33, 142n13, 149n41, 149n44, 150n51

ethos, 12, 82–83, 133–35
Euben, J. Peter, 137n6, 138n28, 142n7
Euripides, 19, 22, 47–52, 52–57, 89

fantasy, 15, 17–18, 39, 80, 99–101, 107–8, 120–27; ; in *Acharnians*, 88, 90; in *Assemblywomen*, 108–13; in *Frogs*, 53, 57; in *Knights*, 93; in *Peace*, 22, 23, 28, 33, 37, 72; in *Wealth*, 113–20
Finley, Moses, 9, 102–3, 105, 111, 138n22
Fraser, Nancy, 103–8, 112

Gutmann, Amy, 3, 137n2

Habermas, Jürgen, 137n2
Heisod, 150n52
Henderson, Jeffrey, 16–17, 51, 72, 118, 128–29
Heracles, 34, 53–55, 75

Hermes, 22, 24, 28, 32, 34, 35, 116

Iraq War, 21–23, 27
Iris, 75
irony, 17–18, 98, 99–101, 107–8, 126–27; in *Assemblywomen*, 110–13; in *Knights*, 94–95; in *Lysistrata*, 22; in *Wasps*, 69; in *Wealth*, 117–22

juries/jurors, 15, 17, 19, 33, 63–71, 72, 103, 128. *See also* lawcourts

Konstan, David, 15, 139n5, 141n34, 144n18, 150n55

lawcourts, 4, 13, 63–64, 68, 70, 72, 79, 83, 131. *See also* juries/jurors
liberalism/liberal democracy, 1, 3, 4–5, 8, 82, 86, 104, 121, 123, 132, 135
Lippmann, Walter, 9–10, 131–32
logos, 74–77, 78, 100
Lysistrata Project, 21–23, 31, 39

madness (*mania*), 23–25, 28, 32–34, 43, 64, 77
Markell, Patchen, 78–80, 106–7
Mitylene Debate, 84–86
Mouffe, Chantal, 3

National People's Party, 62
Nietzsche, 53
nomos, 75
Nussbaum, Martha, 23, 25–26, 140n18

Obama, Barack, 60–61
Ober, Josiah, 4–9, 16, 65, 101, 103, 112–13
oligarchy, 7, 12, 52, 152n11
Olson, Douglas, 100, 138n34, 144n18, 144n22
ordinary citizens, 1–2, 8–11, 13–15, 18–20, 21–23, 41–44, 57–59, 62–63, 81–83, 123–35, 146n16; in *Acharnians*, 87–91; and *archē*, 77–80; and Cleon, 84–86; and cleverness, 95–98; and comic recognition, 120–23; in *Frogs*, 52–57; in *Knights*, 91–95; in *Women at the Thesmophoria*, 47–51

panhellenism, 35, 36–37
parabasis, 14, 31, 34, 52, 58, 71, 75, 86–87, 94, 96–97, 140n28
Peloponnesian War, 12, 23, 32–35, 52, 84, 87–88, 101, 123, 125–26
Pericles, 6, 10, 24, 32, 38, 103, 139n10
Plato, 4, 25–26, 30, 44, 65, 85, 118, 139n14, 144n12; *Apology*, 43, 47; *Gorgias*, 85, 139n10; *Republic*, 26, 131, 149n13
pluralism, 3, 8, 10–11, 94, 134–35
Polyani, Karl, 102–3
populism, 11, 19, 42–45, 47, 51, 57–59, 60–63, 77–80, 81, 98, 129
Poseidon, 75, 115
pragmata, 33, 71–73, 79, 141n29
Prometheus, 75, 150n52

Rancière, Jacques, 19, 23, 25–27, 29–31, 34, 39–40, 65–67, 69–71, 74, 78, 129–30
Rawls, John, 3, 137n2
recognition-redistribution debate, 20, 101, 103–8, 120–22
Reckford, Kenneth, 138n35, 140n20, 141n30, 141n34, 142n16, 143n20, 143n25, 144n19, 145n25, 147n26, 147n30, 149n43, 150n46

Saxonhouse, Arlene, 137n6, 138n28, 139n5, 141n34, 149n43, 150n47
silence, 25–27, 65–66
social justice. *See* recognition-redistribution debate
Socrates, 43–47, 53, 85, 100, 118
Sommerstein, Alan, 15, 99–100, 149n45, 150n47, 151n57
Sophocles, 106–7, 150n51
spectators, as citizens, 9–10, 96–98, 130–33; in the theater, 29–32, 36–38, 42–43, 58–59, 96–98, 108, 128–30
Strauss, Leo, 138n28, 141n32, 142n7, 144n21
Ste. Croix, G. E. M. de, 102–3, 111, 137

Taylor, Charles, 106, 137n8
Thompson, Dennis, 3, 137n2
Thucydides, 10, 28, 38, 84–86, 97, 131

White, Steven, 12, 133–34
Wolin, Sheldon, 4–9, 65, 78, 82–83, 91, 96
Wood, Ellen Meiksins, 103, 105, 112, 150n52

Zeus, 27, 32, 35, 47, 75, 114–17, 120–21, 150n52

Lightning Source UK Ltd.
Milton Keynes UK
UKHW020136030821
388191UK00006B/400